Policing in Natural Disasters

Terri M. Adams and
Leigh R. Anderson

Policing in Natural Disasters

Stress, Resilience, and the Challenges
of Emergency Management

TEMPLE UNIVERSITY PRESS
Philadelphia • Rome • Tokyo

TEMPLE UNIVERSITY PRESS
Philadelphia, Pennsylvania 19122
tupress.temple.edu

Copyright © 2019 by Temple University—Of The Commonwealth System of Higher Education
All rights reserved
Published 2019

Library of Congress Cataloging-in-Publication Data

Names: Adams, Terri M., 1969- author. | Anderson, Leigh R., author.
Title: Policing in natural disasters : stress, resilience, and the challenges of emergency management / Terri M. Adams and Leigh R. Anderson.
Description: Philadelphia : Temple University Press, [2019] | Includes bibliographical references and index. |
Identifiers: LCCN 2018023748 (print) | LCCN 2018025475 (ebook) | ISBN 9781439918388 (E-book) | ISBN 9781439918364 (cloth : alk. paper) | ISBN 9781439918371 (pbk. : alk. paper)
Subjects: LCSH: Police. | Natural disasters. | Emergency management.
Classification: LCC HV7921 (ebook) | LCC HV7921 .A345 2019 (print) | DDC 363.34—dc23
LC record available at https://lccn.loc.gov/2018023748

♾ The paper used in this publication meets the requirements of the American National Standard for Information Sciences—Permanence of Paper for Printed Library Materials, ANSI Z39.48-1992

Printed in the United States of America

9 8 7 6 5 4 3 2 1

For the first responders in our nation and around the world
who know the true meaning of the word *sacrifice*.
T. Adams and L. Anderson

For Retired Sergeant William Lee Anderson,
who made all of *this* and all of *us* possible.
L. Anderson

For the elegant warrior—my mother, Yvonne E. Rahman.
T. Adams

Contents

Introduction — 1

1 A Close-up View of the Disasters, the Police Departments, and the Impact of the Disasters on Police Operations — 11

2 Unusual Circumstances and Unusual Challenges: Dilemmas Faced by Law Enforcement Officers during Disasters — 45

3 Dilemmas with Responding to the Call of Duty: Role Conflict and Role Strain among Law Enforcement Officers during Disasters — 74

4 Missing and Out of Action: Case Study of Post Abandonment in New Orleans during Hurricane Katrina — 101

5 When the Police Become the Criminals: Misconduct among Law Enforcement Officers in the Midst of Disaster — 122

6 Resilience in the Face of It All — 145

7 Picking Up the Pieces: Life after a Disaster — 164

8 Moving Forward: The Role of Management in Mitigating the Challenges that Law Enforcement Officers Face — 192

Index — 219

Policing in Natural Disasters

Introduction

> We rely on law enforcement every day to provide for the safety and security of our communities, and, during disasters, officers are the first on the scene to assist survivors.... It is also important to remember that during a disaster, police have the same concerns as all survivors: Is my family safe and what's the impact on my property? (Fugate 2013, pp. 100–101)

Few phenomena challenge the human spirit or social order of society quite like a disaster (Hoffman and Oliver-Smith 2002). They can completely "overwhelm the coping capacity of the affected communities" (De Goyet, Marti, and Osorio 2013, ch. 61). The impacts of disasters extend beyond the headlines and news feeds on body counts and costs, striking at the core of a community's identity and daily activities. Often overlooked are the short- and long-term effects of these events on the people that society relies on in a disaster—the men and women who serve as first responders (police, firefighters, and emergency medical personnel). The needs of first responders are often neglected or underplayed in dialogues on disaster response and recovery efforts. Little thought goes into the factors that affect their ability to respond to emergencies or into how their disaster work may affect them personally and professionally.

This book provides important insights into the effects of disaster work on law-enforcement officers who served as first responders during some of the worst disasters in modern history. Law-enforcement officers were chosen over other first-responder agents as the focus of the book because they serve as critical actors in mitigation, preparedness, response, and recovery endeavors before, during, and after disasters. They are most often the first to provide immediate assistance to the public, and their presence can serve as a visible deterrent against chaos and violence (Bono 2011).

Generally, first responders are expected to fulfill their duties during an emergency regardless of the magnitude of the disaster. This book provides a unique view into what happens to law-enforcement officers when they are personally affected by a disaster to which they respond professionally. Specifically, the book examines the impact of the disaster on the police departments and the professional and personal lives of officers during the response and recovery phases of a disaster. Doing so can improve understanding of their behaviors during extreme crises and improve the preparedness, mitigation, response, and recovery policies of first responders and emergency managers.

The unprecedented number of natural and manmade disasters since 2005 highlights the need to closely analyze issues that affect disaster response and recovery efforts. It has been argued that society has become increasingly vulnerable to severe weather events (Kunkel, Pielke, and Changnon 1999), and the effects of climate change alone will lead to more extreme weather for the global community (Aalst 2006). Extreme weather may affect the distribution of natural resources, spawn conflict, and pose security threats (Nel and Righarts 2008). Each year since 1990, approximately 227 million people worldwide have been affected by natural disasters (Guha-Sapir et al. 2012). In addition, as terrorist organizations grow and enhance their capabilities, the United States continues to be under threat of manmade disasters (Federal Emergency Management Agency 2005). The risks of both natural and manmade disasters make it imperative that we focus on adequate preparation for future events; this requires a better understanding of the critical issues that affect the behavior of first responders.

The current U.S. homeland security era places its greater demands on the police to serve as first-responder agents (Oliver 2006; 2009). Events such as the terror attacks of September 11 and the Hurricane Katrina disaster brought to the forefront the importance of the role the police play during emergency response. This book—focusing on the nexus of the pertinent and timely issues of emergency response and disaster recovery—explores the seldom-discussed issues in first responder work at a time when the nation has become more aware of the threat of disasters.

Background: The Disasters

All the disasters examined in this book were of epic proportion: they were either large in scale or severely affected communities and the first-responder agencies that serve them. Additionally, the sites selected were chosen for the immense impact they had on affected communities and the potential threats each disaster posed on first responders both professionally and personally. The disasters examined are Hurricane Katrina in New Orleans, Louisiana, and Gulfport, Mississippi (2005); the Tornado Super Outbreak in Tuscaloosa, Alabama (2011); and an earthquake and tsunami in Santiago and Constitución, Chile (2010).

All three disasters were large in scale, but each has its own spatial and temporal dynamics associated with both the unfolding and the duration of the effects on their communities. Each high-consequence event displays subtle differences that provide opportunities to examine the strengths and vulnerabilities of the policing agencies and the officers themselves. In addition, cultural differences between the agencies provide a chance to also add analysis of cultural components among the challenges faced by policing agencies and their officers during disasters, as well as best practices for overcoming these conditions.

Contributions to Theory and Practice

Currently there is a dearth of literature—textbooks or supplemental books—on the challenges faced by law-enforcement officers and law-enforcement agencies during disasters. Most of the existing textbooks focus on the operational functions, culture, and models of policing. Very little attention is given to examining the nuances of the challenges law-enforcement officers face in disaster conditions. This book fills this gap in the literature by providing a comprehensive analysis of the major challenges law-enforcement officers face in such times (i.e., concerns about loved ones, exposure to high fatality rates, inability to maintain normal operational protocols).

The book was inspired by the accounts of triumphs and tragedies shared by the first responders who participated in a research project supported by the National Center for the Study of Preparedness and Catastrophic Event Response—Homeland Security Center of Excellence. The goal of the project was to gain insights from first responders who have firsthand knowledge of disaster work and examine their challenges during major natural disasters and the impact of disaster work on their professional and personal lives. The project sought knowledge from their personal stories.

The ineluctable threat of future natural and manmade disasters makes it imperative that we advance our understanding of the key issues that first responders face and develop meaningful strategies for preparing them for disaster response. This book provides timely insights that advance theoretical understanding of first-responder behaviors and disaster management issues during crises. The book's reliance on the insights provided by police officers who have served during some of the worst disasters in modern history for its analysis contributes significantly to the field of disaster management.

The conflicts between professional and personal responsibilities that first responders may face in responding to a catastrophic event can be considered a distinctive feature of a catastrophic event. The data presented in this book reveal both challenges and best practices in responses to some unique and unprecedentedly widespread disasters. Planners and emergency program managers will be able to use the findings from the book for self-assessment and improvements in their planning.

Description of Study Design and Methods

The work included in this book is a collection of both qualitative and quantitative research, including personal interviews, focus groups, and surveys. We gained access to the study participants through announced requests for volunteers from the departments under examination. The study participants answered questions related to their experiences during the height of the disaster and their experiences afterward. All study participants were assured of their anonymity, explaining that their participation was strictly voluntary and that they could withdraw from the process at any time. For the qualitative component, researchers conducted face-to-face interviews with approximately one hundred study participants as well as three focus groups, during which participants spoke freely about their experiences with the presence and support of other police personnel. For the quantitative component, researchers collected close to nine hundred completed self-administered surveys from additional participants. The survey instrument collected data from each study participant on a range of information, including demographic characteristics, work history, measures of stress, coping strategies, and other work-related questions. It allowed the research team to collect information that would provide an illustration of the challenges that the officers faced and the degree to which their roles as first responders were affected by the disaster.

The qualitative data derived from these instruments provided a nuanced understanding of the nature of the officers' experiences and their ability or inability to process their experiences in order to cope with the stress of disaster work and respond to the crisis and those in need. The face-to-face interviews were designed to obtain contextual information on the study participants' experiences during the disasters. Officers answered questions on their roles as first responders during the disaster and about their actions, sentiments, and thoughts while working as first responders during the crisis. Each officer answered the same set of questions, but the open-ended nature of the interviews allowed the officers to discuss a variety of topics related to the study and how their experiences affected their ability or inability to respond to and cope with the challenges of disaster work. This resulted in the collection of a rich, detailed, in-depth body of information on their experiences, thoughts, feelings, and actions during the disaster. All uncited quotes in this book came from the interviews and focus groups conducted in the study. With the exception of senior officers in the police force and other public officials, pseudonyms were used, where necessary, to protect the anonymity of the respondents.

The common thread that weaves throughout the data reported in this book is the humanity of the people who put themselves in harm's way to protect others and the enduring aftereffects of the disaster on their lives. And while some officers engaged in behavior inconsistent with their role as law-enforcement officers, most upheld their pledge to serve and protect the public. This sense of loyalty was found in participants irrespective of gender, culture, rank, and personal background.

It is important to highlight that some of the respondents were reticent to share details of their experiences, and understandably so. But the vast majority of the participants were willing to share information about their journey through the disaster and were extremely open and frank about the harsh realities they faced during that time. The accounts of their experiences demonstrate the complexities associated with the heroic roles they play, the stress they encounter, and the overall challenges they face in the midst of the disaster. For some, the disaster was over when the recovery plans got underway, but for most the disaster lingered and continued to stay with them for years after the event. This book tells their stories.

While the data provide valuable information, there were some limitations, as with any study of this magnitude and importance. Although the sample collected is representative of the diversity of the police departments examined, a much larger, randomized sample may have provided further insights that could not be obtained from the samples used. In addition, the responses provided by the study participants were based on their memories of past events; hence, some of their recollection of their experiences may not be exact. Despite the study's limitations, the data provide a significant view into the coping practices that fostered resilience among a group of first responders during some of the worst natural disasters in recorded history.

Book Contents and Road Map

This book was guided by the following research questions: (1) How do disasters challenge the typical operational protocols of law enforcement? (2) What are the organizational expectations of law-enforcement officers during times of crisis? (3) How does police culture affect the actions and reaction of law-enforcement officers during disasters? (4) What are the adaptive (e.g., protective and altruistic) and maladaptive behavioral responses that law-enforcement personnel exhibit during a disaster? (5) How does stress affect a law-enforcement officers' ability to function during disasters? (6) What are some of the key challenges law-enforcement officers face after a disaster and how does the disaster experience affect their professional and personal lives? (7) What factors aid law-enforcement officers in reconstructing their lives after a disaster and what protocols can law-enforcement agencies put into place to mitigate the negative impacts of disasters on the well-being of their personnel? (8) What are the similarities and differences in the disaster work experience of law-enforcement officers in different cultural contexts? (9) What can law-enforcement agencies do to train officers to be more resilient during disasters?

Each chapter in this book systematically explores the guiding research questions and introduces the reader to key concepts and phenomena. Together, they provide insights that transform the manner in which crisis and disaster response efforts are conceptualized, specifically when considering the role of law enforcement.

Chapter 1, A Close-up View of the Disasters, the Police Departments, and the Impact of the Disasters on Police Operations, introduces the context for the book and reviews departmental expectations of officers, formal and informal elements of police culture, and the ethos associated with law enforcement. In addition, it provides details on the history and operations of the related police departments that are relevant to understanding their policing practices during disaster events.

Chapter 2, Unusual Circumstances and Unusual Challenges, highlights the challenges law-enforcement officers face in the line of duty. The discussion examines the emotional and behavioral conditions that occur when officers confront extreme challenges. The chapter reviews the literature on police officer responses and discusses the differences between adaptive and maladaptive responses. In addition, the chapter reviews research on stress and post-traumatic stress syndrome among police officers. It examines elements of stress, with a focus on the stress induced by disasters, as well as the resulting post-traumatic stress that often ensues thereafter. Case studies are used to provide examples of the concepts discussed in the chapter.

Chapter 3, Dilemmas with Responding to the Call of Duty, addresses a topic seldom discussed in the literature and highlights challenges and frustrations that occasionally lead to role strain or role conflict among officers, particularly during disasters. These matters are explored using case studies to provide illustrations of the concepts the chapter discusses. The chapter compares the law-enforcement agencies that are a focus of the book to deepen understanding and to widen the lens of perspective.

Chapter 4, Missing and Out of Action, discusses factors that contribute to abandonment of posts of duty, including the issue of abandonment of duty among law-enforcement officers as a response to the extreme stress they experience during disasters. Case studies in the chapter illustrate some of the concepts discussed in the chapter.

Chapter 5, When Police Become the Criminals, explores what happens when law-enforcement officers engage in police misconduct and criminal activities during disasters. Case studies in the chapter illustrate the impact of these events on police organizations.

Chapter 6, Resilience in the Face of It All, in an effort to provide insights into what fosters resilience among law-enforcement officers, uses case studies to highlight resilience and the adaptive responses law-enforcement officers exhibit in response to their exposure to disasters.

Chapter 7, Picking Up the Pieces, picks up where Chapter 3 leaves off and uses survey data and case studies to highlight the ways in which law-enforcement officers attempt to reassemble their lives after a disaster.

Chapter 8, Moving Forward, explores the lessons the first responder community can learn from the experiences of the police officers examined in this book and the ways in which law-enforcement agencies can help alleviate some of the negative impacts of disasters on law-enforcement officers. The chapter explores the topic with data collected from interviews with executives in policing agencies, emergency managers, and psychologists, some of whom have worked with law-enforcement officers during and after disasters.

Acknowledgment

This book was made possible in part by funds provided by the National Center for Preparedness and Catastrophic Event Response, Department of Homeland Security Emeritus Center of Excellence. We would like to extend a heartfelt thank you to the students who provided invaluable assistance on research projects that led to the creation of this book, with a special thank you extended to Jesse Card, Michelle Dovil, Mila Turner, and Nissan Battle.

REFERENCES

Aalst, Maarten. K. 2006. "The Impacts of Climate Change on the Risk of Natural Disasters." *Disasters* 30 (1): 5–18.
Bono, James. 2011. "Police Departments." In *Encyclopedia of Disaster Relief*, edited by K. B. Penuel and M. Statler, 487–488. Thousand Oaks, CA: Sage.

DeGoyet, Claude, Ricardo Z. Marti, and Claudio Osorio. 2013. *Natural Disaster Mitigation and Relief—Disease Control Priorities in Developing Countries*, 2nd ed. NCBI Bookshelf. https://www.ncbi.nlm.nih.gov/books/NBK11792/.

Federal Emergency Management Agency. 2005. *Decision Making and Problem Solving Independent Study Program*. https://training.fema.gov/emiweb/downloads/is241.pdf.

Fugate, W. Craig. 2013. "From the Administrator: Law Enforcement's Role in Responding to Disasters." *Police Chief* 80 (August): 100–101.

Guha-Sapir, Debby, Femke Vos, Reginia Below, and Sylvain Ponserre. 2012. *Annual Disaster Statistical Review 2011: The Numbers and Trends*. Brussels: Center for Research on the Epidemiology of Disasters.

Hoffman, Susanna M., and Anthony Oliver-Smith. 2002. *Catastrophe and Culture: The Anthropology of Disaster*. Santa Fe, NM: School of American Research Press.

Kunkel, Kenneth E., Roger A. Pielke Jr, and Stanley A. Changnon. 1999. "Temporal Fluctuations in Weather and Climate Extremes That Cause Economic and Human Health Impacts: A Review." *Bulletin of the American Meteorological Society* 80 (6): 1077–1098.

Nel, Philip, and Marjolein Righarts. 2008. "Natural Disasters and the Risk of Violent Civil Conflict." *International Studies Quarterly* 52:159–185.

Oliver, Willard. M. 2006. "The Fourth Era of Policing: Homeland Security." *International Review of Law Computers and Technology* 20(1–2): 49–62.

———. 2009. "Policing for Homeland Security." *Criminal Justice Policy Review*, 20(3): 253–260.

World Bank. 2005. *Hazards of Nature, Risks to Development*. http://www.worldbank.org/icg/naturaldisasters/.

1

A Close-up View of the Disasters, the Police Departments, and the Impact of the Disasters on Police Operations

> We're facing the storm most of us have feared.
> —Mayor of New Orleans Ray Nagin

> Hurricane Katrina was the great equalizer. Doctors, lawyers, and other formerly well-to-do residents struggled in the rubble like everyone else to recover what they could and start over.
> —Koch, *Rising from Katrina*

> This will be a day that will go down in state history ... all you can do is pray for those people.
> —James Spann, TV meteorologist in Birmingham, Alabama

These quotes are from newspaper articles that reported the magnitude of disasters that were among the worst in modern times: Hurricane Katrina in 2005 (New Orleans, Louisiana, and Gulfport, Mississippi) and the Tornado Super Outbreak in 2011 (Tuscaloosa, Alabama). This book also explores a third, the Earthquake and Tsunami Disaster in 2010 (Santiago and Constitución, Chile). The disasters were of epic proportion, in that each one was so large in scale that it severely altered the physical landscape, social networks, and economy of the affected communities. In fact, they were so large in scope that they posed a threat to large segments of the population in the disaster sites, including the first responders. This book examines the impact of disaster work on the lives of the police officers who served as first responders to these catastrophic events.

Each of the three disasters exhibited a variety of temporal and spatial dynamics. The extent, breadth, and duration of the disasters from their buildup to their onset affected the preparation, response, and recovery options of local police officers and their departments. The dissimilarities in the disaster types provide an opportunity to better understand not only how the various nuances associated with these events affect disaster work but also the short-term and long-term effects of this work on the lives of the first responders.

While all the disasters are discussed in some form in this book's chapters, Hurricane Katrina is referenced most often because of its dynamic nature. In addition, the authors had access to data on multiple occasions for this first-responder population: more so than for the other disasters examined herein. But each disaster's data provide unique insights, adding important nuances that contribute to our understanding of the challenges each population faces, how these challenges cross cultural boundaries, and the best practices for dealing with them.

The Disasters

Hurricane Katrina: New Orleans, Louisiana, and Gulfport, Mississippi

Late August 2005 was no different from most hot summers in the Gulf Coast region of the United States: southeast Floridians, New Orleanians, and coastal residents of Alabama and Mississippi braced themselves for the onslaught of the third hurricane threat of the season: Hurricane Katrina. Originally landing in Miami and Fort Lauderdale, Florida, on August 25 as a Category 1 hurricane, Katrina continued to build momentum, and by Friday, August 26, the National Oceanic Atmospheric Administration (NOAA) projected that the second landfall would be west of the Florida Panhandle, heading toward the Mississippi and Alabama state lines. Two days later, Katrina was upgraded to a

Category 4 hurricane with the forecast suggesting that the storm surge would flood fifteen to twenty feet above sea level. Later in the afternoon of August 28, NOAA announced that Katrina was a "potentially catastrophic" Category 5 hurricane, with the eye of the storm projected to hit southeastern Louisiana. In the midst of the weather projections, emergency managers, politicians, and heads of first-responder agencies pondered the best strategies to take to prepare for, mitigate damages from, and respond to the forecasted disaster.

In the face of the forecast projections, authorities issued mandatory evacuations for large segments of southeastern Louisiana and the coastal communities in Alabama and Mississippi. Further, schools, community centers, and sports arenas opened as special-needs shelters "of last resort" for residents who could not evacuate, and regional transit authorities sent out buses to pick up residents who needed transportation to shelters. Property owners rushed to board up their homes and storefronts, and residents who had ignored the previous warnings scurried to exit the city or head to the open shelters. First-responder agencies—including the fire department, emergency medical units, and the police—all geared up to enact their pre-hurricane plans. Both the New Orleans Police Department (NOPD) and Gulfport Police Department (GPD) sent officers into communities to spread the word about the mandatory evacuation calls, manage the flow of traffic out of the city, place police vehicles out of harm's way, and station officers at strategic locations within each city. In addition, officers were instructed to make sure their loved ones evacuated the city prior to the storm.

By 6:00 A.M. on August 29, Katrina had made landfall on the Louisiana coast as a Category 4 hurricane, and by 11:00 A.M. it had made another landfall near the Louisiana-Mississippi border as a Category 3 hurricane. The Biloxi-Gulfport region received the brunt of the deadly 120-mph winds, which caused severe damages (see Figure 1.1). Although the sustained winds in New Orleans were not as severe, the levees holding back Lake Pontchartrain were breached in places along the shores of the city (Brookings Institution 2006). As a result of the breaches, 80

Figure 1.1 Aerial view of damaged and destroyed businesses and homes along the coast in the Biloxi-Gulfport area after Hurricane Katrina. (FEMA/Andrea Booher)

percent of New Orleans was under floodwaters, which in some areas reached as high as twenty-eight feet (see Figure 1.2).

Ultimately, Hurricane Katrina turned out to be one of the most devastating disasters in the history of the United States. The storm caused 1,883 fatalities and $108 billion in damages: 86 percent of the fatalities occurred in Louisiana (mostly in New Orleans Parish), 13 percent in Mississippi (mostly in Biloxi-Gulfport County), and 1 percent in other states (including 1 in Kentucky, 2 in Alabama, Georgia, and Ohio, and 14 in Florida). At the peak of the disaster, 200,000 residents were displaced and living in relief shelters, and approximately 114,000 households moved into trailers provided by the Federal Emergency Management Agency (FEMA) that served as temporary homes for months (for some, years) after the disaster ("Hurricane Katrina" 2017). In addition, well over 100 people were reported missing from the Gulf region and remained so for months ("Death Toll" 2006).

Figure 1.2 Neighborhoods and highways throughout the area remained flooded for weeks as a result of Hurricane Katrina. (FEMA/Jocelyn Augustino)

Figure 1.3 Damages caused by the Superstorm Outbreak in Tuscaloosa, Alabama. (FEMA/Tim Burkitt)

Tornado Super Outbreak, Tuscaloosa, Alabama

The Tornado Super Outbreak occurred on April 27, 2011, and spanned several states, mainly Alabama, Kentucky, and central Louisiana. In the span of twenty-four hours as many as 175 confirmed tornadoes occurred, with winds that reached 200 mph (Tanglao and Forer 2011). The devastation of this natural disaster exceeded even national weather predictions and caused at least three hundred deaths. Hundreds of others were injured and thousands were rendered homeless. At the time of the storm, Susan Cobb, a spokesperson for the NOAA, stated, "This happens so rarely, we don't really have a context for it. This many tornadoes on such a wide scale is overwhelming." (Quoted in Brown and Seelye 2011, A19.) The level of destruction that resulted from this outbreak made it one of the worst disasters in the United States (see Figure 1.3) since Hurricane Katrina. As with Hurricane Katrina, the prediction for the severe weather changed over time, but the likelihood of tornadic activity was broadcast to the public several days before the event.

The capricious and volatile nature of tornadoes makes them difficult to predict, as evidenced by the changes in the weather forecasts in the days leading up to the storms. Seven days before the outbreak, NOAA issued a report stating, "The overall tornado threat is low . . . should remain low through Thursday" (National Weather Service 2011). The messages issued a couple of days later predicted strong to severe thunderstorms for the following Tuesday and Wednesday (April 26–27). As time progressed, confidence in the prediction for strong to severe thunderstorms increased, and a threat of tornadoes was announced. Two days before the event, NOAA announced, "All modes of severe weather are possible on Wednesday . . . including tornadoes. . . . Activation of storm spotters and emergency management may be needed Tuesday and Wednesday due to the possibility of severe storms." By April 26, superstorm cells were being predicted across central Alabama. The outbreak was one of the deadliest storms since the 1970s (Simmons and Daniel 2012).

With wind speeds up to two hundred miles per hour, the storms left hospitals, universities, businesses, and other institutions across the affected states in shambles. The tornadoes that raked Alabama alone heavily damaged eighteen schools across the state, according to the Education Department, along with the Hackleburg, Alabama, fire department, police station, and grocery store (Collins 2011). It is estimated that fifty thousand people were without power after the tornado ripped through the region. Across the state of Alabama, the tornadoes destroyed approximately fourteen thousand houses, 37 percent of them in Tuscaloosa, where they destroyed or damaged 5,144 housing units—or 12.6 percent of the city's total of 40,872 housing units. Reportedly, the path of the tornado affected mostly single-family units, medium to small apartments, and student housing. Approximately two thousand people became temporarily homeless as a result of the storm ("Alabama Tornado" 2011). It is estimated that the storms caused between $2 billion and $5 billion in damages in the southern states (Daily Mail Reporter 2011).

Out of all affected states, Alabama suffered most of the damage. According to *Deseret News,* of approximately three hundred people who were killed across six states, more than two-thirds were in Alabama, where large cities bore the half-mile-wide scars that the twisters left behind (Mohr 2011). The city of Tuscaloosa, Alabama, sustained the most significant damage in the state, including sixty-two fatalities and the destruction of homes and businesses.

Earthquake and Tsunami in Santiago and Constitución, Chile

Chile is one of the most seismic nations in the world. On February 27, 2010, at 3:34 A.M., a massive earthquake hit south-central Chile. At 8.8 on the Richter Scale, it was the fifth-strongest earthquake ever recorded. The magnitude of this subduction-induced earthquake may have altered the earth's figure axis and shortened the length of the day by 1.26 millionths of a second (Than 2010). The regions of the country most severely affected were O'Higgins, Maule, Bío Bío, Valparaíso, the metropolitan area of Santiago, and Araucanía, which account for approximately 80 percent of the country (Bárcena et al. 2010). As one of the deadliest earthquakes in recorded history, it triggered a deadly tsunami. More than 2 million people were negatively affected (e.g., lost electrical power, lost access to roadways) and more than 500 people died—as many as 350 lost their lives in Constitución alone. The earthquake resulted in significant infrastructure damage, including the destruction of more than 440,000 buildings, including critical structures such as schools and hospitals. The earthquake and tsunami destroyed 212 bridges and rendered many roadways undrivable.

The strength of the earthquake caused the city of Constitución to move at least ten feet to the west and the capital, Santiago, to move about eleven inches to the west-southwest. More than one hundred temporary villages were set up to provide housing to those whom the earthquake rendered homeless. Although the quake hit the affected communities hard, it was reportedly responsible for fewer than ten deaths. A large number of fatalities resulted from the tsunami, which started less than fifteen minutes after the earthquake and struck the coastal communities.

The first waves hit at 3:48 A.M. in Pichilemu, followed by a wave in Valparaíso. A wave struck Constitución at 4:15 A.M.

The Cities and Their Police Departments
New Orleans, Louisiana, and Gulfport, Mississippi

Before the landfall of Hurricane Katrina, New Orleans was one of the most celebrated southern cities in the United States. Established as a port city in 1718 by French-Canadian nobleman Jean-Baptiste Le Moyne de Bienville, New Orleans sits below Lake Pontchartrain at the mouth of the Mississippi River as it meets the Gulf of Mexico. With its strategic location, New Orleans remains one of the nation's most significant ports. According to data retrieved from the U.S. Census Bureau's American FactFinder, New Orleans was once a densely populated city with a population close to four hundred and eighty-five thousand (484, 674) and more than 27 percent of its families living below the poverty threshold (U.S. Census Bureau 2007). The city's population dropped significantly after Hurricane Katrina to an estimated low of a little over two hundred and thirty thousand in 2006 (Plyer 2016), and the poverty rate dropped to 21 percent (Adelson 2015). Many travelers consider New Orleans to be one of the most distinct southern cities, in that within its city limits one can find a diverse mixture of cultures. Commonly referred to as "the Big Easy," New Orleans has long been known for its nightlife, food, and unique Creole culture.

In a region of the nation known as Hurricane Alley, the city of New Orleans has prepared for and experienced a disproportionately large number of hurricanes over the years. Many cities and towns along the Eastern Seaboard are at risk for hurricanes, but the geographic characteristics of New Orleans make it particularly vulnerable to flooding. With 55 percent of the city's landmass one to ten feet below sea level, the city relies on a levee system to keep back the Mississippi River. Originally established by the French in the eighteenth century, the levee system is managed by the U.S. Army Corps of Engineers, who also extended the system in the nineteenth century and updated it in the twentieth century (Kelman 2007). The city has a long history of teetering between denying its proclivity to flood and actively working to keep the city safe from floodwaters by reinforcing the levee system.

Gulfport lies just sixty-five miles northeast of New Orleans and, like New Orleans, sits along the Gulf of Mexico. With Biloxi, it is the county seat of Harrison County. Two investors cofounded the city in 1898: one the owner of the Gulf and Ship Railroad and the other the owner of the G and SI Railroad. The city was originally established to connect the lumber mills to the coast, but it soon became a promising seaport that contributes significantly to the economy of Mississippi. Over the years, Gulfport's economy has grown to include a healthy casino industry: the city is a popular gambling destination in the South (Gupton et al. 2012).

Before Hurricane Katrina's landfall, Gulfport's population was 72,464, and after Katrina the Gulfport-Biloxi region lost 41,000 people (Whoriskey 2006). Like New Orleans, Gulfport has a long history of tropical storms, is under the threat of a storm every two years or so, and is no stranger to hurricane preparedness.

As expected, the New Orleans and Gulfport police departments reflect the size and scope of criminal threats within their respective communities. The NOPD is a large police department, which employed more than seventeen hundred sworn officers at the time of Hurricane Katrina. The police department has gone through a variety of transformations over the years. It was well known for police misconduct, including police brutality and corruption. The 1986 film *The Big Easy* epitomized the corruption within the department: the story focuses on the life of a "good" officer who compromises his principles by engaging in activities that are not aboveboard but that he and his colleagues consider to be benefits of the job. The production of this film and others, along with many news reports, placed the department under a great deal of scrutiny. In the mid-1990s the misconduct came to a head—drawing the attention of the U.S. Department of Justice—and the NOPD collaborated with the Federal Bureau of Investigation, which launched a series of sting operations designed to weed out the "dirty cops" (Pennington 2006; Moore 2010). (See Chapter 5 for a more detailed discussion.)

In comparison with the NOPD, the GPD is a relatively small department, with fewer than 200 sworn officers on staff. At the time of the Katrina disaster, the department had roughly 170 sworn officers. Unlike the NOPD, the GPD has largely stayed out of the newspaper headlines. While the department has not been entirely free of corruption, unlike NOPD it has largely avoided excessive negative publicity.

Tuscaloosa, Alabama

Located along the Black Warrior River in west-central Alabama, Tuscaloosa is affectionately known as the Druid City because of the numerous Red Oak trees that line the downtown streets. The fifth-largest city in Alabama, Tuscaloosa had more than ninety thousand residents before the onset of the Tornado Super Outbreak in 2011. The city's median household income was $31,874, and close to 30 percent of the population was below the poverty threshold. Tuscaloosa's economy depends on higher education, government agencies, and major manufacturing companies. College football is the main attraction of the city: nonresidents are less likely to flock to the city of Tuscaloosa for its nightlife or recreational activities than is typical of cities of its size. The "Roll Tide" rally call shouted during the football games in the Crimson Tide stadium is emblematic of the city's football culture, which dominates the city's cultural and social scene.

Tuscaloosa is also known for its propensity for severe weather. Although officially located outside tornado alley, it experiences two tornado seasons because of its geographic position: March–May and November–early December. The region is known for having, on average, the largest number of tornado watches and warnings per year in the nation. Consequently, city officials are used to gearing up for and dealing with potential tornadic activities.

The police department of Tuscaloosa is similar in size to that of Gulfport, Mississippi. The department had 286 sworn officers on the force at the time of the disaster and approximately 150 nonsworn personnel. Hence, it is a relatively small police department that has had a number of citizen complaints against its officers over the years, but its level of misconduct was never reported at the level of that of NOPD.

Santiago and Constitución, Chile

There are organizational and structural differences between policing in the United States and policing in Chile. For instance, in the United States there is no national police force, but Chile has both local and national police forces. At the national level, Chile has the Carabineros de Chile, and the Grupo de Operaciones Policiales Especiales (GOPE, Police Special Operations Group), and, like the United States, they have mission-driven federal law-enforcement agencies, such as the Policía de Investigaciones de Chile (Chilean Investigation Police), the Equipo de Reacción Táctica Antinarcóticos (ERTA, Antinarcotics Tactical Response Team), the Gendarmería de Chile (Prison Service), and the Sección de Operaciones Tácticas (SOT, Tactical Operations Section).

The Carabineros are primarily responsible for what are considered normal police operations, such as public order and safety, but they are also responsible for border patrol. The Carabineros also have marine and air units that can be likened to the Coast Guard in the United States, since they can be called to serve in the capacity of a reserve army and operate under the Ministry of Defense during national emergencies. They comprise three geographic units: the Northern Zone, the Southern Zone, and the Central Zone. As in what are typically thought of as subdivisions within a U.S. police department, the Carabineros are supported by the internal and foreign police, health, justice, personnel, and welfare units.

The Investigation Police is a plainclothes law-enforcement organization responsible for criminal investigations and immigration control. This force has its headquarters in the capital city of Santiago and maintains substations throughout the rest of the country. The Carabineros and the Investigation Police are governed by the Interior Ministry.

In addition to the national law enforcement, local jurisdictions have police departments in municipalities throughout the country. These policing units provide services to the local populations that include both law enforcement and public assistance. Unlike police departments in the United States, the local police receive national assistance from the Carabineros during emergencies. The national police force provides first-response and law-enforcement services across the country and receives specialized training to support the populace in times of extreme crisis. During the 2010 earthquake and tsunami, both the national police force and the local police departments served as first responders.

Preparing for What Might Happen: The Big One

Hurricane Katrina

To prepare for a potentially devastating hurricane like Hurricane Katrina, the National Weather Service, the U.S. Army Corps of Engineers, and the Louisiana State University Hurricane Center joined other local, state, and federal government agencies to coordinate a simulated planning and preparedness exercise called Hurricane Pam. The Hurricane Pam exercise was created to devise a common response plan for the Louisiana–Mississippi Gulf region. Conducted in July 2004, the exercise was designed to foster the development of strategies and responses to mitigate the effects of a catastrophic hurricane in the region. The exercise focused on search-and-rescue operations, medical assistance, shelter, temporary housing, school restoration, and debris removal. Over 250 emergency preparedness personnel from fifty local, state, federal, and volunteer organizations took part in the five-day exercise.

The Hurricane Pam simulation projected scenarios more catastrophic than any that had occurred up to that time. The simulation assumed a Category 3 hurricane packing sustained winds of 120 mph with up to twenty inches of rain in southeastern Louisiana, inducing severe flooding that would breach the levees and flood the New Orleans area. The exercise assumed that large segments of the population (300,000 in total) would not evacuate in advance; 500,000 to 600,000 buildings would be severely damaged; close to 100 percent of all forms of communication would be damaged; and that 175,000 people would suffer injuries, 200,000 would become ill, and more than 60,000 would die. In addition, the simulation estimated that 1,000 shelters would be needed for evacuees and that boats and helicopters would be essential for rescue workers to aid residents stranded in floodwaters. One report predicted dire consequences: "a catastrophic flood would leave swaths of southeast Louisiana uninhabitable for more than a year."[1]

Ironically, these words would prove prophetic almost exactly one year and one month after the Hurricane Pam exercise. A number of recommendations were made as a result of the lessons learned from the exercise; unfortunately, many of these recommendations were neither fully explored nor implemented. As stated in a Senatorial Committee Report on Homeland Security and Governmental Affairs (2006):

> As a dry run for the real thing, Pam should have been a wake-up call that could not be ignored. Instead, it seems that a more appropriate name for Pam would have been Cassandra, the mythical prophet who warned of disasters but whom no one really believed. In many ways, the hypothetical problems identified in Pam predict with eerie accuracy the all-too-real problems of Katrina—overcrowded shelters undersupplied with food, water, and other essentials; blocked highways with thousands of people trapped in flooded areas; hospitals swamped with victims

---

1. H.R. Rep. No. 109-377. *A Failure of Initiative: Final Report of the Select Bipartisan Committee to Investigate the Preparation for and Response to Hurricane Katrina*, p. 81.

and running out of fuel for their emergency generators. The list goes on and on.[2]

Unfortunately, the lessons learned from the Hurricane Pam exercise did not translate into any discernible actions. The preparations actually enacted by both the NOPD and GPD during Hurricane Katrina were based on plans that had been used in the past, plans that did not reflect any of the lessons learned from Hurricane Pam.

Tornado Super Outbreak

Ironically, Tuscaloosa went through two federal security exercises that were designed to test the city's emergency response system prior to the Super Storm Outbreak disaster. The first was a tabletop exercise that took place in spring 2009 and involved a simulation of a "dirty bomb" in the Crimson Tide stadium during a football game. Sources report that the chief of the Tuscaloosa Fire Department, Alan Martin, designed the exercise to bring to light problems with the city's emergency response system (Tannenwald 2016).

Because of the findings of this exercise, Chief Alan Martin encouraged Mayor Walter Maddox to support sending city officials to the Community Specific Integrated Emergency Management Course at FEMA's National Emergency Training Center in Emmitsburg, Maryland. In January of the following year, sixty-seven leaders from the Tuscaloosa community were off to Emmitsburg, where they engaged in a weeks-long institute that focused on a series of crisis simulations. The training culminated with a simulation of a massive tornado ripping through the

---

2. Committee on Homeland Security and Governmental Affairs, U.S. Senate. 2006. *Preparing for a Catastrophe: The Hurricane Pam Exercise: Hearing Before the Comm. on Homeland Security and Governmental Affairs.*, 109th Cong. (S. Hrg. 109–403[2006], p. 2). Washington, DC: U.S. Government Printing Office. Retrieved from http://biotech.law.lsu.edu/blaw/FEMA/CHRG-109shrg26749.pdfhttp://biotech.law.lsu.edu/blaw/FEMA/CHRG-109shrg26749.pdf.

city oddly similar to the massive storm that would rip through the city just one year later.

As a result of the training in Emmitsburg, the city moved from using FEMA's Emergency Support Functions system to an incident command system. The mayor went one step further and employed incident commanders—the city's legal affairs administrator and the fire marshal—one to provide administrative skills and the other, public safety knowledge. While the dual-command system had been used in the years preceding the 2011 event, just twelve days prior to the outbreak, the city failed to use the system during a tornado event and the importance of using it became evident. This lesson resulted in the early enactment of the system prior to the Superstorm Outbreak.

Chile 2010 Earthquake and Tsunami

Chile's unique geographic nature makes it prone to natural disasters. It is susceptible to droughts, storm surges, blizzards, volcanic eruptions, wildfires, floods, landslides, tsunamis, and earthquakes. It is one of the most seismic nations in the world and, as a result, has a sophisticated earthquake detection system and national response plan. These efforts are led by ONEMI (Oficina Nacional de Emergencia del Ministerio del Interior y Seguridad Pública—Chile's national emergency service), which is in charge of coordinating the National Civil Protection System. The main mission is to plan and execute disaster-prevention measures and to identify and rehabilitate systems in collective risk situations, emergencies, and natural or human-caused disasters (ONEMI 2011). ONEMI focuses on reinforcing the Emergency and Early Warning System (Centro de Alerta Temprana—CAT—in Spanish) and strengthening the Civil Protection System. It also supports emergency responses to risky situations of various kinds throughout the country (e.g., seismic activity, tsunamis, volcanic eruptions, snow, frontal systems).

The preparation and mitigation activities managed by ONEMI strongly depend on the information provided by the U.S. Geological Survey (USGS) Earthquake Program, which has monitoring stations throughout Chile that provide data to the USGS for real-time updates on earthquake tremors and seismic threats. While currently no long-range systems exist for early earthquake warnings (the most sophisticated system can predict only several seconds in advance), the forewarning systems for tsunamis have greater prediction capabilities; and Chile has a high-tech tsunami warning system that it has used extensively.

In 2010, the tsunami alert system reportedly failed to adequately warn citizens of the risks. This failure has been cited as one of the primary causes of fatalities. In fact, it was reported that no official tsunami warnings were issued during the disaster (Fritz et al. 2011), and government officials reportedly denied the risk, even after the tsunami waves had already crashed into the coastal communities (Soulé 2012), leaving massive destruction in its wake.

Policing during Disasters

Research has shown that the efforts of law-enforcement officers during a disaster often go unnoticed, but they are typically the first responders called to the scene of a crisis and have the most significant involvement in disaster-mitigation activities (Wenger, Quarantelli, and Dynes 1989). Law-enforcement officers play a critical role in emergency-management operations during crisis situations because they are trained to expect the unexpected and to function under extreme duress. Law-enforcement officers serve as critical actors in mitigation, preparedness, response, and recovery efforts before, during, and after a disaster, and other responders rely on them to maintain order. In essence, the police serve an important function every day and provide essential services during critical incidents. According to W. Craig Fugate (2013), the former Administrator of FEMA, "The law enforcement community has two vital roles in responding to disasters: to provide for the safety and security of the community and to be first responders during times of crisis" (p. 101).

When an impending disaster is forecast and emergency preparedness activities are delegated, the police are often called on to assist with evacuation efforts, control the flow of traffic, and perform crowd control, as well as notify the public of mandatory evacuation orders, which may include going door to door to deliver the call to action. In addition, at minimum, their predisaster plans include (1) establishing memorandums of understanding with neighboring jurisdictions to assist in ensuring their continuity-of-operations plan can proceed with the necessary resources, (2) working with the local emergency operations center to determine how the police department will fold into the overall response and recovery plan established for the jurisdiction, (3) stocking up on supplies and moving sensitive materials to protected locations, (4) setting up triage in safe spaces, and (5) instructing personnel on what actions to take during an impending disaster.

It is also important to note that a police department official may be the designated incident commander for the disaster. This places the department in more of a leadership role along with the elected executive for the jurisdiction and the head of the emergency-management agency. Therefore, the police department plays an integral role in the decision making on both intergovernmental collaboration and response to the disaster, which adds to the strain on the department.

The police provide important functions during the preparedness and mitigation phases of a disaster, but they also serve an important role during the response and recovery phases. Generally, they play a key preventative role after a disaster by serving as protectors of property through their presence in business districts: they mitigate looting and other crimes. They also provide protection to critical incident sites and provide protection of citizens through community patrols. Further, the police play an active role in rescue missions during the response phase of a disaster.

Most local and state governments now have funds allocated to disaster planning and preparation efforts, and the federal government has a wealth of resources to assist. In addition to a number of grants and technical assistance programs, as of 2016,

FEMA offered twenty-five training courses for law-enforcement personnel. Though each of the grants and technical assistance programs has its own goals and objectives that police department recipients must achieve, it is important to recognize that this new funding and overall technical support for police departments has resulted in many organizational changes within law-enforcement agencies across the country. One key change has been in the organizational structure of law-enforcement agencies with the creation of bureaus or units focused solely on efforts related to homeland security, such as planning and preparing for both human-caused and natural disasters.

With this new assistance, law-enforcement agencies can create and execute comprehensive emergency-preparedness programs, and the Hurricane Katrina crisis started a national conversation on policing and emergency preparedness and response. More and more local and state governments are realizing both the unique organizational and intergovernmental role of local law-enforcement agencies and the unique experiences individual police officers bring to a disaster response. Such clarity was not present in 2005.

During the Hurricane Katrina disaster, the Tornado Super Outbreak disaster, and the 2010 tsunami disaster, the police departments played pivotal roles in assisting the citizens of their respective cities during the mitigation, response, and recovery phases of the disaster. Each police department primed its officers with information on the risk of the impending disaster and attempted to provide mitigation strategies to them (e.g., moving a family out of the path of the storm, moving vehicles to high levels). The mitigation strategies could not, however, shield the officers from most of the negative effects of the disaster on their personal and professional lives.

This truth is perhaps most evident in the role of police departments as paramilitary organizations. A strong and consistent hierarchical management structure is an integral part of ensuring that rank-and-file officers are grounded organizationally in the goals to be achieved and how and when procedures are to be executed. Unfortunately, with the elimination of communication tools and the destruction of other key resources during a disaster, this level of control was not guaranteed and management could not consistently communicate status updates to officers. This breakdown resulted in incongruent actions based on the discretion of individual officers during crisis response. Cohen, March, and Olsen (1972) argue that "where goals and technology are hazy and participation is fluid, many of the standard procedures of management collapse" (p. 2).

In the three disasters highlighted here, breakdown in hierarchical communication resulted in a misalignment of objectives, inconsistent presence and direction from management, and an added layer of stress for responding officers as the foundation in which their training was grounded was, at best, fractured during a time when they needed the guidance most. Chapter 2 expands the particulars associated with their levels of engagement with mitigation and response activities, but in an effort to provide a foundation of understanding for the manner in which police functioned during Hurricane Katrina, the Superstorm Outbreak, and the 2010 Earthquake and Tsunami disasters—and the effects of strain on the officers—the following section discusses the role of stress in policing.

All Stressed Out: Stress and Policing

The literature thoroughly documents the fact that law enforcement is a particularly stressful occupation (Goodman 1990; Violanti, Marshall, and Howe 1985), one that sometimes provokes characteristic coping strategies (Anshel, Robertson, and Caputi 1997). Stress is the body's reaction to external or internal stimuli. Stress can affect a person physically, emotionally, and mentally. "It is defined as a response to a perceived threat, challenge, or change; a physical and psychological response to any demand; and a state of psychological and physical arousal" (Mitchell and Bray 1990, p. 195).

Stress in police work can result from a number of stimuli: external stressors (e.g., frustrations with the criminal justice system, lack of public support), organizational stressors (e.g., departmental policies and procedures, paperwork, inadequate reward system), personal stressors (e.g., family conflict, financial problems), and operational stressors (e.g., intensity of responsibilities, unit morale). According to Dempsey and Forst (2013), stressors among police officers include poor training and poor pay, substandard equipment, lack of opportunity, role conflict, exposure to brutality, fears about job competence and safety, lack of job satisfaction, and fatigue.

Some of the dangers associated with policing cause stress. In particular, the loss of a fellow officer to violence and the taking of someone's life in the line of duty are among the top stressors experienced by officers (Comen and Evans 1991; Violanti and Aron 1993). The lengthy number of hours an officer works in a shift within a compressed work week (typically ten-hour schedules) also contributes to high levels of stress. Comen and Evans (1991) have also cited the bureaucratic nature of police organizations as a stressor for officers. Other research has found that the paramilitary nature of police organizations causes alienation from family and friends and the larger society (Golembiewski and Kim 1990), which can also increase stress levels.

The nature of the work in which law-enforcement officers engage exposes them to extreme circumstances that can result in high levels of stress. Such incidents are often termed *critical incidents* and are traumatic major events that can cause tremendous stress (e.g., a shooting that results in loss of life, disaster work). Stress that results from a critical incident can be a major force shaping an officer's career long after the incident is over. Such events can lead to posttraumatic stress syndrome and use of negative coping strategies. These issues are discussed in more depth in Chapter 2.

Some of the effects of the stress officers share in the profession shape police culture. Stress has been linked to the cynicism, suspiciousness, and emotional detachment that are aspects of police culture. These responses to stress can serve as barriers that officers erect to protect themselves from the emotional and psychological trauma of facing the ugly realities they encounter on the job. The stress can also lead to reductions in efficiency or can even lead to what has been referred to as retirement on the job (Cox, McCarney, and Scaramella 1987) or cause absenteeism and early retirement. Job-related stress can also lead to other negative behavioral patterns such as excessive aggressiveness, which can trigger abusive behavior and even police brutality. According to Zillmann (2013), stress "is a more likely contributor to impulsive, angry aggression" (p. 46).

Other negative coping mechanisms include alcohol and drug abuse. Stress has also been linked to marital discord and divorce among police officers, who have high rates of divorce. Stress is also believed to be associated with a host of physical health problems such as sleep disturbance, respiratory ailments, cardiovascular disease, ulcers, weight gain, and other health problems (Manzoni and Eisner 2006). As stated by Anshel (2000), "The failure to cope effectively with stress results in increased rates of heart disease, stomach disorders, divorce, alcohol and drug abuse, and suicide, as compared to the norms for the general population" (p. 376). Most insidious are the mental effects of stress that have been linked to the development of posttraumatic stress disorder and suicide. Police officers have higher suicide rates than any other profession (Friedman 1967; Kelling and Pate 1975).

Because policing is considered one of the most stressful occupations, it is assumed that officers' threshold for stress is higher than that of others outside their occupation, largely because they are routinely subjected to highly stressful situations. Studies have shown, however, that police officers tend to engage in maladaptive coping strategies such as absenteeism and substance abuse, which in turn leads to long-term chronic stress (Hurrell 1995). Moreover, according to Woody (2006), this stress often leads to severe emotional and physical consequences that cause a vast number of officers to need mental health services.

As previously noted, people respond to stress in a variety of ways and seek to manage their stress using coping strategies. Some negative responses to job stress include increased alcohol use, which is related to a higher rate of psychiatric symptoms (Ballenger et al. 2001). Burnout is another negative response to long-term job stress, and alcohol use typically increases when officers experience feelings of being overwhelmed (Cherniss 1980; Burke et al. 1984; Burke and Deszca 1986; Suresh et al. 2013).

Stress during Disasters

As noted above, police officers deal with stressful situations every day. To a certain extent, stress is an inherent part of their job and determines the type, amount, and method of training that they receive. One would assume that the occupational stress law-enforcement officers experience would prepare them for the stress experienced during a disaster. But the stress experienced during a disaster is more intense than what is generally experienced and is all-consuming. A police officer, whose job is to respond to stress-related events, is trained to gain control of the situations they encounter. The circumstances generated by a disaster, however, can be so complicated that they cannot be controlled or completely understood.

In order to properly understand the challenges a police officer faces during a disaster, it is essential to understand the nature of critical incidents. Critical incidents are defined as psychologically distressing events outside the range of usual human experiences (Wollman 1993). According to Spina (2005), the threat of a critical incident is always present because of the nature of police work. Blau (1994) adds that a critical incident has several characteristics that affect the way a police officer responds: (1) the event is unexpected; (2) the event is a threat to an officer's existence or well-being; (3) the event may include an element of loss (e.g., loved one, physical ability); and (4) the event may result in an abrupt change in the officer's values, confidence, or ideals. For this reason, a disaster can be considered the ultimate critical incident.

For a police officer acting as a first responder, the perception of the critical incident becomes increasingly distorted. This distortion causes a form of stress known as critical-incident stress. Schein et al. (2006) define critical-incident stress as a normal reaction in healthy people to an unusually traumatic event.

They further state that it is a typical response, but that does not mean there is an absence of pain; the pain alerts the individual to the fact that the situation demands attention and is part of the human drive toward survival. Critical-incident stress is simply a heightened state of arousal that results from exposure to a traumatic event (Everly and Mitchell 1997).

In a mass crisis where resources are unavailable and the emergency responders are personally affected by the critical incident physically, emotionally, or mentally, the first responder may become aware that he or she may not be able to respond on instinct. This impact stage, as the disaster has begun to take place, is commonly referred to as the "acute trauma phase" simply because, at this time, "fear and tension are extremely high . . . the focus is on survival and enduring the event intact" (Halpern and Tramontin 2006, p. 20). Schein et al. (2006) address this concern in further detail, describing three main characteristics of an emergency worker affected by the crisis: (1) the relative balance between one's thinking and emotions becomes disrupted, (2) one's usual coping methods fail to work, and (3) mild to severe impairment occurs in the individual or group involved in the crisis.

According to Halpern and Tramontin (2006), morale and tension are high in this stage as survivors and helpers focus their energies on productive but taxing activities such as search and rescue. The post-impact or recovery stage is the phase at which one achieves some sense of normality or stability; it is also, however, a time during which people fully realize what has happened. This realization can cause some emergency workers to suffer from mental illnesses such as depression and, most commonly, post-traumatic stress disorder (PTSD).

As previously noted, civilians assume that a police officer's threshold for stress is higher than those who do not choose it as an occupation. They serve several crucial functions during disasters that make them susceptible to elevated stress levels, mental strain, and physical exhaustion, all of which can affect their capacity to think clearly and work effectively. Some first responders exhibit signs of critical-incident stress at the height of a critical incident; these individuals find it difficult to focus and perform their jobs. Some show signs of being overwhelmed, while others can mask the emotions they are suffering internally. As the previous discussion highlighted, individuals who suffer from acute stress or anxiety may struggle to function effectively. Individuals who suffer from acute stress and depression may be at risk for committing suicide or abandoning their post. Exposure to a major disaster can cause people to fear the loss of life personally, and confrontation with one's mortality can lead to negative and maladaptive behaviors (Arndt et al. 1999; Pyszczynski, Greenberg, and Solomon 1999). Some of the maladaptive responses include suicide, panic, flight, and disaster syndrome. While these responses have typically been rare (Tienney 2008), as in most of the disaster sites examined in this book, the stories collected from the Katrina disaster illustrate that some individuals do respond in such a manner. Chapter 3 further explores these issues.

The Impact of Stress on Police

The literature informs us that when people encounter large traumatic events, such as a natural disaster, they can experience short-term and sometimes long-term emotional and psychological effects. Depression, acute stress, and PTSD may develop as a consequence of participation in disaster rescue efforts (Fullerton, Ursano, and Wang 2004). The onset of these conditions can occur immediately after a critical incident or up to a year after serving as a first responder. Critical-incident stress debriefings are a useful tool for reducing the levels of stress among disaster and rescue workers (Everly and Boyle 1999; Hokanson and Wirth 2000). Some, however, have questioned whether the process is valid and whether it reduces stress among first responders (Begley 2003; Kenardy et al. 1996).

PTSD is a type of anxiety disorder that someone may exhibit after having been exposed to a traumatic event. The three major symptoms of PTSD are (1) reliving the event in such a manner that it disturbs daily activities, (2) avoidance, and (3) arousal. Research has shown that those most at risk for a traumatic stress response are disaster workers who were exposed to or experienced life-threatening danger or physical harm, extreme environmental destruction, loss of home and community, loss of contact and support from loved ones, intense emotional demands, extreme fatigue or sleep deprivation, and deleterious weather conditions (West et al. 2008).

According to a study that the Centers for Disease Control and Prevention and the National Institute for Occupational Safety and Health (2009) conducted, 26 percent of NOPD officers surveyed reported symptoms of major depression. The depression was associated with minimal family contact, family member injury, witnessing an assault, living in an uninhabitable house, and isolation from regular NOPD assignments. Studies (e.g., Briere and Elliott 2000; Galea, Nandi, and Vlahov 2005; Harville, Jacobs, and Boynton-Jarrett 2015) that have examined disaster exposure on the general population have found that personal loss is a major risk factor for depression (West et al. 2008). It is also important to note that, according to Galea et al. (2005), the rate of PTSD is lower among rescue workers than it is among "direct victims of disasters" (p. 84). Some studies report that between 30 percent to 40 percent of disaster victims will experience PTSD, compared to a rate of 10 percent to 20 percent among rescue workers (Schlenger et al. 2002; Turner et al. 1995; Havennar et al. 1997). Other studies show the rate of PTSD among rescue workers to be as low as 5 or 6 percent to a high of 32 percent (McFarlane et al. 2009; Fullerton et al. 2004; Guo et al. 2004; North et al. 2002). Javidi and Yadollahie (2012) found a PTSD rate of 30–40 percent among direct victims of a disaster and 10–30 percent in rescue workers. Other research, however, has found that emergency responders are at a higher risk of PTSD (e.g., Bryant and Harvey 1995; Fullerton et al. 2004; Ginexi et al. 2000). Whether responders are ultimately found to be more or less at risk for PTSD than nonresponders, it is clear that responders are yet personally affected by a disaster: they, too, are direct victims.

Interviews with law-enforcement officers who have experienced various disasters within diverse social and cultural contexts (e.g., New Orleans, Louisiana; Gulfport, Mississippi; Tuscaloosa, Alabama; Santiago and Constitución, Chile) have revealed that many still suffer the effects of disaster response years after a disaster. During several of the interviews conducted by the authors of this book, some of the first responders articulated a deep sense of sadness about their time working as a first responder, and it is evident that the wounds of a disaster do not easily heal for some.

These battle scars of disaster work are caused by the various emotional responses that are associated with being a victim of a disaster, but some of the injuries cannot be quantified. Many officers have lived experiences that they carry deep within themselves, a fact that we further expound on in Chapter 6. Hence, even if PTSD is not experienced by most of the officers working during a disaster, it is critical to highlight that the effects of these events on the officers do not end after the recovery process begins in the affected sites: sometimes these officers are still in a recovery phase for years after the disaster. As one officer in Gulfport, Mississippi, stated,

> It goes back to as a police officer you are always dealing with situations, you're used to stressing, you're used to trying to figure things out on the run. We're always faced with the unknown, even though you do the same job day in and day out it's always different people, which makes it unknown. So, the ability to think quick on the feet [and] prior experience gives you that, it provides you with the ability to be a problem solver. Well, this put everybody to the test and some it even broke them during the test.

It is also imperative to highlight that research has shown that "despite the heavy toll of work-related stressors on the morale and psyche of police officers, when under stress they are reluctant to seek professional psychological help as its use implies weakness, cowardice, and an inability to perform the job effectively" (Levenson 2003). The desire to keep up the appearance of being emotionally and psychologically strong appears to be a long-standing tradition within the field of policing, and it is common for officers to avoid seeking mental health care from professionals. Chapter 7 addresses the topic in more depth.

Although many officers experience acute stress, not all emergency workers develop mental health problems. In fact—according to authors Halpern and Tramontin (2006) in their book *Disaster Mental Health: Theory and Practice (Crisis Intervention)*—emergency workers, including firefighters, police officers, and paramedics, are less likely to develop PTSD than members of the public. They further explain that only 1 percent of rescue workers developed post-disaster panic disorders, in comparison with 6 percent of the civilian survivors. With research suggesting that a significant percentage of emergency workers do not exhibit high rates of PTSD, it can be concluded that it is possible to overcome trauma and experience through personal growth (Tramontin and Halpern 2007). This is commonly referred to as posttraumatic growth, or PTG. Tedeschi and Calhoun (1996) defined posttraumatic growth as "positive psychological change experienced as a result of the struggle with highly challenging life circumstances" (p. 455). Research has shown that persons who claim that trauma was beneficial gave the following reasons: (1) stronger religious convictions, (2) more enjoyment of life, (3) a new appreciation for life, (4) discovery of new possibilities for themselves, (5) a feeling of more personal strength and (6) more appreciation for others (Tedeschi and Calhoun 1996). Chapter 6 further addresses these issues.

Conclusion

When disasters strike, they have the power to displace all sense of normality, including the operations of law-enforcement agencies. Disasters of certain types can drastically affect the ability of law-enforcement agencies to respond effectively to the crisis at hand. The challenges that an agency confront depend on the scope of the disaster and the effect it has on the infrastructure, landscape, and distribution of resources. Disasters also affect law-enforcement officers both professional and personally.

The professional effects range from operational to logistical and organizational. The depths of the effects depend on the type of disaster and the scope of the devastation. Most of the police agencies examined in this book had to contend with the loss of communication capabilities, loss of multiple police stations and police headquarters, and a scarcity of adequate food and water supplies. In some of these cases, the agencies also had to deal with an absence of basic equipment, lack of housing, and a drastic reduction in sleep. The dearth of the resources can acutely affect the normal operational protocols of law-enforcement operations. It can also disrupt the hierarchical order of a department and affect how the officers feel about their roles in the disaster response.

Although police officers are often used to dealing with stressful situations, the weightiness of the circumstances presented during a disaster intensifies stress levels among the officers. This heightened sense of stress can affect the behavioral responses of officers during disasters. Although the majority of officers can function appropriately and carry out their responsibilities, some officers find it difficult to manage the strains imposed on them during these events and engage in maladaptive behaviors, including absenteeism and misconduct. While most of these responses have been cited as a nonissue within first-responder communities during disasters, such issues arose during the Hurricane Katrina disaster. Currently, there are no public reports of absenteeism or misconduct among the officers who served during the Superstorm Outbreak or the 2010 Chilean earthquake and tsunami.

KEY TAKEAWAYS FROM THIS CHAPTER

1. Three major conditions affect recovery operations: (1) the expanse of the geography affected by the incident, (2) the duration of the preparation period, and (3) the timing of the onset of the disaster.
2. The critical factor that most affects preparation and mitigation activities is the amount of time between

the prediction of the critical incident and the onset of the event. Consequently, preparation and mitigation activities are possible before the onset of some disaster types (e.g., hurricanes, tornadoes) but not for others (e.g., earthquake, terrorist attacks).
3. There are both maladaptive and adaptive behavioral responses to the extreme stress caused by disasters.
4. Of all the police departments examined in this book, NOPD is the largest police department: it is more than twice the size of the other departments discussed (e.g., GPD, and the Carabineros de Chile). It also has a complicated history, part of which has been marked by a reputation of corruption, which may account for some of the manifestations of stress that are discussed later herein.
5. Police who serve as first responders to disasters are at risk of both short-term and long-term adverse emotional and psychological effects. Police officers who serve as first responders are at risk of PTSD acute stress and depression. Some first responders, however, experience the opposite of PTSD—PTG.
6. While there is mixed evidence on the validity of critical-incident stress debriefings, some have considered it a useful tool to use during disasters.

DISCUSSION QUESTIONS

1. Reflect on the distinguishing features of the disasters examined in this book (Hurricane Katrina, the Superstorm Outbreak, and the Earthquake in Constitución, Chile). How do you think the differences in the spatial and temporal characteristics affected the ability of the communities to prepare for the impending disasters?
2. How do the preparedness and mitigation activities of police officers before a disaster differ from their traditional responsibilities?

3. Which disaster type appears to be the most difficult to prepare for and why?
4. What are the differences and similarities between the stress police officers typically experience in the line of work and during a disaster?
5. What is PTSD, and is there conclusive evidence that suggests it should be an expected response to disaster work?

REFERENCES

"Alabama Tornado Disaster Leaves Thousands without Homes in Birmingham, Tuscaloosa." 2011. *Huffington Post*, May 5. https://www.huffingtonpost.com/2011/05/05/alabama-tornado-disaster-_n_858130.html.

Arndt, Jamie, Jeff Greenberg, Sheldon Solomon, Tom Pyszczynski, and Jeff Schimel. 1999. "Creativity and Terror Management: Evidence That Creative Activity Increases Guilt and Social Projection following Mortality Salience." *Journal of Personality and Social Psychology* 77:19–32.

Ballenger, James C., Jonathan R. Davidson, Yves Lecrubier, David J. Nutt, Thomas D. Borkovec, Karl Rickels, D. J. Stein, et al. 2001. "Consensus Statement on Generalized Anxiety Disorder from the International Consensus Group on Depression and Anxiety." *Journal of Clinical Psychiatry* 62 (Supp. 11): 53–58.

Bárcena, Alicia, Antonio Prado, Laura López, and Joseluls Samaniego. 2010. *The Chilean Earthquake of 27 February 2010—an Overview*. Santiago, Chile: Comisión Económica para América Latina y el Caribe.

Begley, Sharon. 2003. "Is Trauma Debriefing Worse Than Letting Victims Heal Naturally?" *Wall Street Journal*, September 12. http://online.wsj.com/article/0,,SB10633129057000400,00.html.

Blau, Theodore. H. 1994. *Psychological Services for Law Enforcement*. New York: Wiley.

Briere, John, and Diana J. Elliott. 2000. "Prevalence, Characteristics, and Long-Term Sequelae of Natural Disaster Exposure in the General Population." *Trauma Stress* 13 (4): 661–679.

Brown, Robbie, and Katharine Q. Seelye. 2011. "A Chaotic Flurry of Twisters That Spread Devastation Fast and Wide." *New York Times*, April 28.

Bryant, Richard A., and Allison G. Harvey. 1995. "Posttraumatic Stress in Volunteer Firefighters: Predictors of Distress." *Journal of Nervous and Mental Disease* 183 (4): 267–271.

Cohen, Michael D., James G. March, and Johan P. Olsen. 1972. "A Garbage Can Model of Organizational Choice." *Administrative Science Quarterly* 17:1–25.

Comen, Greg, and Barry Evans. 1991. "Stressors Facing Australian Police in the 1990s." *Police Studies* 14:153–165.

"Death Toll from Katrina Likely Higher Than 1,300." 2006. Associated Press, February 10. http://www.nbcnews.com/id/11281267/ns/us_news-katrina_the_long_road_back/t/death-toll-katrina-likely-higher/.

Everly Jr., George S., and Stephen H. Boyle. 1999. "Critical Incident Stress Debriefing (CISD): A Meta-analysis." *International Journal of Emergency Mental Health* 1 (3): 165–168.

Everly Jr., George S., and Jeffrey T. Mitchell. 1999. *Critical Incident Stress Management (CISM): A New Era and Standard in Crisis Intervention.* Ellicott City, MD: Chevron.

Friedman, Paul. 1967. "Suicide among Police." In *Essays in Self-Destruction*, edited by E. S. Schneidman, 414–449. New York: Science House.

Fritz, Herman. M., Catherine M. Petroff, Patricio Catalan, Rodrigo Cienfuegos, Patricio Winckler, Nikos Kalligeris, Robert Weiss, et al. 2011. "Field Survey of the 27 February 2010 Chile Tsunami." *Pure Applied Geophysics* 168 (11): 1989–2010.

Fugate, W. Craig. 2013. "From the Administrator: Law Enforcement's Role in Responding to Disasters." *Police Chief* 80 (August): 100–101.

Fullerton, Carol S., Robert J. Ursano, and Leming Wang. 2004. "Acute Stress Disorder, Posttraumatic Stress Disorder, and Depression in Disaster or Rescue Workers." *American Journal of Psychiatry* 161 (8): 1370–1376.

Galea, Sandro, Arijit Nandi, and David Vlahov. 2005. "The Epidemiology of Post-traumatic Stress Disorder after Disasters." *Epidemiology Review* 27 (1): 78–91.

Ginexi, Elizabeth M., Karen Weihs, Samuel J. Simmens, and Danny R. Hoyt. 2000. "Natural Disaster and Depression: A Prospective Investigation of Reactions to the 1993 Midwest Floods." *American Journal of Community Psychology* 28:495–518.

Golembiewski, Robert T., and Byong-Seob Kim. 1990. "Burnout in Police Work: Stressors, Strain, and the Phase Model." *Police Studies* 13:74–80.

Goodman, Alan M. 1990. "A Model for Police Officer Burnout." *Journal of Business and Psychology* 5 (1): 85–99.

Gupton, Herbert M., Evan Axelrod, Luz Cornell, Stephen F. Curran, Carol J. Hood, Jennifer Kelly, and Jon Moss. 2012. "Support and Sustain: Psychological Intervention for Law Enforcement Personnel." *Police Chief Magazine*, July 16. https://doc.uments.com/download/s-support-and-sustain-psychological-intervention-for-law-enforcement.pdf.

Halpern, James, and Mary Tramontin. 2006. *Disaster Mental Health: Theory and Practice.* Belmont, CA: Brooks/Cole.

Harville, Emily W., Marni Jacobs, and Renee Boynton-Jarrett. 2015. "When Is Exposure to a Natural Disaster Traumatic? Comparison of a Trauma Questionnaire and Disaster Exposure Inventory." *PLoS ONE* 10 (4). https://doi.org/10.1371/journal.pone.0123632.

Hurrell, Joseph J. 1995. "Police Work, Occupational Stress and Individual Coping." *Journal of Organizational Behavior* 16:27–28.

Javidi, Hojjatollah, and Mahboobeh Yadollahie. 2012. "Post-traumatic Stress Disorder." *International Journal of Occupational and Environmental Medicine* 3 (1): 2–9.

Kelling, George L., and Mary Ann Pate. 1975. "The Person-Role Fit in Policing: The Current Knowledge." In *Job Stress and the Police Officer: Identifying Stress Reduction Techniques: Proceedings of Symposium, Cincinnati, Ohio, May 8–9, 1975*, edited by W. H. Kroes and J. J. Hurrell, 117–129. Bethesda, MD: U.S. Dept. of Health, Education, and Welfare, Public Health Service, Center for Disease Control, National Institute for Occupational Safety and Health, Division on Biomedical and Behavioral Science.

Kenardy, Justin A., Rosemary A. Webster, Terry J. Lewin, Vaughn J. Carr, Philip L. Hazell, and Gregory L. Carter. 1996. "Stress Debriefing and Patterns of Recovery following a Natural Disaster." *Journal of Traumatic Stress* 9 (1): 37–49.

Koch, Kathleen. 2010. *Rising from Katrina: How My Mississippi Hometown Lost It All and Found What Mattered*. Bay Saint Louis, MO: John F. Blair.

Levenson, Richard L., and Lauren A. Dwyer. (2003). "Peer Support in Law Enforcement: Past, Present, and Future." *International Journal of Emergency Mental Health* 5 (3):147–152.

Manzoni, Patrik, and Manuel Eisner. 2006. "Violence between the Police and the Public: Influences of Work-Related Stress, Job Satisfaction, Burnout, and Situational Factors." *Criminal Justice and Behavior* 33 (5): 613–645.

McFarlane, Alexander C., Penny Williamson, and Christopher A. Barton. 2009. "The Impact of Traumatic Stressors in Civilian Occupational Settings." *Journal of Public Health Policy* 30 (3): 311–327.

Mohr, Holbrook. 2011. "Tornadoes Devastate South, Killing at Least 297." *Deseret News*, April 29. http://www.deseretnews.com/article/700131129/Tornadoes-devastate-South-killing-at-least-297.html?s_cid=rss-5.

Pyszczynski, Tom, Jeff D. Greenberg, and Sheldon Solomon. 1999. "A Dual-Process Model of Defense against Conscious and Unconscious Death-Related Thoughts: An Extension of Terror Management Theory." *Psychological Review* 106 (4): 835–845.

Schein, Leon. A., Henry I. Spitz, Gary M. Burlingame, and Phillip R. Muskin (Eds.). 2006. *Psychological Effects of Catastrophic Disasters: Group Approaches to Treatment* (Shannon Vargo, Collaborator). New York: Haworth Press.

Simmons, Kevin M., and Sutter Daniel. 2012. *Deadly Season: Analyzing the 2011 Tornado Outbreaks*. Boston, MA: American Meteorological Society.

Soulé, Bastien. 2012. "Coupled Seismic and Socio-political Crises: The Case of Puerto Aysen in 2007." *Journal of Risk Research* 15 (1): 21–37.

Sterud, Tom, Erlend Hem, Øivind Ekeberg, and Bjorn Lau. 2007. "Occupational Stress and Alcohol Use: A Study of Two Nationwide Samples of Operational Police and Ambulance Personnel in Norway." *Journal of Studies on Alcohol and Drugs* 68 (6): 896–904.

Tanglao, Leezel, and Ben Forer. 2011. "Tornadoes and Storms Tear through South; at Least 292 Dead." *ABC News*, April 28. http://abcnews.go.com/US/tornadoes-storms-tear-south-292-dead/story?id=13474955.

Tannenwald, David. 2016. *Ready in Advance: The City of Tuscaloosa's Response to the 4/27/11 Tornado*. Cambridge, MA: Harvard Kennedy School Institute of Politics.

Tedeschi, Richard G., and Lawrence. G. Calhoun. 1996. "Post-traumatic Growth Inventory: Measuring the Positive Legacy of Trauma." *Journal of Traumatic Stress* 9:455–471.

Tramontin, Mary, and James Halpern. 2007. "The Psychological Aftermath of Terrorism: The 2001 World Trade Center Attack." In *Trauma Psychology: Issues in Violence, Disaster, Health and Illness*, edited by E. K. Carll, 1–32. Westport, CT: Praeger.

Violanti, John M., and Fred Aron. 1993. "Sources of Police Stressors, Job Attitudes and Psychological Distress." *Psychological Reports* 72:899–904.

Violanti, John M., James R. Marshall, and Barbara Howe. 1985. "Stress, Coping, and Alcohol Use: The Police Connection." *Journal of Police Science and Administration* 13 (2): 106–110.

Wenger, Dennis E., E. L. Quarantelli, and Russell R. Dynes. 1989. *Disaster Analysis: Police and Fire Departments: Final Report #37*. Newark: University of Delaware Disaster Research Center.

West, Christine, Bruce Bernard, Charles Mueller, Margaret Kitt, Richard Driscoll, and Sangwoo Tak. 2008. "Mental Health Outcomes in Police Personnel after Hurricane Katrina." *Journal of Occupational and Environmental Medicine* 50 (6): 689–695.

Whoriskey, Peter. 2006. "Katrina Displaced 400,000, Study Says." *Washington Post*, June 7. http://www.washingtonpost.com/wp-dyn/content/article/2006/06/06/AR2006060601729.html.

Woody, Henley Robert. 2006. "Family Interventions with Law Enforcement Officers." *American Journal of Family Therapy* 34 (2): 95–103.

Zillmann, Dolf. 2013. "Cognition-Excitation Interdependences in Escalation of Anger and Angry Aggression." In *The Dynamics of Aggression: Biological and Social Processes in Dyad and Groups*, edited by M. Potegal and J. F. Knutson, 45–71. Mahwah, NJ: L. Erlbaum Associates.

2

Unusual Circumstances and Unusual Challenges

Dilemmas Faced by Law Enforcement Officers during Disasters

In the early morning hours of Monday, August 29, holed up about eight long city blocks away from Clarkson at the Hyatt, was Deputy Chief of Police Warren Riley, his face bitten by anguish. About five inches of water was already flowing down South White Street behind the NOPD headquarters, and the storm had just started kicking in. The telephones and radios were still working; in the first twenty-three minutes after wind speeds exceeded 80 mph, there were more than six hundred 911 calls, mostly from New Orleans East, the rest of the Ninth Ward, and Lakeview. His dispatchers were overwhelmed: roofs were blowing off, levees were breaching, storm surges were topping flood walls, sewers were backing up, homes were being destroyed, and people were dying. The NOPD saved the SOS tapes—the most heart-wrenching historic artifact of the entire Katrina saga. Just imagine the agony of being a dispatcher, receiving a 911 call with a woman screaming that her son or daughter was going to die, and all you could do was say, "After the storm." The NOPD was going to need therapists and psychiatrists when the atmosphere settled—a trainload of them. An impatient

Riley paced about like a caged tiger, tormented that he couldn't do anything to help these poor drowning souls. (Brinkley 2006, pp. 138–139)

The above text was taken from Douglas Brinkley's *The Great Deluge*. It exemplifies the extreme nature of the challenges faced by first responders during major crises. This chapter examines the experiences of law-enforcement departments and their officers in the line of duty during Hurricane Katrina; the Tuscaloosa, Alabama, Tornado Super Outbreak; and the Chilean earthquake and tsunami disasters with a particular focus on the events in New Orleans because of the idiosyncrasies of the crisis in this city. This chapter addresses the following questions: (1) How do disasters challenge the typical operational protocols of policing? (2) How do police departments come back from the brink of collapse? (3) What are the behavioral responses of officers affected by an extreme crisis?

The Impact of Disasters on Standard Police Operations

A considerable number of definitions have been developed to characterize disasters; for the purposes of this book, we use the definition developed by Charles Fritz, who is considered a pioneer in disaster research. According to Fritz (1961), a disaster is "an event concentrated in time and space, in which a society or one of its subdivisions undergoes physical harm and social disruption, such that all or some essential functions of the society or subdivision are impaired" (p. 655). Disasters of a certain magnitude and scope can have devastating short- and long-term effects on individual victims and on the social and economic order of society. From the annihilation of modern technological tools to the loss of basic resources such as clean water, disasters force the normal systems of society out of balance.

First responder agencies are not immune to the devastating effects of disasters. The police departments examined in this book experienced a plethora of negative impacts, including the loss of staff, contact with loved ones, essential equipment, access to resources, and communication capabilities. The departments also suffered from major infrastructure damages, including the loss of police stations in Tuscaloosa, Alabama, and Constitución, Chile, and the loss of both police headquarters and police stations in New Orleans, Louisiana, and Gulfport, Mississippi.

The myriad challenges faced by the police departments during the disasters made it impossible to operate with normal standards and protocols. In some cases, the departments reverted to the days before the advent of modern tools that typify contemporary policing. In his book *Why Law Enforcement Organizations Fail*, O'Hara (2005, p. 7) argues that "law enforcement agencies fail because of deeply rooted and largely hidden defects of [organizational] structure, culture and collective behavior [that] are embedded in the everyday life of any organization." As officers sought to rely on the instructions, policies, and procedures on which they were trained and that they utilized daily to execute their job duties, as the personal stories of officers attest, it became clear early on in the disasters that that training would prove irrelevant. In fact, in each of the cases examined here, normal police operations were severely disrupted in their (1) standard operational procedures, (2) normal modes of communication, (3) hierarchical order in the chain of command, and (4) ability to respond to calls for service.

Together, the effects of these challenges can accumulate to such an extent as to severely hamper the ability of police to function effectively. In fact, a disaster of a certain size and kind can throw the entire system into a crisis. This observation suggests that more attention needs to be paid to the link between the individual stressors that police officers face during disaster response and the planning that happens at the organizational level to prepare officers for alternative forms of discretionary decision making during nonroutine response assignments such as disasters. To provide an example of what this process might look like, the next section of the chapter briefly reviews the events that took place during the Hurricane Katrina disaster and underscores the differences between the impact of this disaster on the police departments in New Orleans and Gulfport and the impact of other disasters examined herein.

When Disaster Strikes, Chaos Follows

The Hurricane Katrina Disaster

Hurricane Katrina hit the city of New Orleans on Monday August 29, 2005, just after 6:10 A.M., setting the city's police department into a chaotic tailspin. Within the first twenty-three minutes of the storm, the NOPD received over six hundred emergency calls for service from citizens (Superintendent W. Riley, personal communication, August 2007; Brinkley 2006). The high winds and heavy rainfall made it impossible for the department to respond to calls, setting the stage for what would be the beginning of a frenzied and exhausting time for the NOPD (W. Riley, personal communication, August 2007).

After Katrina had swept past New Orleans, the officers were mostly unaware of the impact of the storm on the city: as some officers reported, they believed the city had endured the hurricane with minimal damage (police Lt. Marlon DeFillio, personal communication, August 2006; Adams and Stewart 2014). Soon thereafter, the officers began to notice that the floodwaters began to rise instead of receding, indicating this was not like other recent storm experiences (M. DeFillio, personal communication, August 2006; Adams and Stewart 2014). Before dawn on August 29, 2005, over 80 percent of the city was under as much as twenty feet of water (EMAC 2006).

The floodwaters and high winds devastated the city, and the NOPD was not impervious to the devastation. The police headquarters, three of the district police stations were flooded, and many of the department's police vehicles became inoperable from flood damage. As we discuss below, the department also found itself without the necessary boating equipment needed for the storm's aftermath: the boats could not be reached because they were kept in storage in the Lower Ninth Ward, which suffered damages from a break in the city's levee system. (See

Figure 2.1 A break in the levee that caused a neighborhood to flood. Neighborhoods throughout the area remained flooded as a result of Hurricane Katrina. (FEMA/Jocelyn Augustino)

Figure 2.1.) In addition, the city's communication system was destroyed, and backup power generators also failed, leaving much of the city without electricity.

In addition to the infrastructural challenges, the department was beset with pleas for help from the citizen's as well as fellow officers. According to Superintendent Riley (personal communication, August 3, 2006), some officers who were preparing for the storm at home or in other locations around the city found themselves in the midst of rising floodwaters. In the wake of the disaster, the NOPD rescued ninety-one officers (Adams and Stewart 2014). Over 80 percent of force members lost their homes, and 30 percent of them did not know the whereabouts of loved ones after the storm passed over the city (Adams et al. 2011).

The damaged infrastructure of the department also severely hampered the flow of communication and disrupted the chain of command during the disaster. Some officers found themselves stranded and some reported having no directives for actions to take immediately after the disaster. This complication was exemplified by the description of one officer's experience during Katrina: "Everything was in chaos. I could not locate my supervisor. . . . Basically, it was every man for himself." The inability to communicate frustrated the officers and made it difficult for the department to dispatch orders and fully assess the situation. The NOPD found itself beset with multiple challenges during Hurricane Katrina that critically restricted the department's capabilities, and many of its officers found themselves facing circumstances that extended beyond their training.

Although Gulfport, Mississippi, did not receive the same level of news coverage as New Orleans, it also experienced catastrophic conditions as a result of the storm. The storm hit the shores of Gulfport on August 29, 2005, with the storm surge reaching the shorelines a little after 6:00 A.M. The right quadrant of the storm, carrying the strongest winds and the peak storm surge, hit Gulfport at 11:00 A.M., leaving massive destruction in its wake.

Overall, Gulfport experienced storm surges up to 24.5 feet, with sustained winds of 46 to 104 mph, resulting in a tremendous amount of damage. In Mississippi, there were 238 fatalities, approximately 169,000 houses were destroyed, and other houses sustained significant damage. Many of the houses were flooded up to the second or third floors, with some structures completely submerged in water. The force of winds and rain moved others completely off their foundations. Many businesses in the city of Gulfport experienced major damage as well. For example, the casinos, which were once located on barges off the shores of the city, were moved by the storm surges onto the city's streets and onto Highway 10. The city was also littered with snapped trees and debris, and the toppling of the trees, power lines, and cellphone towers resulted in the loss of communication systems.

In essence, the city of Gulfport was turned upside down. Consequently, the officers of the GPD found themselves mired by the devastation caused by Katrina. As with the NOPD,

Katrina also destroyed the GPD police headquarters, electrical power was unavailable, cell phones were inoperable for days after the storm, and police substations were also destroyed. Likewise, many of the officers in Gulfport lost their homes, were unsure whether their loved ones were safe, and were without a functioning communication system, further complicating the functions of the police department. In addition, large pieces of debris and trees clogged roadways, hampering the ability of first responders and volunteers to aid victims of the storm. In some instances, the debris and downed power lines made traveling across the cities extremely difficult, and it was nearly impossible to reach some locations. Hence, the police department had to wait for the debris to be cleared before they could enter a community to provide assistance.

The fundamental difference between the levels of devastation experienced in the two cities was that multiple breaks in the levee system protecting the city from Lake Pontchartrain caused most of the severe damage in New Orleans and made that damage more widespread. In Gulfport, damages were principally the result of storm surges and high winds, creating a dividing line in Gulfport that marked the locations with the most severe damages. Katrina caused a tremendous amount of destruction in both Gulfport and New Orleans: consequently, most of the officers of both police departments were either affected personally or were plagued with professional challenges by the disaster.

The disruptive impact of Hurricane Katrina on the police agencies of New Orleans and Gulfport illustrates the unpredictable nature of disasters and the obstacles they can put in the way of operations of policing agencies. While different in scale and scope, the Tornado Super Outbreak and the 2010 earthquake and tsunami provide additional examples of the unpredictable nature of disasters.

The Super Outbreak Disaster

The devastation caused by the Tornado Super Outbreak followed the comparatively narrow but long path of the EF 5 tornado that touched down in Tuscaloosa, Alabama, on April 29 2011. Dubbed the "Monster Storm," the storm was a mile wide with a trail of destruction three hundred miles long. Along with the destruction of hundreds of homes and businesses, the storm severely damaged a police station and wiped out the headquarters for the city's Emergency Management Office, the Red Cross, and the Salvation Army. The loss of these agencies challenged the disaster-response protocols that relied on the Emergency Management Office. The city also suffered from gaps in its communication systems from damage to the power lines and communication towers from the storm. The storm left massive amounts of debris in the streets, making it almost impossible to move from one city block to another in some neighborhoods.

The Earthquake and Tsunami Disaster in Chile

The 2010 Earthquake and Tsunami disaster in Chile affected a larger geographic landscape than the other disasters. Unlike the Katrina or Tornado Super Outbreak disasters, the earthquake was not predicted, and therefore neither the first-responder agencies nor the public took any preparation or mitigation actions before the event. Seasoned first responders are aware of the risk for tsunamis after earthquakes, and soon after the earthquake, tsunami warnings were issued along the shores of Chile. The Chilean Navy's emergency plans allow officials in each port to sound alarms automatically when a rise in the sea is detected without waiting for an order from above. However, the effectiveness of the warning systems has come under criticism. Major public officials such as President Verónica Michelle Bachelet played down the threat of the risk of tsunami, saying large waves were expected but not a tsunami ("Chile Minister" 2010; Sabloff 2010). Hence, despite the warning systems that are in place, the conflicting messages given to the public reduced the effectiveness of this system.

More than 2 million people were affected by the Chile disaster, and more than 500 people died—as many as 350 lost their lives in Constitución alone. The earthquake resulted in significant infrastructure damage, including the destruction of over 440,000 buildings, critical structures like schools and hospitals among them. A total of 212 bridges were destroyed and many roadways were rendered undrivable.

The strength of the earthquake caused the city of Constitución to move at least 10 feet to the west and the capital Santiago moved about 11 inches to the west-southwest. The government and the Chilean Red Cross set up over 100 temporary villages to provide housing to those who were rendered homeless by the earthquake. Although the quake hit the affected communities hard, it was reportedly responsible for fewer than 10 deaths. A large number of fatalities resulted from the tsunami, which started less than 15 minutes after the earthquake, striking the coastal communities. The cities of Santiago and Constitución suffered different impacts from the earthquake and tsunami. Constitución experienced more destruction of its built environment, major gaps in its communication systems, and a direct hit from the tsunami. Santiago, slightly more inland, also suffered from multiple fatalities and major infrastructure damage, including damage to its airport; a highway bridge and buildings collapsed; but it was not in the path of the tsunami.

The Bottom Line

All four of the examined disasters resulted in the loss of access to modern technologies that provide both conveniences and the communication and infrastructure resources that first-responder agencies rely on, complicating their ability to fulfill their normal policing duties and first responder responsibilities. Differences in disaster type, however, affected the preparation and mitigation efforts of first-responder agencies differently. Hurricanes and tornadoes can be predicted days in advance, but there are still no reliable methods of predicting earthquakes, and the warning time for a tsunami threat within the affected earthquake zones is twenty minutes or less. Regardless of such organizational challenges, police agencies have to be responsive to the needs of the community. As Reiss (1971) has indicated, the police are "the major emergency arm of the community in times of personal and public crisis" (pp. 1–2). Hence, it is expected that they will be present and fully engaged in responding to a disaster.

Finding Order Creatively Out of Chaos

The events of a disaster can force policing agencies to shift from relying on traditional methods of policing to developing alternative methods. One of the greatest harmful impacts of Katrina on both the NOPD and the GPD was the loss of traditional communication capabilities. The Tuscaloosa Police Department and the Constitución Police Department also suffered from a loss of communication capabilities, but the interruption was not as widespread as what the NOPD and the GPD suffered.

Both the NOPD and the GPD relied on nontraditional approaches to mitigate the challenge. For example, when faced with the inability to use both landlines and cell phones during Hurricane Katrina, the NOPD used a mutual aid channel to communicate (First Response Coalition 2005). Mutual aid channels or mutual aid frequencies are public safety spectrum bands that are set aside by the Federal Communication Commission for interagency public safety coordination (Federal Communication Commission 2018; Szalajeski 2007). Unfortunately, the fire department needed to use the same spectrum, and the urgent need for both agencies to use the spectrum at the same time diminished the ability of both to communicate effectively. The inability to use the regular modes of communication and the secondary mutual aid channel system forced the NOPD to establish an alternative communication system that relied on runners to physically deliver messages between police units and top management (M. DeFillio, personal communication, August 2006; First Response Coalition 2005). The NOPD's predicament and its solution illustrates dynamism of a disaster's effects and the need for departments to be able to develop alternative methods for critical departmental functions.

The loss of communication and damaged infrastructure punctuate the need to be flexible throughout the system in both police departments. In the case of the NOPD, the reliance on messenger-based methods of communication after the storm slowed the flow of information between the police units and top officials. This required isolated officers and district commanders to rely on their own assessments of the crisis within their scope of vision. As a result, mid- and lower-level ranking officers had to step up and play a more active leadership role (Terry Ebbert, former New Orleans Homeland Security Director, personal communication, August 2006), and rely on the little information available to them to carry out response missions and make decisions at the lowest level. Interviews with GPD officers also revealed that mid- and lower-level officers within that agency took it upon themselves to develop their own "form of communication through talkabouts [two-way radios]" in response to the confusion on the radio traffic (anonymous interview, 2010). As one officer stated, "Officers took this initiative on their own minus administration" (anonymous interview, 2010). As hierarchical paramilitary organizations, police departments are very traditional organizations and do not usually rely on lower- and mid-level leadership to such an extent. The shift in responsibility did not reflect the hierarchical order of the force, but instead reflected what was necessary in a time of a crisis.

Another unusual circumstance police agencies may find themselves in during a major critical event is insufficiencies in supplies, including basic equipment, food, and water. For example, the NOPD stored their powerboats used for hurricane events along the docks in the Lower Ninth Ward, which was affected heavily by storm surge as well as breaks in the city's levee system. Consequently, the boats could not be retrieved, which was a major setback to the effective operations of the force. Some officers reported commandeering boats from citizens in the wake of the storm to conduct rescue and response missions (M. DeFillio, personal communication 2006). In addition, many of the department's police cars were submerged underwater by the massive flooding, rendering them inoperable. In short, the department had a major transportation crisis.

The loss of normal modes of transportation also came up as an issue during the disasters in Tuscaloosa and Constitución. Officials in Tuscaloosa reported having difficulty traversing the city's streets as a result of the debris that blocked major roadways. Officials with ONEMI in Chile reported that for the first couple of days after the disaster, Constitución could be reached only by plane. This greatly challenged emergency response efforts, as first responders had to take circuitous routes to provide support to the public and first responders agents.

While the absence of the proper equipment and transportation poses serious challenges, three of the most basic issues that can negatively affect the quality of life of officers during a crisis are the absence of food, water, and clean and dry socks. In a disaster, an officer may be required to work around the clock for several days at a time, with little or no rest. Both NOPD and GPD officers reported having to sleep for short periods of time while sitting against a wall, and during the early days of the disaster many worked with very little food. They reported having only the limited supplies they brought with them before Katrina's arrival, as they waited out the storm in various locations in the city. Those who did bring food brought enough for three days (standard practice in the case of severe storms), but they had to share their rations with their less-prepared comrades during the crisis. Lack of basic supplies, limited intake of nutrition and water, and sleep deprivation combined to create hazardous conditions for the officers as they were pushed to their limits. Despite the lack of resources, most police officers participated fully in the recovery efforts, but the magnitude of the crisis called for outside assistance.

Helping Hands: The Impact of Outside Agencies on the Functions of Local Police Departments during Disasters

In most major disasters, including Hurricane Katrina, outside assistance and resources are needed to aid with response and recovery efforts. Such support comes in a variety of forms and the type provided often depends on the magnitude of the disaster. In instances where the event is of such proportions as to require federal assistance, the governor of a state may—under provisions in the Stafford Act (§401)—ask the regional Federal Emergency Management Agency (FEMA) office to request that the president of the United States declare a federal state of emergency for the affected areas. Once the declaration has been made, FEMA sets up a central field office to coordinate efforts (Federal Emergency Management Agency 2018). In situations where the president has declared a state of emergency, FEMA can provide relief through individual assistance, public assistance, and hazard mitigation. Individual assistance includes temporary housing, disaster grants, low-interest loans, and other resources. Public assistance includes providing fiscal aid to local and state governments to fund recovery and rebuilding plans. FEMA provides mitigation funds for decreasing risks of future disasters.

In the case of the Katrina disaster, Governor Kathleen Blanco of Louisiana declared a state of emergency three days before Katrina's landfall, and Governor Haley Barbour of Mississippi made a declaration the following day. At 11:00 a.m. on August 29, 2005, FEMA director Michael Brown dispatched one thousand workers to the affected region but gave them two days to report for duty. At 1:45 p.m., President George W. Bush declared a federal state of emergency, which made federal funding available.

While FEMA assistance provides resources that help benefit first-responder agencies, the agencies often need more direct assistance during a disaster. In most instances, additional boots on the ground are needed to fill in the gaps of first-responder agencies that are strapped for resources and need additional staff to meet the growing demands on their organizations. In some cases, police departments in other jurisdictions around the nation or outside the United States will send a cadre of officers to an affected area, and often individual police officers will decide to show up ready to provide assistance to private citizens. This support is often appreciated because it provides the department with extra officers to assist with recovery efforts; at the same time, the officers can sometimes pose challenges for the agencies as well.

The onslaught of volunteers can sometimes complicate an already complex set of circumstances for departments in the midst of dealing with the demands of the disaster. Unlike fire departments, the laws and protocols that police departments follow differ from jurisdiction to jurisdiction and the rights granted to a police officer in one jurisdiction do not translate to another jurisdiction in the United States (this would not be an issue in Chile and other nations that have a national police force). Consequently, the police department receiving the volunteers must carefully remind the newcomers of the limits that are placed on their ability to serve as law-enforcement officers in the disaster area.

In some instances, a department can have a previously established mutual aid agreement already in place with outside law-enforcement agencies, which can expedite the assistance and streamline the process of integration and jurisdiction management. This arrangement is a general conceptual agreement that outlines interagency provision of support before, during, or after a critical incident. The law-enforcement agencies create such agreements to ensure that assistance will be readily available in times of crisis. These agreements are made between different levels of government and various types of organizations, including governmental agencies, private businesses, and nonprofit organizations. In general, the agreements are made to address emergency medicine, police, fire, and emergency management issues (Henstra 2010; Logan 2011).

In some cases, the state legislature must approve by the mutual aid agreements. In other cases, during an emergency situation, a simple handshake establishes a mutual aid agreement. Established agreements need regular updating and must provide specific policies and protocols for facilitating interagency coordination, as well as training and exercises to support these coordinated plans (Logan 2011). In situations where a hosting policing agency has not executed a mutual aid agreement with the department that wishes to provide assistance, it may draft a memorandum of understanding to outline agreements between the agencies. In some instances, police officers just show up on the scene to volunteer. FEMA director Michael Brown issued a statement on the afternoon after Katrina's landfall asking first responders not to report to the city without proper coordination between the state and local officials, but many showed up anyway without such coordination.

Despite the fact that volunteer police officers are most often welcome, they may present additional burdens to the local department. Some officers arrive without the necessary supplies to support themselves, requiring the receiving department to provide food and shelter for the volunteers. As noted earlier, in some instances, the resources are scarce, and it can be quite challenging for a department to provide adequate food, water, and shelter for its regular staff and volunteers—a challenge compounded by the needs of volunteer police officers. This situation contrasts with more formal provision of police support: when agencies send out volunteers they provide food and other supplies.

All the same, the extra personnel perform an invaluable service to the receiving agencies. During the Hurricane Katrina disaster, a blitz of volunteers showed up to support relief efforts within disaster recovery areas, including Gulfport and New Orleans. A total of 725 officers assembled by the U.S. Immigration and Customs Enforcement came to assist the Gulf Coast (Davis and Tang 2006), and hundreds of officers from near and far came to assist the NOPD. The assistance was well received by most of the department. One officer in Gulfport said, "Seeing the line of blue lights coming in from Florida was the coolest sight. . . . They understood what was going on and could [sic] really helped." Thus, despite the challenges the volunteers impose on receiving departments, overall they are a welcome source of assistance.

Although the outside policing units advanced the response capabilities of the NOPD during Katrina, the National Guard and the U.S. Army served as the primary stabilizing agents during the disaster (Adams and Stewart 2014). Before Katrina's landfall, U.S. military units geared up to respond to the impending disaster (Berthelot 2010). Activated by the declaration of a state of emergency by Louisiana's governor Blanco, that state's

National Guard prepared to join in addressing the fallout of Katrina. The Louisiana National Guard also experienced the wrath of the storm: they spent the first twenty-four hours after the storm's landfall repairing the damages from fifteen-foot floodwaters that severed communication capabilities and disabled high-water trucks, and the headquarters staff had to scramble for their lives while evacuating to the Superdome. Subsequently, other National Guard units were dispatched as reinforcements from other states, including 922 Army National Guard and 8 Air National Guard personnel the first day, with more added during the following days of the disaster, totaling upward of 5,770 troopers (Shane and Shanker 2005). The National Guard was the first military force in New Orleans, playing a pivotal role in the search and rescue missions, distribution of food and water, fuel distribution, medical services, and order maintenance (Davis et al. 2005).

The National Guard also provided direct assistance to the TPD during the Tornado Super Outbreak disaster. The morning prior to the outbreak, Alabama governor Robert Bentley declared a state of emergency, which authorized the assistance of over one thousand National guard troops. The National Guard provided assistance with medical services, law enforcement, and debris removal. The National Guard provided services that were as invaluable to the community in Tuscaloosa as those they provided to the Gulf region during the Katrina crisis.

Decisive as the National Guard's assistance is in a disaster, sometimes supplemental personnel are needed. Once the levees broke in New Orleans hours after Katrina's landfall, it became apparent that additional forces were needed, and forces from the U.S. Army came in. Some regarded their presence, under the command of Lieutenant General Russell Honoré, to be the most effective factor in establishing order and peace in the city. Unlike the National Guard, the U.S. Army moved into the city heavily armed, which caused mixed feelings among the city residents, who viewed that display as hostile (Adams and Stewart 2014). Many others, including Terry Ebbert, the director of Homeland Security at the time, welcomed the military presence and believed it was necessary to restore order in the city (Adams and Stewart 2014). Public perception aside, the military can serve to restore order during a disaster; in some countries, their role is vital. (See Chapter 8.) For example, in Chile, the national police force routinely works alongside local police agencies during events that require assistance. For this reason, the national police force has the same rights and privileges in their ability to restore order as the local officers, and they are not seen as an outside source of brute force.

Impact of the Disasters on the Officers: Behavioral Responses of Law Enforcement Officers

Besides the systemic effects on a police department, the turmoil that ensues from a disaster can pose serious personal challenges to the officers and affect their behavioral responses to it. Some of the challenges and behavioral responses exhibited during the Katrina disaster were exposure to extreme levels of devastation, threats to personal safety, feelings of isolation, decreased ability to rationalize and make decisions, role conflict and role strain, role abandonment, and misconduct. All these factors mitigate the officer's ability to fulfill the role of first responder during a disaster.

Exposure to Extreme Levels of Devastation

A disaster not only challenges the objective performance of law-enforcement officers during the crisis, it also affects them on a personal level. The onslaught of out-of-the-ordinary destructive events can lead to confusion, frustration, sadness, and an overall sense of bewilderment. As previously noted, both Gulfport and New Orleans were heavily hit by Katrina. Some officers described the early hours after the storm as being eerily quiet in the areas of the cities they patrolled. In Gulfport, the devastation caused by the storm was immediately evident; in New Orleans it became apparent only gradually. Officers in both departments describe confronting scenes they had never witnessed before and an experience of sensory overload. Human bodies floating in floodwaters, grief-stricken children and adults, and stranded victims wading in the water were frequent sights. These images were etched into the psyche of the officers, causing some deep emotional distress and cognitive dissonance.

In addition to the human suffering, the officers also faced having to orient themselves to the drastic changes in the landscape of the affected communities. Homes were submerged in water and pushed off their foundations, rooftops were blown onto city streets, cars were lodged inside houses, trees were felled and blocked roadways, and broken glass and debris from houses and businesses littered the streets. In many instances, this destruction consumed entire neighborhoods. Many of the officers noted that no training can prepare one for dealing with such high levels of devastation. As one officer noted, "Climbing over debris, GPS-ing dead bodies—can't train for that."

When confronted with dreadful imagery, one has to readjust oneself mentally to the change in the landscape and the level of human suffering. This necessary readjustment can be emotionally taxing. The devastation caused the officers fear, exhaustion, and a sense of great loss, which can cause sadness and despair and at least dramatically increase stress levels (Lazarus 2006). Chapter 7 discusses these issues in more detail.

Threats to Personal Safety

In addition to the psychological risk officers encounter during a critical incident, the chaos produced by disasters also put officers in perilous situations. The nature of the peril depends on the nature of the disaster and the mitigation strategies instituted ahead of time. An earthquake or technological disaster gives no forewarning and catches people off guard. In the event of a weather-related catastrophe, warnings are usually issued, which allows preparation and mitigation activities to take place, some of which serve to reduce the storm's impact on a police department's resources, equipment, or staff. For instance, before Katrina made landfall, the NOPD and GPD officers had time to assist with the evacuation of residents from the city to places of refuge. In addition, they had time to move equipment out of the expected path of the storm, stock some resources, instruct officers to facilitate the movement of their loved ones out of the city, and place staff members in strategic safe places. These activities serve to reduce the potential danger a first responder may face and reduce the time for reestablishing departmental capabilities and functions. But even when the potential risks are known, it is impossible to know the total magnitude of the impact of the coming event on the landscape, infrastructure, general environment, or the department and its staff.

Having predisaster protocols is necessary, but it is important to be flexible to adapt to new potential dangers caused by a disaster event. For instance, following normal prestorm protocols, a number of the officers with the NOPD were waiting out the storm in their homes when Katrina hit the city, many of whom became stranded and needed to be rescued (Adams and Stewart 2014). Other officers had to be rescued from police stations and other places that flooded unexpectedly and stranded them. As noted earlier, ninety-one officers were rescued after Katrina's landfall, many of whose lives were threatened by rising floodwaters. Among the innumerable hair-raising incidents the NOPD experienced during Katrina, the incident that opened this chapter highlights the fact that first responders are often vulnerable to the hazard that they are tasked to respond to.

The previous example is but one instance of the precarious situations officers can sometimes find themselves in during a disaster. During the 2010 earthquake in Chile, many of the police officers found themselves fighting for their own lives while trying to respond to the disaster. One Carabinero recounted in an interview this harrowing scenario:

> We evacuated people for about one hour. We moved all the residents to a safe area on top of a hill and then went down to the coast to evaluate the situation.... While me and two other Carabineros were doing this, the first wave came in. The sea dragged me about 800 meters inland and

> I struggled for about 40 minutes in the water. . . . While in the water my feet were entangled in some plastics. The wave dragged me until I was washed away to a hillside.

The officer was able to extricate himself and went on to continue his work as a first responder after struggling to save his own life.

Not all officers can endure the chaos of a disaster and keep their wits about them, focusing on their objectives as first responders. Chapter 6 explores in greater detail the adaptive responses and coping strategies some officers employ to increase their mental and emotional resilience during a disaster.

Isolation

Some disasters and some agencies' predisaster protocols may place an officer in an isolated position without the aid of fellow officers to help make important decisions about how to respond to events. While police officers frequently work independently, they can usually communicate with other officers to seek assistance through various modes. For some officers, the absence of their fellow officers, coupled with the uncertainty and instability of the environment, affects their situational awareness. This combination of circumstances can lead to a heightened sense of disorientation and despair, which in turn affects their decision-making and performance capabilities. Under even normal circumstances, individuals make decisions based on the limits of the situations they are facing. A decision maker may lack vital pieces of information to make an informed decision. In a disaster, however, heightened levels of stressors can especially hamper decision-making processes, particularly if one is isolated from the chain of command and other sources of information.

So, while police officers are trained to operate autonomously, and are often called on to make important decisions in the line of duty, the situations they face during a disaster are outside the realm of what they are used to confronting. More experienced officers may fare better in these situations than their less experienced counterparts (Alison et al. 2015). A lack of experience may thus make a difference in the degree to which the disaster affects officers and their ability to function appropriately during the disaster. As one officer with the GPD pointed out,

> Years of experience made me stronger. Just the normal training of a police officer and the years of experience helped me . . . to be mentally tough. Not necessary formal training, but the experience of being [a] police officer over the years. . . . I think the veterans were able to handle this a little better than the youngsters . . . ; people with 5 or 6 years. The people who had been here 15–20 years, I'm not saying it didn't faze them, because it did, but we were able to cope with it a lot better than guys who had only been here 3 or 5 years. It affected them a lot more.

In sum, the more years one has on the force, the more experience one tends to have in coping with difficult challenges and making rational decisions with just the information and knowledge at hand. Being separated from veteran officers can, therefore, severely limit the ability especially of less experienced officers to operate effectively during disasters.

Decreased Ability to Rationalize and Make Decisions

Whether from a lack of experience or other factors, the inability to think rationally about what to do in the midst of a chaotic situation is another challenge that some officers face during a crisis. Generally, people attempt to make the best decisions possible, but in the face of constraints, decision makers forgo optimal solutions for satisfactory solutions as situations limit both their access to information and their capacity for rational decision making (Simon 1955). In the example of the Katrina disaster, it is easy to see how the infrastructure damage, officers abandoning their posts, inaccessibility of resources, fellow officers' suicides, and in some cases, concerns about the safety of loved ones created very stressful circumstances that would make it challenging to think rationally (Adams et al. 2011). NOPD officers were subjected to many stress-inducing events besides. Further, a situation that is heavily laced with uncertainty and tragedy can intensify feelings of despair and impair decision-making capabilities (Sims 2007).

The chaos of a disaster can lead some officers to feel distraught and out of balance to the point that they develop fatalistic views of the situation before them. During the Katrina disaster, two NOPD officers committed suicide during the early days of the disaster, reflecting the harrowing conditions they faced. While police in general have the highest rates of suicide among all municipal professions (Violanti, Vena, and Marshall 1986), the fact of two suicides during that relatively short period highlights the bedlam during the disaster. They also served to add to the emotional trauma of the other members of the force. Research has shown that the loss of a fellow officer increases stress among law-enforcement officers (Comen and Evans 1991; Violanti and Aron 1993). The accumulation of these stressors and traumas works to inhibit officers' decision-making capacity. Chapter 4 further explicates these issues.

Role Conflict and Role Strain

Further complicating decision making during disasters are the issues of role conflict and role strain. Large and widespread disasters can pose a threat to everyone who lives or works in the geographic space, thus potentially including the loved ones of first responders. In widespread disasters, a responder may have concerns about the welfare of his or her loved ones. Such concerns can lead to what is often referred to as role conflict, which is the feeling of being torn between fulfilling one's role as a first responder and fulfilling other roles one plays in one's life. It can be difficult for officers to focus on the job when they have concerns about those they love. Some of the officers who participated in the Katrina disaster expressed a sense of role conflict while serving as first responders.

In addition, the multiple needs caused by the disaster can cause a responder to feel uncertain about which of several responsibilities to carry out or which to carry out first. That is, an officer can be unsure about which responsibilities should take precedence over others in a long list of competing role-related requirements—e.g., that of law enforcer, rescue worker, service provider—during a disaster. This is called role strain; Chapter 3 discusses it and role conflict more fully.

Post Abandonment

One of the most problematic matters from an emergency management perspective is post abandonment among emergency respondents. A number of NOPD officers reportedly left their posts for extended periods of time during the Katrina crisis, and review of the disciplinary hearing case files of the officers who were accused of abandoning their posts reveals many reasons for officers leaving their posts, including role conflict, role strain, and fear. These actions brought to light an issue that was previously regarded as a nonissue within the first-responder community. It nevertheless exists as a maladaptive response to disaster work and is a serious potential facet of crisis management. Chapter 4 discusses the issue in more detail.

Misconduct

The decisions officers make during crises sometimes conflict with the standards and goals of the department. Although most people engage in altruistic behavior during a crisis event, there are exceptions. The degree of the infractions varies but can include both illegal acts and acts that are not exactly criminal but are a misuse official powers. For example, during the Hurricane Katrina disaster, according to the Washington *Post* and other news outlets, a number of NOPD officers participated in taking personal possession of nonessential items (e.g., televisions, watches, jewelry) from stores.

According to an interview conducted by the Washington *Post*, spokesperson Deputy Superintendent DeFillio contended that "out of the 1,750 officers we're looking into the possibility that maybe 12 officers were involved in misconduct" (Nossiter 2005). There were reports of more malicious acts that members of the NOPD committed. A retired schoolteacher was reportedly beaten by officers in response to asking a simple question about curfew during the early days of the storm (Frailing and Harper 2012). Several legal charges were brought against NOPD officers, including four cases relating to civil-rights violations, which resulted in criminal charges against twenty officers (Frailing and Harper 2012). One of the most horrible acts was the shooting of six unarmed citizens, two of them fatally injured, which was covered up by the officers, who were later found guilty (Maggi 2005; Robertson 2011).

Some reports indicate that NOPD officers were ordered to take a no-nonsense approach to crime fighting after Katrina. They were ordered by Mayor Ray Nagin to switch from search and rescue to fighting crime, and, when National Guard troops arrived in the city, Governor Blanco announced at a press conference that they "are fresh back from Iraq, well trained, experienced, battle-tested and under my orders to restore order in the streets. They have M-16s, and they are locked and loaded. These troops know how to shoot and kill, and they are more than willing to do so if necessary, and I expect they will" (ABC News 2005, as cited in Frailing and Harper 2012, p. 304). Frailing and Harper (2012) report that the governor's statement can be interpreted as a "by any means necessary" approach to handling crime in the city. The use of such rhetoric can amount to a possible *posse comitatus* violation, and at the very least it can be regarded as a statement that condones the use of excessive force. Chapter 5 covers police misconduct in more detail.

The many aspects of the noted impacts of a disaster on behavioral responses of law-enforcement officers are either an expression of or result of the stress they endure during extreme crisis events. The next chapter discusses the role of stress in a law-enforcement officer's life and how stress caused by disaster work affects their functions during and after participating in disaster response efforts.

Conclusion

When disasters strike, they have the power to knock out all sense of normality, including the operations of law-enforcement agencies. Some disasters can drastically affect the ability of law-enforcement agencies to respond effectively to the crisis. The disaster may present challenges to authorities from the effect it has on the infrastructure, landscape, and distribution of resources. Disasters also affect individual law-enforcement officers professional and personally.

The professional impacts range from operational to logistical and organizational. The depths of these impacts depend on the type of disaster, the span of its impact, and the scope of the devastation. Local authorities and first responders struggled with serious organizational challenges in all the disasters examined. All three of the disaster types reduced communication capabilities and disrupted swift rescue responses to needs in their communities. In the case of Hurricane Katrina, most of the police agencies had to contend with the loss of communication capabilities, loss of multiple police stations and police headquarters, and a scarcity of adequate food and water supplies. In some of these cases, the agencies also had to deal with an absence of basic equipment, lack of housing, and a drastic lack of sleep. These challenges acutely affected the normal operational protocols of law-enforcement operations. Disasters can also affect the hierarchical order of a department and how the officers feel about their roles in the disaster response.

Although police officers are often used to dealing with stressful situations, the weightiness of the circumstances during a disaster intensifies stress levels among the officers. The heightened stress can affect the behavioral response of officers. Some officers find themselves affected by role conflict and role strain, but most are able to overcome these issues and other related stressors caused by the crisis. Although the majority of officers can function appropriately and carry out their responsibilities, some officers find it difficult to manage the strains imposed on them during disasters and engage in maladaptive behaviors, including absenteeism and misconduct. While maladaptive responses have generally been a nonissue in first-responder communities during disasters, some such responses occurred during the Hurricane Katrina disaster but not among the police who responded to the Superstorm Outbreak in Tuscaloosa, Alabama, or the earthquake and tsunami in Chile.

KEY TAKEAWAYS FROM THIS CHAPTER

1. The size and scope of a disaster can cause a loss of human resources, equipment, and communication, which in turn can plunge a policing agency to into chaos.
2. Nontraditional approaches to accomplishing a standard policing task may be necessary to meet the needs of the community during a disaster.
3. The size and scope of a disaster may require a police officer to work around the clock, taking as few breaks as possible until a semblance of order is reestablished in the affected community.
4. Governmental entities are tied to a set of strict regulations, which sometimes cause gaps in relief efforts.
5. Previously established mutual-aid agreements between police departments can serve to expedite the processes of assisting with a critical incident.
6. Volunteers serve an essential function during disasters, but they do bring with them an additional set of organizational challenges.
7. Disaster work can pose severe personal and professional challenges to officers and affect their behavioral responses to their work.

DISCUSSION QUESTIONS

1. What kinds of police operations are most affected by a disaster? Which one do you believe most affects their ability to fulfill their law-enforcement duties during disasters?

2. What essential operational protocols of a police department are more likely to be sustained during a disaster? Why do you think they can be maintained?
3. What mitigation activities would you suggest a police department routinize at the onset of a disaster to ensure its ability to assist with rescue missions during a critical incident?
4. What kind of assistance can FEMA provide first-responder agencies during a disaster? Does FEMA provide direct aid to first-responder agencies during a disaster?
5. What challenges are posed on policing agencies when they accept volunteers from police from other jurisdictions?
6. What are the types of behavioral responses one can expect from a police officer who has served as a first responder during a disaster? Which do you think may have the most detrimental effects on someone's personal life?

REFERENCES

Adams, Terri, Leigh Anderson, Milanika Turner, and Jonathon Armstrong. 2011. "Coping through a Disaster: Lessons from Hurricane Katrina." *Journal of Homeland Security and Emergency Management* 8 (1). https://doi.org/10.2202/1547-7355.1836.

Adams, Terri, and Larry Stewart. 2014. "Chaos Theory and Organizational Crisis: A Theoretical Analysis of the Challenges Faced by the New Orleans Police Department during Hurricane Katrina." *Public Organization Review*, June. http://link.springer.com/article/10.1007/s11115-014-0284-9/fulltext.html.

Alison, Laurence, Nicola Power, Claudia von den Heuvel, Michael Humann, Marek Palasinksi, and Jonathan Crego. 2015. "Decision Inertia: Deciding between Least Worst Outcomes in Emergency Responses to Disasters." *Journal of Occupational and Organizational Psychology, 88*, 295–321.

Berthelot, Roberta. 2010. *The Army Response to Katrina*. Carlisle, PA: Army Heritage Education Center.

"Chile Minister Says Navy Erred on Tsunami." 2010. Associated Press, February 28. http://www.nbcnews.com/id/35637211/ns/world_news-chile_earthquake/t/chile-minister-says-navy-erred-tsunami/.

Comen, Greg, and Barry Evans. 1991. "Stressors Facing Australian Police in the 1990s." *Police Studies* 14:153–165.

Davis, Lynn E., Jill Rough, Gary Cecchine, Agnes Gereben Schaefer, and Laurinda. Zeman. 2005. *Hurricane Katrina: Lessons for Army Planning and Operations.* Santa Monica, CA: RAND.

EMAC. 2006. *Emergency Management Assistance Compact (EMAC) 2005 Hurricane Season Response after Action Report*, edited by Barry Leonard. Darby, PA: Diane Publishing Company.

Federal Communication Commission. 2018. *National Interoperability Channels.* Accessed May 31. https://www.fcc.gov/general/national-interoperability-channels.

Federal Emergency Management Agency. 2018. *The Declaration Process.* Accessed May 31. http://www.fema.gov/declaration-process.

First Response Coalition. 2005. *Interoperability Failures Following Hurricane Katrina.* Accessed December 1. https://transition.fcc.gov/pshs/docs/advisory/hkip/public-comments/FRCFail.pdf.

Frailing, Kelly, and Dee Wood Harper. 2012. "Fear, Prosocial Behavior and Looting: The Katrina Experience." In *Crime and Criminal Justice in Disaster*, 2nd ed., edited by D. W. Harper and K. Frailing, 101–121. Durham, NC: Carolina Academic Press.

Fritz, Charles E. 1961. "Disasters." In *Contemporary Social Problems*, edited by R. K. Merton and R. A. Nisbet, 651–694. New York: Harcourt.

Harper, Dee Wood. 2012. "The New Orleans Police Department during and after Hurricane Katrina—Lessons Learned." In *Crime and Criminal Justice in Disaster*, 2nd ed., edited by D. W. Harper and K. Frailing, 285–310. Durham, NC: Carolina Academic Press.

Henstra, Daniel. 2010. "Evaluating Local Government Emergency Management Programs: What Framework Should Public Managers Adopt?" *Public Administration Review* 70 (2): 236–246.

Hokanson, Melvin, and Bonnita Wirth. 2000. "The Critical Incident Stress Debriefing Process for the Los Angeles County Fire Department: Automatic and Effective." *International Journal of Emergency Mental Health* 2 (4): 249–257.

Lazarus, Richard. 2006. *Stress and Emotion: A New Synthesis.* New York: Springer.

Maggi, Laura. 2005. "Lack of Communication during Katrina Proved Crippling." *New Orleans Times-Picayune*, September 15.

Nossiter, Adam. 2005. "New Orleans Probing Alleged Police Looting." Associated Press, September 30. http://www.washingtonpost.com/wp-dyn/content/article/2005/09/29/AR2005092901975.html.

O'Hara, Patrick. 2005. *Why Law Enforcement Organizations Fail: Mapping the Organizational Fault Lines in Policing.* Durham, NC: Carolina Academic.

Reiss, Albert, J. 1971. *The Police and the Public.* New Haven, CT: Yale University Press.

Robertson, Campbell. 2011. "Officers Guilty of Shooting Six in New Orleans." *New York Times*, August 5. http://www.nytimes.com/2011/08/06/us/06danziger.html.

Sabloff, Nicholas. 2010. "Chile Earthquake, Tsunami 2010: Latest Update, Video." *Huffington Post*, February 27. https://www.huffingtonpost.com/2010/02/27/chile-earthquake-tsunami_n_479393.html.

Shane, Scott, and Thom Shanker. 2005. "When Storm Hit, National Guard Was Deluged Too." *New York Times*, September 28. http://www.nytimes.com/2005/09/28/us/nationalspecial/when-storm-hit-national-guard-was-deluged-too.html.

Simon, Herbert, A. 1955. "A Behavioral Model of Rational Choice." *Quarterly Journal of Economics* 59:99–118.

Sims, Benjamin. 2007. "'The Day after the Hurricane': Infrastructure, Order, and the New Orleans Police Department's Response to Hurricane Katrina." *Social Studies of Science* 37 (1): 111–118.

Szalajeski, Jim. 2007. "Look for Success Where It Can Be Found." *Urgent Communications*. http://urgentcomm.com/mag/look-success-where-it-can-be-found.

Violanti, John M., and Fred Aron. 1993. "Sources of Police Stressors, Job Attitudes and Psychological Distress." *Psychological Reports* 72:899–904.

Violanti, John M., John E. Vena, and James R. Marshall. 1986. "Disease Risk and Mortality among Police Officers." *Journal of Police Science and Administration* 14:17–23.

3

Dilemmas with Responding to the Call of Duty

Role Conflict and Role Strain among Law Enforcement Officers during Disasters

> There was chaos, no communication. The situation was hell! We were stuck in the hospital. [The] captain said before we go we have to save the people: I didn't want to at first, but it was the best decision. The captain was strong. I didn't know where my family was, yet I had to save other people. Didn't know for three weeks, I was helping other people, couldn't help my family. [The] hardest part was not knowing where my family was . . . helping people but could not help my family . . . police helped my Momma.
> —Anonymous

> Sure, there was role conflict. I lost everything I owned, but I'm still, or even at the time was, married to the department.
> —Anonymous

As Chapter 2 emphasized, first responders may sometimes find themselves facing unusual circumstances and challenges that affect their ability to respond. The above quotes, from an NOPD officer and a GPD police officer, both of whom served during the Hurricane Katrina disaster, illustrate the strain law-enforcement personnel face when they are personally affected by a disaster during which they are expected to respond professionally. For some, the challenges faced during the disaster did not cause emotional turmoil, while others struggled with internal conflicts over their responsibilities.

This chapter discusses the seldom-addressed reality of first responders experiencing direct and indirect victimization during and after their response to high-consequence events. They are direct victims when they live in or have strong ties to the community affected by the disaster and indirect victims when they bear witness to destruction and human suffering. The confluence of such factors confronted during a full-scale emergency can lead to role strain and role conflict, which can ultimately affect a law-enforcement officer's ability to effectively fulfill his or her duty during a high-consequence event. This chapter deconstructs the meaning and interpretation of role conflict and role strain as they relate to the feelings and actions of first responders during the extreme events under examination. A case study is used to illustrate the concepts and addresses the following questions: (1) What are role conflict and role strain? (2) How are they manifested among law-enforcement officers during major crisis events? (3) What factors affect differences in prioritizing the roles that are played during a disaster?

Defining Role Conflict and Role Strain

> I left. Maybe it was [the] wrong decision. Deep down in my heart if I had to do it again for my family, I would do it again.
> —NOPD Officer

The concept of role is a construct that is used to signify a position or status within a structure rather than the person occupying the position. It denotes a pattern of expectations and responsibilities associated with a position, including attitudes and behaviors (Lipman-Blumen 1973). Both formal and informal roles (e.g., occupational, familial, societal) exist for individuals within society and the specific expectations associated with each role can be explicit or implicit (Sarbin and Allen 1968; Stryker and Statham 1985). In many cases, problems emerge from this mélange of various roles individuals hold, resulting in role conflict or role strain.

Role Conflict

When the expectations of the role and the needs or values of the individual occupying the role are not aligned, a person experiences conflict, which is commonly described by the term "role conflict." While the term has been conceptualized in numerous ways in the literature—with dissent about what the term constitutes—for the purpose of this chapter, Getzels and Guba's (1954) definition of role conflict will be utilized. Getzels and Guba define role conflict as occurring when "situations are so ordered that an actor is required to simultaneously fill two or more roles that present inconsistent, contradictory, or even mutually exclusive expectations" (p. 165). Role conflict also occurs when the expectations of a role are out of line with the person's ability to meet the requirements of the role or roles, especially when the person cannot reconcile the expectation with his or her ability (Wilcox 1994).

Regardless of the nature of the expectations associated with the roles a person occupies, expectations are deeply associated with one's social identity and group affiliations. Tajfel and Turner (1979) note that an individual's self-concept derives from the person's personal identity and social identity. According to social identity theory, one's sense of self extends beyond one's identity and is often embedded within group memberships (Ashforth and Mael 1989); and most people have multiple group identities such as race, gender, class, occupation, hobby (Stryker and Statham 1985; Tajfel 1978). The strength of the identity's impact on the normal daily functions of one's existence may influence the level of loyalty or the priority of the identity in one's life or overall self-concept. One or more identities may emerge as being more significant than others at a given time or in a given context (Turner et al. 1987).

The roles that a person occupies in society reflect the person's multiple group memberships. With each role comes expectations of the occupant about what is appropriate to the performance of the role, which derive from beliefs, duties, obligations, rights, and privileges (Sarbin and Allen 1968). Often one or more roles that one occupies are not aligned with his or her self-concept, or are otherwise misaligned with other roles he or she holds simultaneously, a situation that may manifest as a role conflict. Multiple expectations associated with each role can cause a person to feel unsure about which expectation to fulfill, particularly when those expectations are in opposition to one another—leading to a circumstance in which an individual feels that in order to fulfill the obligations of one role one must reject those of another.

Role Strain

Although related, there are distinct differences between role strain and role conflict. Some scholars refer to the difficulty of fulfilling role obligations—whether or not the individual does, in fact, fulfill the obligations—as role strain (Rogers 1986). According to Goode (1960), role strain occurs when one experiences a sense of being overwhelmed by the demands of the roles they fulfill. He argues that there are four key factors associated with role strain: (1) Role demands are not always pleasurable and conforming with the role may not always be automatic. (2) Different roles may require different sets of obligations that may cause conflict. (3) Different norms may be associated with different roles. (4) Sometimes an individual may participate in role sets that cross into relationships with different people that may pose conflicting or distracting obligations. A person has to manage his or her system in a manner that reduces the possibility of role strain. As Goode (1960) states, "The individual cannot satisfy all demands fully, and must move through a continuous sequence of role decisions and bargains, by which he attempts to adjust these demands" (p. 495).

Though both role strain and role conflict involve stresses or incongruence among multiple roles or responsibilities, the two concepts are quite distinct. Role conflict occurs when a person believes there is an obligation to choose between two or more conflicting roles, and the two cannot be fulfilled simultaneously. Role strain, on the other hand, refers to instances where the competing demands of responsibilities within or between roles threaten to overwhelm the person occupying them. There is indeed a sort of conflict in both, but in role conflict the conflict lies primarily within incongruent identities associated with certain roles, while in role strain the conflict primarily regards competition between various roles and responsibilities for limited time, attention, and resources. With role strain the person can usually perform the duties associated with the roles but has some degree of difficulty fulfilling the obligations. With role conflict, the person may have to choose to abandon, temporarily or permanently, a role and its related responsibilities. Various situations and social context may provide opportunities for both role strain and role conflict to occur during disaster response and recovery.

Role Conflict and Role Strain in the Context of Disaster Response

As previously noted, evidence regarding the experience of role conflict among emergency workers is mixed. Some research suggests that they are capable of fulfilling their duties without experiencing internal conflicts between professional and personal duties. The literature contains discussions, for example, of when personal responsibilities may override professional duties. Killian (1952) suggests that primary group membership would override secondary group membership during times of disaster and predicted that role abandonment was possible among emergency workers. He also noted a less common form of role conflict exists when people are faced with choosing between "playing the heroic role as a rescue worker" and performing basic but necessary "occupational roles" (p. 312). For example, first responders may feel torn between fulfilling basic service roles such as managing crowd sand the heroic role of rescuing victims. This less common form of role conflict that Killian describes is often called a type of role strain instead, acknowledging the fact that the requirement to choose between the two subroles lies less in a fundamental incongruence between them than in a lack of sufficient resources and time to perform both subroles satisfactorily.

Rogers (1986) also recognized the issue of role conflict in crises but insisted that complete role abandonment due to role conflict in emergency situations occurs rarely. Rogers discovered that first responders' proximity to a significant other, "both victims and socially related," during the impact of an event is related to the "type of emergency response possible and the nature of any associated conflicting role expectation" (p. 37). Rogers's study identified nine potential types of conflict between family and responder roles, which depended on the location of first responder personnel at the time of the crisis and the individual's knowledge of the disaster's impact. The physical location of a first responder at the time of a disaster determines which role takes precedence over the other roles. Hence, if a person is physically close to their family at the time of the disaster, he or she will respond to those role expectations, which is likely to be followed by the expectations of their work roles and vice versa. Thus, first responders reported minimal role conflict when they immediately responded with their emergency organization, eliminating the onset of role conflict at least during the initial stage of a disaster. Ultimately, Rogers suggests that role conflict could be minimized through role adjustment, which occurs when role expectations are ranked, and the values of each role are shared commonly among members of groups. Likewise, Barton (1969) suggested that a community could put pressure on responder personnel to stay and work by making direct personal appeals to responders, offsetting their concerns for their family.

A further distinction in the study of role conflict is the source of the conflict. Numerous studies have analyzed family-role and work-role conflict, which examines the incongruous pressures that arise within either domain (e.g., Coverman 1989; Kahn and Wolfe 1964; Kopelman, Greenhaus, and Connolly 1983; Pietromonaco, Manis, and Frohardt-Lane 1986; Pleck, Staines, and Lang 1980). Studies have shown that multiple role involvement and overload can affect job and family life satisfaction (Coverman 1989; Kopelman et al. 1983; Pleck et al. 1980). Killian (1952) raised the issue of the potential challenges of multiple group membership in times of disaster in the early 1950s. His study of various disasters in southwestern U.S. communities confirmed several other findings that most individuals choose loyalty to primary groups (e.g., family and friends) over work, community, and other secondary member groups when faced with making an immediate choice during a disaster. Furthermore, he observed that conflicting group memberships and contradictory role expectations significantly influenced individual behavior in a time of crisis because emergency situations allowed potential conflict and contradictions among various roles to manifest themselves.

Other researchers have noted a lack of evidence that role conflict occurs or presents a significant dilemma in disaster situations. Reviewing interviews collected from organization officials on four separate disaster agents, Dynes (1986) discovered that, out of a sample of 443 people who worked for "emergency relevant organizations," there were no reports of abandonment of duty for family role obligations. Further, less than 1 percent indicated that they were delayed in reporting to work. Hence, regardless of where individuals were at the time of the disaster, they responded to the needs generated by the crisis. Dynes's work lends support to the concepts of "role moratorium," "role reduction," and "role simplification," wherein the only tasks performed are those that are relevant to the emergency situation while irrelevant functions and duties are eliminated or temporarily suspended.

Dynes's finding is similar to that of White (1962), who found that individuals usually respond to the most immediate needs of those around them after a disaster, whether the needs are professional or familial in nature. In a comprehensive study, White examined members of various ranks within several disaster-related organizations and found that, of the entire sample, 89 percent reported that they participated in the disaster relief efforts and none abandoned disaster work to be with their families. Individuals enacted whichever role they felt was germane at the moment. White further noted that the type of disaster agent (e.g., flood, earthquake, tornado, fire, bombing) may play a role in responders' reactions, as some situations require critical work performance (e.g., fighting a fire) to ensure the safety of family or community. Hence, the way a person responds and whether role conflict affects them may depend on the type and scope of the critical incident the person faces.

Recent literature finds more evidence that role conflict is a potential issue for first responders. Trainor and Barsky (2011) reported that although role conflict did not appear to be an issue among first responders, role abandonment (i.e., leaving an assigned post without permission) cannot be considered a nonissue for first-responder agencies during disasters. Adams and Turner (2014) found that several law-enforcement officers who served during Katrina indicated they experienced role conflict. Among those who did not, some seemed to contradict their assertion when they described the situations they faced during the disaster. Although the officers examined did not report abandoning their post, many of the officers reported feeling a conflict between the roles they play within their family and as law-enforcement officers. The study found that some of the officers were creative in their quest to fulfill their multiple roles, some of which included taking unauthorized time away from their formal professional duties to attend to perceived personal responsibilities.

Although some scholars note that role conflict and role abandonment occurred (Adams and Turner 2014; Killian 1952; Trainor and Barsky 2011), some argue that role conflict and abandonment of duty among disaster workers is rare (Dynes 1986; Rogers 1986; White 1962). Instead, the more common experience is that of role strain: that is, the difficulty in fulfilling multiple role obligations, though one may still meet the behavioral expectations inherent in the role. Findings may depend on the nature of the emergency on which the data are based, as well as the type of reporting agent used in the study. For instance, Dynes (1986) interviewed organization officials, who, in their professional roles as administrators of organizations may be less inclined to acknowledge the existence of role conflict or reveal that role abandonment occurred among their employees. In addition, a disaster may cause less role conflict if it does not immediately affect the responder or their loved ones at the time of the event. Thus, first responders may be more susceptible to role conflict when the magnitude of the disaster is so enormous and sudden that it affects a large enough portion of the community to include the responder's family.

It is also important to note that most of the previous examinations of role conflict have focused on its expression in role abandonment. As a result, role abandonment has been conflated with role conflict, as if role conflict only exists within the context of role abandonment. As noted earlier, however, role conflict occurs when people feel compelled to simultaneously fill two or more roles that are inconsistent, contradictory, or mutually exclusive (Getzels and Guba 1954). Therefore, an individual may experience role conflict and have difficulty in resolving such conflict and not resort to completely abandoning professional responsibilities. Instead, the individual, unable to resolve the conflict or unwilling to abandon the conflicting role(s), may remain at his or her post but experience deep guilt or cognitive dissonance. In sum, the concept of role conflict should be understood as a condition that does not necessarily translate into actions that result in role abandonment.

While there have been a number of studies examining role conflict among first responders, there is a dearth of studies examining role strain. It is important to note that while role conflict and role strain represent different issues, the concepts overlap a bit. Figure 3.1 provides an illustration of the differences and similarities between these concepts.

Research has found first responders may rank-order their priorities during a disaster and concentrate on the roles that appear to be the most important at any given moment. Other scholars have examined the performance of particular groups of people during crises to determine where role strain exists and how they attempt to manage it. For example, Bradfield, Wylie, and Echterling (1989) note that ministers of churches who respond to the needs of people during disasters experience role strain. Although not usually referred to as first responders, ministers often provide much-needed services to those in need during disasters, sometimes filling multiple roles. In addition to

```
Role Conflict              Role Strain

Internal Conflicts         Internal Conflicts

Conflict between           Conflicts between
professional roles         professional and
                           personal roles

Feelings of                Role reduction
Inadequacy
```

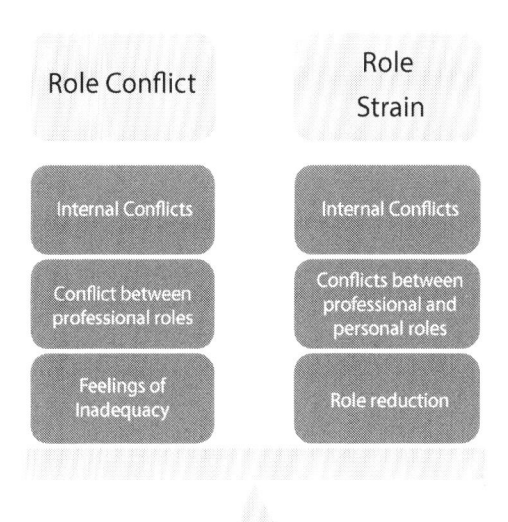

Figure 3.1 Conflicts between professional roles and roles outside the profession.

offering spiritual guidance during a disaster, clergy also provide resources, establish communication networks, and sometimes provide rescue assistance. This accumulation of responsibilities in their role as a clergyperson can be daunting. Bradfield et al. (1989) state, "responding to a disaster may be especially problematic when the assumption of new roles is not accompanied by a decrease in other role responsibilities" (p. 398). According to Bradfield et al., the ministers interviewed in their study reported that they were originally energized by the multiple roles they fulfilled during the disaster relief but later experienced adverse effects, including feeling fatigued and guilty about not being able to meet all the demands of their multiple roles. These are symptoms that are strongly associated with role strain.

Other studies have found the condition of stacked obligations to be less problematic. In her work examining the role of women in disasters, Fothergill (2004) found that as the expectations of women providing aid during the Grand Folks flood in 1997 increased, they remained able to negotiate the demands of all their roles. She argued that these women experienced what Sieber (1974) calls "role accumulation," but instead of feeling overwhelmed, they felt empowered by the performance of their various duties. These women did not experience role strain while performing their disaster work.

As this review of the literature suggests, there are conflicting findings on the occurrence of role conflict and the manifestation of role strain among emergency workers. It appears that role conflict is a nuanced issue, and the expression of it through role abandonment depends on certain factors. The type of agent that causes the disaster may affect response decisions, as some situations require a more urgent response to ensure the safety of loved ones or the community (White 1962). Hence, the way a person responds and whether or not role conflict affects him or her personally may depend on the type of incident faced. In addition, whether a first responder experiences role strain among the varied responsibilities associated with multiple roles depends strongly on the nature of the events in a disaster as well as the responder's experience with managing multiple role expectations. Individuals usually respond to the most immediate needs of those around them after a disaster whether the perceived needs are professional or familial (White 1962). Finally, the prioritizing of required duties can serve to stave off feelings of role strain.

Taking a Closer Look: Evidence of Role Conflict and Role Strain among Law Enforcement Officers in Two Disasters

To explore more fully the nuances associated with role strain and role conflict among police during disasters, this section of the chapter uses a case-study approach to deconstruct these phenomena among police officers who served during the Hurricane Katrina and the 2010 Chile earthquake and tsunami disasters. While the disaster types are different, their impact is similar in scale and scope, especially considering the tsunami in the equation of the Chilean disaster. Similarities between the two include the impact of the event across multiple jurisdictions; great physical damage to infrastructure, homes, and businesses; and the disruption of daily life activities.

Both Hurricane Katrina and the 2010 Chile earthquake and tsunami caused a tremendous amount of damage and destruction and severely challenged the operations of the police departments. Consequently, many of the officers who worked for the police departments were either affected personally or were presented with professional challenges by the disaster, if not both. The impact on these officers make each community of first responders excellent subjects for examining role conflict in the face of a high-consequence event.

As described in the Introduction, to assess the degree to which the storm affected officers' ability to respond to the call of duty, officers who served as first responders to the Hurricane Katrina and Chile earthquake and tsunami disaster were asked to volunteer to participate in a survey and face-to-face interviews. (See the Introduction for more information on the study design.) Although all the respondents reported fulfilling their professional roles during the disaster, upon further examination, the interview data revealed that almost half the officers interviewed reported feeling conflicted between their work and family obligations during the disaster. While a few of the officers interviewed said that they did not experience role conflict, the personal stories they shared about their experiences indicated they experienced at least some degree of role strain among their multiple priorities during the disaster.

As we have mentioned, these two disasters are ideal topics of study because of their magnitude and breadth of destruction. Hurricane Katrina was one of the most destructive weather events in U.S. history, a truly high-consequence event that was severe and pervasive enough to affect the police agency as well as individual officers' personal lives in major ways. Responders unmistakably perceived it as a threat to their families, friends, and property. The 2010 Chile earthquake and tsunami disaster was also a major one, with more than 2 million people affected by the combined disasters. The city of Concepción moved at least ten feet to the west, and the capital, Santiago, moved about eleven inches to the west-southwest. It is important to note that the Tuscaloosa Tornado

Super Outbreak disaster is not included in this discussion because the spatial attributes of the disaster did not pose the same level of threat to the officers as the other disaster sites. In fact, the Tuscaloosa Police Department officers interviewed did not report having the same level of concern for their loved ones and property as the officers in the other disaster sites.

Case Study 1: New Orleans and Gulfport

This section of the case study reviews the participants' responses to face-to-face interview questions on their experiences during Hurricane Katrina, but the focus of the discussion is on role conflict. Many themes emerged among individuals, who indicated that they experienced role conflict during the Katrina crisis. The most common theme was a general concern for the whereabouts of loved ones. The majority of those who experienced role conflict indicated that concerns for the safety of their loved ones was foremost in their minds as they performed their roles as first responders during the disaster. One of the central causes for concern was not knowing the status of their loved ones (e.g., whether they were in a safe location). Over a third of the GPD officers and nearly all the NOPD officers indicated that there was no communication between themselves and their loved ones, which caused them great concern. As one GPD officer stated, "I mean, of course you want to be there for your family, and take care of them, but you have to be here doing this. There were days you didn't even, I mean, my family went out of town, there were days . . . about two or three weeks before I could even talk with them to let them know I was OK, and make sure they was [sic] OK." Others conveyed the sentiment that the familial concerns obstructed their ability to focus on their professional responsibilities. As one NOPD officer stated, "Yes, I know I am a police officer and I had a duty to perform, but I could not perform that duty because I was thinking about my family."

Some individuals who experienced feeling conflicted, particularly those concerned about their loved ones, dealt with the conflict either by putting off thoughts about their concerns, seeking permission to leave, or leaving without permission. They often experienced denial as they tried to divert their attention to the work at hand instead of reflecting on worries and concerns outside their job as law-enforcement officers. One GPD officer stated, "You always thought about your family's well-being, but you tried to put it in the back of your mind." When officers sought permission to leave, the requests were reportedly denied. Their family responsibilities clearly remained a high priority, and some officers took time out to check on loved ones during their work hours. One noted that he "stole time" from the police department to get personal affairs in order.

A few of the respondents pointed out that they had concerns about their property during the disaster. There appeared to be a general understanding that they could not do much to save their homes from the impending damage. One GPD officer said, "There would've been no way I could've saved my house. We got four foot of water.... I might've thought if I knew that big a storm surge was coming I might've moved a li'l higher because above four foot in your house if you look around there's not much." Others reported that, while they had concerns about loved ones and property damage, the assistance provided by other family members is what dwarfed their sense of role conflict. As one GPD officer stated, "My dad patched up the roof, and my uncle cut up the tree in the yard and stuff like that; but it's my house, so they're doing repairs to my house, they're fixing my house and I'm out on the street doing my job, and if it wasn't for them doing what they did at my house, I couldn't have done what I did out on the street because I would have really felt torn, I needed to be at home doing these things. So if not for family . . ." Though some officers felt conflicted in their professional and familial responsibilities during the disaster, assistance provided by others helped to mitigate this discord with a few of the officers.

Those officers who indicated that role conflict was not an issue for them during the Katrina disaster provided several reasons for their ability to focus on the tasks at hand. Among the reasons were not having any concerns about the safety of loved ones, having a sense that their loved ones understood their professional duties, and having clear priorities. Some responders knew that their loved ones were in a safe place inside the affected area (e.g., hospital, shelter) or had no family members in the disaster zone. Having a sense that family members understood the officers' job requirements and professional duties appeared to be important for some of the officers who did not experience role conflict. As one respondent stated, "I can say that because of my wife—the relationship we have and the understanding and support I get from her—made it, you know, where [role conflict] wasn't a factor for me."

Some of the respondents who reported they did not experience role conflict stated they did not experience conflict because their commitment to their profession overrides their family responsibilities. As one officer said that it was "very sick to say, but most of us—because of our personalities, and what we do and why we do what we do—we have a tendency to put our job before our families." Another officer echoed this sentiment, saying he "put family second before, during, and after [Katrina]." These officers believed their role as law-enforcement officers superseded the roles they played within their family units.

Others experienced the opposite valuation, noting that they did not experience role conflict because their professional responsibilities did not take precedence over their family responsibilities. As one GPD officer stated, "People realize that you have to take care of your family first and your job second." Aside from the officers who reportedly "stole time" to deal with family needs, most of the officers who prioritized family did not indicate how their feelings were manifested during the height of the disaster.

The data collected on the NOPD and GPD officers showed role strain to be more of an issue among the NOPD officers than among the GPD officers. Most of the GPD officers interviewed said they had focused on addressing the immediate concerns in front of them and expressed high levels of confidence about the value of the disaster work they performed, whereas the NOPD.... This difference in experiences may be due to the differences in the degree to which the disaster directly affected the personal lives of the officers, as well as differences in the organizational leadership styles and the different levels of chaos that ensued after the storm.

It is interesting to note that while they reported differences in perceived levels of role strain, almost all the officers in both departments voiced having a sense of role conflict while serving in the Katrina disaster. The weight of that conflict appeared to vary among the responders. A majority of the responders reported that, while they were able to fulfill their professional responsibilities during the Katrina disaster, the inability to communicate and know the whereabouts of loved ones proved to be emotionally difficult. This appeared to be the case even among officers who mentioned that they knew the location of their family members. The inability to provide direct assistance to them at the time of the disaster caused some discord in their conscience, and it may have created dissonance within their personal lives beyond the scope of the disaster. The major cause of this conflict was fear and concern about the whereabouts and safety of loved ones.

Case Study 2: Constitución, Chile

As Chapter 1 notes, the police force in Chile is composed of both local police departments and the national police force. The national police force (GOPE) provides services across the country and receives special training to assist in times of extreme crisis. During the 2010 Chile earthquake and tsunami, both the national police force and officers with the local police departments served as first responders. This chapter includes analyses of data that were collected from the law-enforcement officers who worked in Constitución, Chile, during the disaster. The city of Constitución was one of the hardest hit by the earthquake because of its proximity to the quake's epicenter. The city was also hit by tsunami waves that reached over twenty-eight meters in height (Olsen et al. 2012). Thousands were rendered homeless as the tsunami destroyed wooden-framed and poorly constructed masonry houses (Olsen et al. 2012). The police department headquarters was under threat during the tsunami and so were the homes of most of the officers.

The analysis of the survey data collected on the police officers in Chile showed that, as with the officers in Gulfport, over half those surveyed reported being concerned about their loved ones during the earthquake and tsunami disaster. But unlike the case of the Gulfport officers, well over half of the Chilean officers (56 percent) did not believe that their law-enforcement responsibilities conflicted with their family obligations. As with the Gulfport officers, all the Chilean responders indicated that they fulfilled their professional obligations throughout the disaster.

The interview data of the police officers in Chile show both similarities and differences in concerns among the officers. As noted earlier, the data set for this study site includes both officers of the local police department in Constitución, Chile, and Special Operation Officers, a special unit of GOPE, who are relocated to various regions of the country to serve when needed. Therefore, some of the sample consisted of both local officers who had family members living within the immediate area of the earthquake and tsunami and others who were not local residents of Constitución. Nevertheless, most of the sample indicated that they did have concerns about the welfare of their loved ones at the time of the disaster, probably because of the widespread impact of the disaster.

The officers who did not have loved ones living in the most affected areas may have had a level of concern for their loved ones may that was different from the level of concern among the Gulfport, Mississippi, officers. The fact that a special organization takes care of GOPE officers' family members in times of need seems to have minimized their level of concern. Some of the officers reported that they knew their families were being taken care of. As one asserted, "The Carabineros institution was very supportive and protective to our families. Therefore, we knew our relatives were fine." These officers noted that the Carabineros provided basic supplies to their families and close relatives. If in some cases an officer had not known whether loved ones were in trouble, the officer knew that, if it was needed, an identified unit was designed to take care of their family members. In sum, while they could not be confident that their family members were not affected by the disaster, they could be assured that their needs were being addressed.

Those who knew their families were safe were able to focus their attention squarely on the tasks before them. One officer said, "Knowing that my family was doing well made me feel emotionally calm and able to dedicate myself to work. We always knew this would happen, but no one imagined an earthquake and tsunami of such a great magnitude." Knowing that their families were safe seemed to allow the officers the ability to focus on their role as police officers during the disaster.

Generally, the national police officers fared better than the officers of the Constitución police department. Many of these officers were born and raised in Constitución, and many of them had family members who resided in the city. Their loved ones were among the many who needed to evacuate before the tsunami hit the city. Like some of the officers in Gulfport, some of the officers in Constitución reported that their concerns about their loved ones dominated their thoughts. An officer stated, "those colleagues that did not have contact with their families were slowed down." Officers who were not aware of the whereabouts of their loved ones were affected by their concerns, which affected their job performance. For these officers, the high degree of uncertainty about the safety of their loved ones caused anxiety.

Like the Gulfport, Mississippi, officers, some of the Chilean officers indicated that they did not feel conflicted about meeting their professional obligations. One captain with the local police department shared that, after the earthquake hit, she immediately jumped out of bed, grabbed her bathrobe, and ran to the police department. When asked whether she felt conflicted about her responsibilities she said, "I left my daughter in my home but my mother and sisters were very close. I knew they were out of any danger and far away from the tsunami zone."

What is interesting about the captain's response is that she indicated that her home was one block away from the police station, which was very close to the evacuation zone. Therefore, although she didn't consider the direct risk associated with the threat of a tsunami while fleeing her home to attend to the duties of her job, her home and family were at risk from a tsunami. Instead of feeling worried about the risk associated with leaving her home and her daughter, she felt the pull toward performing her role as a police officer. It appears that she left feeling confident that her nearby family members would look after her daughter, thus alleviating any major concerns. Later in the interview, she noted that she returned to find her family once she finished with the rescue operations. She stated, "My only concern was whether they had food and water since we were without basic utilities for about ten to eleven days. Once the rescue activities were under control, I dedicated myself to assist the needs of my family." This officer clearly put the needs of her family second to the role she played as a law-enforcement officer during the crisis. But she was quick to rededicate herself to her family role once she fulfilled her role as a police officer.

Taking a Deeper Look: Law Enforcement Officers in Extreme Crises

Role strain during crisis events has not emerged as a frequent issue among the studies conducted on first responders. Rogers (1986), for one, suggests that individuals may meet behavioral expectations of their professional roles even when they find it difficult. The mixed findings among the data collected on the NOPD and GPD officers makes it important to further unpack this issue and review its implications for first response. The mixed findings may also be explained by Goode's (1960) argument regarding individuals' ability to "role bargain," wherein one goes through a process of alternating role behaviors to reduce role strain.

Yet disaster situations contain complications that can interfere with coping mechanisms like alternating role behaviors. Granted that the work of police officers is always multifaceted, the role becomes even more involved during disasters, and they may be required to perform search and rescue work and serve as law enforcers simultaneously. Despite some degree of overlap in the skills needed to perform police work and rescue operations, the two differ in the attitude and focus they require.

Having to enforce the law when these efforts seem to be taking the place of life-saving rescue activities, as in the case of NOPD officers during the Katrina disaster, can lead to cognitive dissonance among police officers. According to cognitive dissonance theory, people have a tendency to need consistency among their attitudes and beliefs (cognitions) and they feel uncomfortable when there is inconsistency (dissonance) between their attitudes and their behaviors (Festinger 1957). Having one's work performance out of harmony with one's values can cause stress and psychological discomfort. Under this type of inner conflict, most people will do as instructed as a result of positional obedience, normalization, or emotional trading. Positional obedience involves the justification of an action because it is in response to an order of an authority figure. Normalization is the process of internally explaining the action: it is not something that one wants to do, but it is part of the job. Last, emotional trading is the process of assessing that future rewards are worth the costs of compromising one's beliefs. Despite the fact that people often develop ways to circumvent their psychological discomfort, the effects of the resulting inner turmoil can manifest in negative behaviors.

When cognitive dissonance is not addressed, people often engage in maladaptive behaviors that can manifest themselves at the workplace. Such behaviors include increased absenteeism from work, withdrawal and disengagement from work-related activities, diminished job performance, and negative or inappropriate behaviors in the workplace. Festinger (1957) argues that in addition to "try[ing] to reduce the dissonance and achieve consonance," people will also actively seek to avoid the dissonance, which can ultimately serve to increase it.

All these behaviors can negatively affect the morale of the department and consequently the response and recovery efforts. On the surface, it appeared that, by and large, the NOPD and GPD officers accomplished what was needed with little regard for what they might prefer to do. However, it is possible that the call to switch from a focus on rescue missions to a focus on crime fighting caused cognitive dissonance among the NOPD officers. As noted earlier, research has shown that first responders often rank order their priorities, and for some officers, rescue missions should be prioritized over crime-fighting activities. This shift in official priorities, and a concomitant reconsidering of personal priorities as a result, may have contributed to the maladaptive behaviors that the NOPD officers exhibited during the Katrina disaster that Chapter 4 discusses.

Another impingement on an officer's ability to operate effectively is unmet fundamental needs while working at full capacity during a disaster. Lack of sustenance, water, and sleep presented themselves as pivotal issues for the NOPD officers that adversely affected the officers' ability to function. Lack of sleep arose as an issue among the GPD officers as well, but the majority of those interviewed did not convey major concerns about a lack of food or water. Lack of food, water, and sleep has been noted as major concerns among first responders in other major disasters (Toge and Adams, unpublished manuscript). The duration, intensity, and scope of the disaster determine the accessibility of needed resources. In the case of New Orleans, the breaks in the levee system caused the floodwaters to be sustained at high levels for several days, which made it more challenging to provide needed supplies to first responders. These differences in conditions helps to explain why these officers may have reported high levels of role strain than the GPD officers. Despite role strain's importance as an issue, role conflict is discussed more often in the first responder literature because it is often assumed to be more likely to lead to role abandonment. The internal struggle of having to decide whether to attend to personal responsibilities or to professional responsibilities is difficult to navigate for officers in times of crisis (Adams and Turner 2014). This will particularly be an issue for officers who are not able to communicate with or know the whereabouts of loved ones who live or work in the disaster zone. As illustrated in data discussed above, role conflict can lead to anguish, despair, and internal conflicts over priorities. But role conflict does not necessarily lead to role abandonment; role conflict reflects emotions and thoughts which do not have to translate into the action of abandoning one's role or post (Adams and Turner 2014). Role conflict and role abandonment are not synonymous. Chapter 4 discusses the issue of role abandonment in more detail.

The fact that the overwhelming majority of the officers chose to fulfill their professional duties despite their feelings of conflict opposes Killian's (1952) thesis that primary group membership supersedes secondary group membership during a crisis. The choice of whether to prioritize one's family or professional role during a crisis may be influenced by the individual's self-concept. Officers differ in their role prioritization, the priority largely depending on the weight each role plays in his or her self-identity. For officers who chose their professional roles over family roles, their personal and social identity appeared to be heavily rooted in their identity as a police officer.

For some individuals, prioritizing familial versus professional roles does not cause conflict as they are confident in their priorities, while others find it difficult. The findings from the NOPD and GPD data lend support to Major's (2003) argument that individuals do not have identical expectations in their roles as roles become "personalized." Some of the officers in the study divulged that the expectations they had for themselves as officers required that they place that role above the roles they played within their families. Other officers revealed that the expectations they had for themselves in the roles they play within their families were more important.

The findings also suggest that many of the officers fully embraced their roles as first responders, pointing to another potential response of officers during an extreme crisis—role enhancement (see Ahrens and Ryff 2006; Sieber 1974). It appeared that, for some, the importance of their professional roles became more apparent during the crisis. As previously noted, a few of the officers clearly indicated that the role as a police officer took precedence over the roles they played in their personal lives during the crisis. Borrowing the concept of the "heroic role as a rescue worker" from Killian (1952, p. 312), this role may serve as a means of role enhancement for some officers. This finding may reflect the fact that the "heroic role" reinforces their identity as law-enforcement officers, which serves to mitigate feelings of role conflict and role strain during crisis events. The finding may also reveal that for some officers their primary group membership resides with the police department.

Conclusion

The preponderance of literature examining role conflict within first-responder communities suggests that it does not exist among first responders. The measurement of this phenomenon, however, has largely been through an examination of the expression of the conflict through role abandonment. This chapter sought to examine the issue of role conflict through an analysis of the perceptions of first responders and their descriptions of how described behaviors manifested the conflicts. If the conflict did not lead to role abandonment among most of the responders examined in this book, the findings still suggest that role conflict is a complicated issue that could cause discord among first responders when they are personally affected by the disaster to which they are expected to respond. As Chapter 4 elucidates, some police officers did abandon their posts during the Hurricane Katrina disaster. Therefore, it cannot be considered a nonissue, but rather one that needs further examination.

This chapter thus illustrates that the traditional definition of role conflict as it relates to the first-responder communities should be expanded. The concept of role conflict within the context of the first-responder community should not be reduced to the single expression of it through role abandonment. The term should be used to denote the feelings caused by conflicting sets of responsibilities broadly, which can lead to discord within the psyches of the first responders. Role conflict can occur within first-responder communities when an event is so catastrophic that it affects responders and causes them to feel torn between professional and familial obligations. While it can manifest itself as role abandonment, or momentary role abandonment, abandonment does not have to occur for one to feel conflicted about responsibilities, and ultimately lead to what Rogers (1986) refers to as role strain, where one finds it difficult to fulfill role expectations despite meeting the behavioral expectations.

Currently, little research directly examines role strain among first responders generally and police specifically. Scholars who have considered the issue describe it as a feeling people sometimes experience when they are overwhelmed by responsibilities associated with one of their roles. Some use it to describe the feeling people get when they feel they are incapable of fulfilling responsibilities of all their several roles. Neither of these issues appeared as a major concern for most of the first responders examined in this chapter. The issue was brought up, however, among the NOPD officers who reportedly abandoned their post during the Katrina disaster. (See Chapter 4 for more information.)

KEY TAKEAWAYS FROM THIS CHAPTER

1. The concepts of role conflict and role strain are sometimes used interchangeably, but they are distinct. Role conflict is more likely than role strain to lead to role abandonment. It is essential to look for signs of stress within officers during high-consequence events to try to stave off negative responses of role conflict or role strain among the officers.
2. Concern for loved ones during a disaster adds additional emotional strain on officers that can lead to feelings of role conflict. The establishment of programs that provide immediate support for officers and their loved ones, which an officer can access during their rest breaks, at the time of a critical incident can work to reduce their level of strain. When officers know the whereabouts of their loved ones, they are more likely to feel comfortable with performing their roles as first responders.
3. While some officers feel a degree of conflict during a disaster when forced to choose between fulfilling their roles as police officers and fulfilling the roles they play in their personal lives, others do not feel any conflict. Those whose identity is firmly rooted in their role as a law-enforcement officers are less likely to feel role conflict.

4. Being required to fulfill law-enforcement responsibilities instead of what may be perceived as more important lifesaving tasks can cause role strain and cognitive dissonance. These feelings must be addressed during critical incident debriefing sessions with commanding officers before they lead to maladaptive behavioral responses.

DISCUSSION QUESTIONS

1. What are the differences between role conflict and role strain? Which do you think is most likely to be experienced by a police officer during a disaster? Why?
2. Imagine you are a police officer who is required to work during a major disaster in your hometown. Do you believe you would experience role conflict? Why or why not?
3. Are there any organizational factors that affect the differences in how police officers feel about the roles they may play during a disaster?
4. What types of behavioral responses may be manifested by a police officer who experiences role strain during a disaster?
5. What factors do you think most influenced the differences in the manifestation of role conflict among the police officers in the two departments examined in this chapter?

REFERENCES

Adams, Terri, and Milanika Turner. 2014. "Professional Responsibilities vs. Familial Responsibilities: An Examination of Role Conflict among First Responders during the Hurricane Katrina Disaster." *Journal of Emergency Management* 12 (1): 45–54.

Ahrens, Christina, and Carol Ryff. 2006. "Multiple Roles and Well-Being: Sociodemographic and Psychological Moderators." *Sex Roles* 55 (11–12): 801–815.

Ashforth, Blake E., and Fred Mael. 1989. "Social Identity Theory and the Organization." *Academy of Management Review* 14 (1): 20–39.

Barton, Allen H. 1969. *Communities in Disaster: A Sociological Analysis of Collective Stress Situations.* Garden City, NY: Doubleday.

Bradfield, Cecil, Mary Lou Wylie, and Lennis G. Echterling. 1989. "After the Flood: The Response of Ministers to a Natural Disaster." *Sociological Analysis* 49 (4): 397–407.

Coverman, Shelley. 1989. "Role Overload, Role Conflict, and Stress: Addressing Consequences of Multiple Role Demands." *Social Forces* 67 (4): 965–982.

Dynes, Russell R. 1986. *The Concept of Role in Disaster Research*. Newark, DE: University of Delaware Disaster Research Center.

Dynes, Russell R., and E. L. Quarantelli. 1986. "Role Simplification in Disaster." In *Role Stressors and Support for Emergency Workers: Proceedings of a 1984 Workshop Sponsored by the National Institute of Mental Health and the Federal Emergency Management Agency*. Center for Mental Health Studies of Emergencies (U.S.), National Institute of Mental Health (U.S.).

Festinger, Leon. 1957. *A Theory of Cognitive Dissonance*. Stanford, CA: Stanford University Press.

Fothergill, Alice. 2004. *Heads above Water: Gender, Class, and Family in the Grand Forks Flood*. Albany: State University of New York Press.

Getzels, J. W., and E. G. Guba. 1954. "Role, Role Conflict, and Effectiveness: An Empirical Study." *American Sociological Review* 19 (2): 164–175.

Goode, William J. 1960. "A Theory of Role Strain." *American Sociological Review* 25 (4): 483–496.

Kahn, Robert L., Donald Wolfe, Robert P. Quinn. 1964. *Organizational Stress: Studies in Role Conflict and Ambiguity*. New York: Wiley.

Killian, Lewis M. 1952. "The Significance of Multiple-Group Membership in Disaster." *American Journal of Sociology* 57 (4): 309–314.

Kopelman, Richard E., Jeffrey H. Greenhaus., and Thomas F. Connolly. 1983. "A Model of Work Family and Interrole Conflict: A Construct Validation Study." *Organizational Behavior and Human Performance* 32:198–215.

Lipman-Blumen, Jean. 1973. "Role-Differentiation as a System Response to Crisis: Occupational and Political Roles for Women." *Social Inquiry* 43: 105–129.

Major, Debra. 2003. "Utilizing Role Theory to Help Employed Parents Cope with Children's Chronic Illness." *Health Education Research: Theory and Practice* 18 (1): 45–57.

Olsen, Michael J., Kwik Fai Cheung, Yoshiki Yamazaki, Shawn Butcher, Maria Garlock, Solomon Yim, Sarah McGarity, et al. 2012. "Damage Assessment of 2010 Chile Earthquake and Tsunami using Terrestrial Laser Scanning." *Earthquake Spectra* 28 (S1): S179–S197.

Pietromonaco, Paula. R., Jean Manis, and Katherine Frohardt-Lane. 1986. "Psychological Consequences of Multiple Social Roles." *Psychology of Women Quarterly* 10:373–382.

Pleck, Joseph H., Graham L. Staines, and Linda Lang. 1980. "Conflicts between Work and Family Life." *Monthly Labor Review* 103:29–32.

Rogers, George Oliver. 1986. "Role Conflict in Crisis with Limited Forewarning." *Journal of Applied Psychology* 3 (1): 33–50.

Sarbin, Theodore R., and Vernon L. Allen. 1968. "Role Theory." In *Handbook of Social Psychology*, 2nd ed., vol. 1, edited by G. Lindzey and E. Aronson, 488–567. Reading, MA: Addison-Wesley.

Sieber, Sam, D. 1974. "Toward a Theory of Role Accumulation." *American Sociological Review* 39 (August): 567–578.

Stryker, Sheldon, and Anne Statham. 1985. "Symbolic Interaction and Role Theory." In *Handbook of Social Psychology*, 3rd ed., vol. 1, edited by G. Lindzey and E. Aronson, 311–378. New York: Random House.

Tajfel, Henri. 1978. "Interindividual Behavior and Intergroup Behavior." In *Differentiation between Social Groups: Studies in the Social Psychology of Intergroup Relations*, edited by H. Tajfel, 27–60. London: Academic.

Tajfel, Henri, and John Turner. 1979. "An Integrative Theory of Intergroup Conflict." In *The Social Psychology of Intergroup Relations*, edited by W. G. Austin and S. Worshel, 33–47. Monterey, CA: Brooks/Cole.

Trainor, Joseph E., and Lauren E. Barsky. 2011. *Reporting for Duty? A Synthesis of Research on Role Conflict, Strain and Abandonment among Emergency Responders during Disasters and Catastrophes*. Newark: University of Delaware Disaster Research Center.

Turner, John C., Michael Hogg, Penelope Oakes, Stephen Reicher, and Margaret Wetherell. 1987. *Rediscovering the Social Group: A Self-Categorization Theory*. Oxford, U.K.: Basil Blackwell.

White, Meda Miller. 1962. *Role Conflict in Disasters: Not Family but Familiarity First*. Chicago: University of Chicago.

Wilcox, Victoria L. 1994. "Burnout in Military Personnel." In *Military Psychiatry: Preparing in Peace for War*, edited by L. B. Davis, C. M. Quick, and S. E. Siegel, 30–49. Washington, DC: U.S. Department of the Army and Borden Institute.

4

Missing and Out of Action

Case Study of Post Abandonment in New Orleans during Hurricane Katrina

> At least 200 officers walk away.
> —Seattle Times

> Law officers, overwhelmed, are quitting the force.
> —New York Times

> Katrina made police choose between duty and loved ones.
> —USA Today

As highlighted by the above headlines from some of the nation's most well-circulated newspapers, role abandonment emerged as a critical issue during the Katrina disaster. Several news outlets reported that more than two hundred police officers from the NOPD abandoned their posts during the crisis. The reported post abandonment challenged the longstanding belief within the first-responder community that first responders never or rarely forsake their responsibilities during crisis events (e.g., Dynes 1986; White 1962).

While post abandonment is considered uncommon, the fact that NOPD lost close to 10 percent of its police force during the Katrina crisis signals a need for the first-responder community to take the issue seriously. It also suggests that post abandonment can represent a distinctive emergency management concern during a catastrophic event. For this reason, it is important to understand the underlying factors that influenced the officers' decisions to leave their posts during one of the most cataclysmic events in the nation's history.

This chapter discusses the issue of post abandonment and the underlying factors that led officers to leave their assigned duties during the Hurricane Katrina crisis. It examines the stories behind the headlines, exploring the reasons why the officers chose to abandon their obligations. The chapter also presents a theoretical analysis of the decision-making processes that led the officers to forsake their professional duties at the height of one of the worst disasters to affect the nation. Specifically, the chapter addresses the following questions: (1) What constitutes abandonment of duty? (2) What factors contribute to the abandonment of duty? (3) How is post abandonment manifested among first responders? (4) What decision-making processes contribute to post abandonment? These questions are addressed through an analysis of characteristic stories expressed through the testimonies of officers who were sanctioned by the NOPD, as well as through interviews of officers who served during the Katrina disaster.

Absence in the Line of Duty

Typically, post abandonment is defined as the act of leaving one's assigned job responsibility without receiving permission from a superior. The notion is very similar to the military acronym AWOL—absent without leave—which, according to the *Uniform Code of Military Justice* Article 86 ("Absence without Leave" 2018, n.p.), occurs when a member of the armed services, without authority, "(1) fails to go to his appointed place of duty at the time prescribed; (2) goes from that place; or (3) absents himself or remains absent from his unit, organization, or place of duty at which he is required to be at the time prescribed." There is little discussion of this issue in the policing literature, and, as Chapter 3 notes, the research on first-responder behaviors discusses it in connection with role conflict. Nevertheless, Adams and Turner (2014) suggest that these issues are not synonymous with each other, as role conflict can exist without manifesting itself as role abandonment. This section reviews research that examines the issue of post abandonment among first responders—as well as military personnel, as this phenomenon is more commonly researched within that population.

There has been significant debate over whether role abandonment is an issue among first responders. Lewis Killian was one of the first researchers to suggest that role abandonment occurs among emergency workers. In his examination of the emergency response to a tanker explosion that resulted in over 4,000 injuries and 512 deaths in Texas City, Texas, Killian (1952) reported, "the great majority of persons . . . involved in such dilemmas [of family versus work] resolved them in favor of loyalty to the family or, in some cases, friendship groups" (p. 311). Thus, emergency responders who feel conflicted about their roles will place their familial roles above their first responder duties. Subsequent work does not support Killian's observation. White (1962) finds that role abandonment did not arise as an issue in her study of several organizations involved in disasters. Similarly, Dynes (1986) reports that no disaster workers abandoned their posts in an examination of over 443 disaster workers. In addition, Rogers (1986) notes that post abandonment is rare, and instead argues that role strain is more common (see Chapter 3). Adams and Turner (2014), however, posit that, although role abandonment is rare, first responders engage in temporary role abandonment, sometimes using creative strategies to take care of non-job-related responsibilities during disasters. In addition, Trainor and Barsky (2011) suggest that the possibility of role abandonment should not be regarded as a nonissue within the first-responder community.

In addition to role abandonment among emergency workers, a number of scholars seek to elucidate the reasons soldiers go absent without leave. Among military personnel, abandonment of duty can occur for many reasons. Avins (1962) examines the case of those who deliberately chose to abandon their mission as a means of avoiding hazardous duty. Woodbury (1921) argues that psychological issues (i.e., impaired mental health) and familial obligations lead to the desertion of duty among soldiers, as well as the use of drugs and alcohol as a means of coping with the pressures of serving in the military. Other research reports that the primary reason for the abandonment of duty is personal and family problems, including feelings of devaluation and difficulty assimilating to the military lifestyle (Ramsberger and D. Bruce Bell 2002). Neurosis and lack of moral support from colleagues have also been linked to desertion (Rose 1951). Similarly, Walzer (1967) finds that group interpersonal relationships and conflict are causes of desertion. Additional personal characteristics linked to the abandonment of duty are lack of discipline (Vargas 1987), underdeveloped morality (Penton 1950), and youthfulness and a lack of education (Woodbury 1921). One of the most counterintuitive findings is that of Eisenberg (2005), who finds that some soldiers with high levels of patriotism feel that desertion is the only honorable means of leaving the military when faced with having to meet familial obligations. Other research, however, suggests that the higher the level of patriotism a soldier has, the greater the chance that the soldier will remain on his or her post (Patterson 2005).

While some scholars have described the connection between personal attributes and abandonment of duty, others have focused on organizational characteristics. Dobie (2005) reports that desertion is considered a last-resort option for soldiers who seek to escape their military duties, a desire that has been linked to the recruiting process, basic training, and the control and aggressiveness characteristic of the military. Resentment resulting from a variety of reasons, including having to work while injured, serving on less-than-exciting missions, and growing antipathy toward the war they were fighting have been correlated with desertion (Dobie 2005).

Post Abandonment during Katrina

Most of the research on post abandonment has focused on military personnel: the scant research on its incidence among first responders finds it uncommon in that community. Most police departments have strict protocols for seeking permission for the relief of duty during a noncrisis incident, and the requirements are more stringent during a crisis. For instance, during a hurricane, NOPD officers can only receive permission to be relieved of their duties from the superintendent or a deputy superintendent. For this reason, anyone who did not receive direct permission from one of these officers was deemed to be in violation of departmental codes during Hurricane Katrina.

As noted in this chapter's introduction, during the Katrina disaster a number of media outlets reported up to two hundred officers missing from the NOPD (Sims 2007; Treaster 2005). Superintendent Warren Riley contradicted these early figures in a congressional hearing, testifying that 147 officers left or abandoned their post sometime during the storm.[1] He asserted that the original media reports included officers who had to be rescued from the disaster (Griffin and Phillips 2005). As Riley stated, "When we lost telephone service and radio communication, some officers were stranded on their rooftops for four to five days, stranded in areas around the water due to rising water or displaced into other units or divisions" (as cited in Griffin and Phillips 2005). In short, some of the early figures of post abandonment included these stranded officers. At the time, NOPD officers were not required to report for duty until their appointed shift time, and some were waiting out the storm at home and found themselves stranded and in need of assistance after the breaches in the levee system. In total, 91 officers had to be rescued (Adams and Stewart 2015). The superintendent's figures showed that 8 to 11 percent of 1,750 officers abandoned their post during the disaster (Adams and Stewart 2015).

Reasons for Leaving: The Stories behind the Headlines

> No, sir. I didn't say it was anyone's fault. I'm saying that no one was prepared for this. If I had a crystal ball, then I would have been there of course.
>
> —Anonymous

---

1. *Hurricane Katrina: Managing Law Enforcement and Communications in a Catastrophe: Hearing Before the S. Comm. on Homeland Sec. & Gov't'l Affairs*, 109th Cong. (2006) (testimony of Warren J. Riley, Sup. of the New Orleans Police Dep't).

This section of the chapter presents a case study analysis to explore the reasons why the officers who abandoned their post opted to do so. The hearing records of the NOPD officers who were charged with abandoning their posts during the Katrina disaster provide insight into why these officers made that decision. During the hearings, the officers were asked about the circumstances of their cases, and the responses to the myriad questions provide data on why. The cases selected for this discussion typify the pre- or postdisaster experiences of the officers who abandoned their posts. Pseudonyms are used in place of the actual names to protect the identity of the officers; but the details provided on each case reflect actual events.

Several of the officers indicated that their reasons for leaving were many. Such was the case for Walker Kendall, who was a NOPD patrol officer for twenty-five years at the time of the Katrina disaster. Kendall reported for duty in the 2nd District at his scheduled shift time prior to Katrina's landfall, but he fled the city two days later and was absent from the department for two days. According to Kendall's testimony, he attempted to get permission to be relieved of his duties but was unsuccessful in overcoming the communication barriers. He felt compelled to attend to the needs of his family, as he was unable to convince his wife and sister-in-law to evacuate the city before the storm. According to Kendall, his family was left at home with a manual-transmission truck, and neither his wife nor his sister-in-law was capable of driving it. He used his absence to evacuate his family to Dallas, Texas, he testified.

While Kendall attested that he left to take care of his family, he also admitted that fear was a determining factor in his decision to flee the city. During his appeal trial, he disclosed the following: "I mean, like I say, everybody had their own circumstances that they had to deal with during Katrina. Some—you know, some panicked. A lot—I mean, a lot of us panicked. I'm not going to lie and say that, you know I wasn't a little bit upset or scared about what was going on." Essentially, Kendall acknowledged that fear played a role in why he left his post. Despite appealing the sanction, he was suspended without pay for thirty days.

An additional pressing concern influencing the officers' decisions to leave was the issue of child care. Child care was a principal concern for female officers, as it was for Nanette Karle. At the time of Katrina's landfall, Karle had been an officer with NOPD for three years and was assigned to the 2nd District at the time of Katrina's landfall. She waited for the storm to pass at one of the local hotels. That hotel also fell victim to floodwaters, so Karle assisted in efforts to relocate the hotel guests to a hotel in Baton Rouge. After arriving in Baton Rouge, she spoke with her immediate supervisor, who, she reported, did not assign her any duties, but she actively participated in evacuating hotel guests on her own initiative.

On day three of the disaster, Karle decided to leave her post without permission to retrieve her daughter from what she considered to be unsecure circumstances. According to Karle, her husband was out of town and could not get a flight back to the city. Meanwhile, an elderly aunt was caring for their child. Karle testified that after several attempts to reach her sergeant, she was overcome with concerns about their daughter. She decided to leave her post to pick up her daughter and take her to their nearest relative in Atlanta, Georgia. Karle hitched a ride to Atlanta, where she stayed for nine days. She maintained that while absent she continued to call her sergeant and eventually reached him, whereupon she received oral permission to take care of what she needed to take care of and return to work afterward. Karle was passionate in her description of why she chose to leave:

> I've been on the job for seven years. I'm a very good officer, a very good officer. My work speaks for itself. It wasn't about me being a coward. It was not about me being scared, because I've worked in the St. Bernard, Iberville, and Lafitte Housing Developments.... I'm considered one of the toughest even among the men, so it wasn't about me being scared. My main objective was to take care of my four-year-old daughter. I was abandoned as a child, and I didn't want my daughter to feel that way. And that was my reason for leaving, my only reason for leaving.

Hence, Karle's decision to leave was based on her perception that it was her best option for addressing the needs of her family. She received a sanction of suspension without pay for fifty-five days, which she appealed, but her appeal was denied.

As in Karle's case, some officers who knew the whereabouts of their nearest and dearest loved ones felt pressured by calls from those loved ones to leave their posts and evacuate the city. This was an issue faced by Melinda Davis, who had only been on the force for one year at the time of the Katrina disaster. She was fired for leaving her post without permission for twenty-one days. According to Davis, neither she nor her immediate family members were aware of the seriousness of the storm until she had a conversation with her partner in the 8th District, who mentioned that "we have a big storm coming" on the evening of August 27. She noted that her mother evacuated, but her husband decided to stay behind with their family, which included five children, at a local motel because he did not want to leave her behind. She said, "Me and my husband we [were] thinking it was just gonna be a storm like it was last year, cause it didn't actually hit and we didn't have to stay [at the hotel] overnight."

Davis testified that she worked for a week after the disaster, but she started getting sick and felt drained. She testified that the pleas from her family to leave the city, including her mother stressing that she was not feeling well, began to wear on her. As she described in her testimony, "I think had I done things differently and if my family could have gotten out of the city I would have been able to stay and perform my duties no doubt. But to be there and see them, their emotions and the suffering, that took a toll on me so I was just drained. I just couldn't take it." Davis explained that once she made the decision to leave, she searched for a ranking officer and eventually found her sergeant. She indicated that she was not quitting, but she felt she had to evacuate her family out of the city, and she would return. According to her, the sergeant responded, "I understand, kiddo, you got to do what you got to do."

Davis asserted that she requested permission to return to work on September 15 but was denied permission by her captain, and thus she was prevented from working. She appealed her termination, and her appeal was granted. Davis was reinstated and provided her back pay, and her penalty was reduced to a 105-day suspension.

Unlike the previously mentioned cases, some of the officers were not on duty at the time of the storm. Such was the case for Lionel Lyons, a fifteen-year veteran on the force and member of the K-9 Unit. While the department was gearing up for the storm, he was on vacation, but he returned to work a day before the storm at the request of his captain. According to Lyons, his sergeant instructed him to go home and secure his family and await a call on where to meet the next day. He reported that he never received a call from his sergeant, and his house was deluged with floodwater. In his testimony, he asserted that he waited for assistance on the roof of his house as he made several attempts to contact his sergeant. He stated, "By this point, I'm stuck on the roof . . . and I'm calling him. I'm trying to communicate, and nobody's responding. I called dispatch. They tell me a boat is on the way. The boat never come [*sic*]."

Lyons went on to report that he was eventually rescued by a CNN crew, and he later ran into someone from Wildlife and Fisheries who agreed to return him to his unit to retrieve his dog, all while they were rescuing flood victims from the rooftops of their homes. After being united with his dog, Lyons ran into a police officer from the 6th District station who took him back to the 6th District. Once he reached the station, he was put in contact with his sergeant. In his testimony, Lyons related this conversation with his sergeant: "'We feel it's best, though, that you stay here because your dog is . . . secure in the station, we have nowhere to house your dog.' He said, 'but it's up to you.' The captain never ordered me to report to duty." As a result of what he perceived as an indication to stay put, Lyons stayed at the police station with his dog for a week after Katrina. The commander of the K-9 Unit testified that Lyons was instructed to report back to his unit, and he was suspended for fifteen days for a violation of the internal regulation regarding instructions from an authoritative source. Lyons appealed the ruling, but the appeal was denied.

The above cases illustrate that the duration of the absenteeism and the reasons for it varied among those who left. Many of the officers left for two days or less. Among these officers, some used the time to evacuate family members who had not evacuated during the time when they were first instructed to before the hurricane's landfall. Others left the city to look for loved ones at evacuation sites outside the city, either before or after the onset of the storm and resulting disaster. Some of the officers left for more than a week, and, in one of the reviewed cases, an officer left for fifteen weeks.

The most common thread running through a majority of the cases of post abandonment was concern for the wellbeing of loved ones. This finding is similar to previous research that has noted family problems to be a cause of military personnel leaving without permission (e.g., Ramsberger and Bell 2002; Woodbury 1921). This finding supports Wilcox's (2012) loyalty conflict argument, as these officers felt torn between their conflicting loyalties toward their family and their profession. (See Chapter 3 for a more detailed discussion on this topic.) As Chapter 3 notes, role conflict occurs when individuals feel conflicted about which duties from which role (e.g., professional role, family role, community role) they should try to fulfill during a disaster when those duties or roles are incongruous with one another.

Most of the officers discussed in the previous chapter did not abandon their posts during the disaster in which they served. Certain cases in this review of data collected from the NOPD hearings, however, reveal that some officers left because they felt conflicted. The ability to navigate between competing roles sometimes leaves individuals feeling as if they have more loyalty toward their loved ones than their occupation. Under that light, some officers who left the department to attend to the needs of their loved ones did so out of loyalty to those they love. For some of them, leaving their post seemed to be the only option that made sense.

The other frequently cited cause of post abandonment—miscommunication between superior officers and the lower-ranking officers—has not previously been noted in the literature.

In several of the post abandonment cases reviewed, the officers cited miscommunication issues as a contributing factor in why they left their assigned post during the disaster. The failure of regular communication channels served to complicate the situation, making it nearly impossible for the officers to reach their superiors by phone. In the absence of normal modes of communication, many of the officers were faced with having to make potentially life-altering decisions in the midst of an extreme situation. The cases that highlight miscommunication as an essential reason for the officers' failure to report to work bring to light another important factor: overreliance on directives from superiors. As Chapter 2 asserts, it is imperative that officers of all ranks have the ability to lead in times of crisis. Because the police have to function autonomously and regularly employ independent discretion, it would be expected that they be capable of making decisions during a crisis without relying on orders from ranking officers. These cases illustrate that this assumption cannot be taken for granted.

The above-described cases of post abandonment among the New Orleans police officers during Hurricane Katrina illustrate that abandonment can happen at any point during a disaster. Some officers chose to flee their post during the initial phase of the disaster, which looks chiefly like a result of acute fear. The cases reviewed demonstrate, however, that abandonment is most likely to occur after the initial phase of a crisis. That is, post abandonment appears to be more likely to occur in the response phase of a disaster. The decision to leave one's post during this phase appears to be largely in response to concern for loved ones and results from a deliberate decision-making process that reflects the desire to attend to the needs of loved ones.

While most of the officers who left received a formal sanction by the department, many also faced informal sanctions by their peers. Fellow officers perceived those who left their posts but returned within a two days differently from those who left for more than a few days. Those who left for longer periods of time were regarded as cowards by some of the officers who stayed on post for the duration of the disaster. Some of the officers reported being treated differently by their fellow officers when they returned to the department. Many of the officers who were interviewed who did not leave their posts during the disaster reported feeling that they could not trust those who left to watch their back in tight situations in the line of duty. One officer stated the following:

> People did make distinctions, I don't know if everyone, and I know there are some people who are back on the job, that I know for certain left because they were scared and I mean I don't have resentment for them. I do reserve my safety around them because I know what they did in that situation. What happens is I'm going to second guess them, if I'm on the line with them; then again, you have to prove yourself. This was a situation nobody had ever been through before in our lifetime or our professional lifetime.

As noted in the above statement, an important distinction was made between those who were perceived to have left for legitimate reasons such as seeking to assist family members and those who left for reasons that were perceived as being illegitimate. After the disaster, those who served during the Hurricane Katrina were given special pins to mark their service during the disaster. One officer interviewed noted that the significance of the pin was considerably reduced when he saw officers who left their post during the disaster wearing the pin. The symbolism of post abandonment appears to have had a lasting effect on the officers of NOPD.

While the dust has settled, and most have gotten on with their lives, some still regard the actions of those who left their posts as being questionable and the ties that bind them together are not as strong. As underscored in the officer's statement above, some of the officers who left their post acquired a reputation of being untrustworthy. The inability to trust those who left their posts during the disaster affected how their fellow officers perceive and treat them, and trust and the ability to depend on a fellow officer are essential elements in policing. Embedded in police culture are ideals of solidarity, brotherhood/sisterhood, and bravery (Skolnick 1994). These ideals include a variety of axioms such as "watch out for your partner," "don't give up on another cop," and "getting the job done" (Reuss-Ianni 1983). Thus, looking out for each other and not turning your back on another officer are core elements in the ideals of policing, elements that abandoning one's post can undermine.

The Reasoning behind the Actions

Because abandoning one's post runs counter to traditional police ethics, it is important to understand the processes behind decision making during highly intense crisis events that could lead to the perception that post abandonment is the most favorable choice. Of the many theories and concepts that describe decision-making processes, three of the most relevant to decision making in the midst of a crisis are crisis decision theory, bounded rationality theory, and the concept of panic flight.

Crisis decision theory draws on research findings on coping, health behaviors, and decision making to define the process of how individuals respond to negative life events. Developed by Sweeney (2008), crisis decision theory posits that decisions made under crisis circumstances occur in three stages. As highlighted in the coping literature (see Folkman and Lazarus 1980; Lazarus and Folkman 1984), people seek to appraise the situation and make assessments of the negative impacts of the event during the first stage. In the second stage, individuals choose a set of response options that fit the "controllability" of the circumstances faced from among the available response options. Sweeney (2008) argues that limited time, finances, personal abilities, and social support can prevent a person from selecting the optimal response strategy. The process is further complicated when a person has multiple response options, which can be overwhelming to choose between. In the last stage of the process, people evaluate the pros and cons of response strategies. When evaluating a possible response to a crisis, the decision maker takes three factors into consideration: resources needed to service response and rescue efforts, direct consequences, and indirect consequences. Direct consequences are things that could improve circumstances or make them worse. The responses the individual believes to be more likely to lead to positive circumstances are more attractive than others. Evaluation of indirect consequences includes an appraisal of the following factors: emotions, public image, potential impact on other areas of one's life, and impact on others.

The three stages can be experienced as a nonlinear, unordered process: as Sweeney (2008) asserts, one can either get stuck at one stage or revert to a previous stage at any time. Sweeney also notes that decision-making processes are further affected by "social context, personal motivations, and automatic processing" (p. 61). Sweeney's theory offers useful insights on the stages that decision makers go through when faced with a crisis, but it does not fully explicate how decisions are made within imposed limitations.

Bounded rationality theory describes how people are forced to make decisions within a limited set of circumstances. The theory asserts that human behavior contains both rational and irrational elements (Simon 1956). Most people make decisions that are based on limited information, limited cognitive capabilities, and within a limited timeframe. The decision maker does his or her best to select the best choice within these constraints but does not behave as an entirely rational actor. When a person confronts a need to make a decision, the person will either replicate previous responses or take a new course of action if facing circumstances he or she has never experienced before (Fiori 2011). Circumstances that are outside the norm are riddled with uncertainty, forcing people to make a nonoptimal decision within the scope of a set of unknowns—a process referred to as "satisficing" (Simon 1956). Thus, bounded rationality theory describes what people do when they make a decision within a set of limits that may or may not be sensible when viewed outside the constraints (March 1978).

There are many unknowns in the midst of a disaster such as Hurricane Katrina: the amount of information available is limited, time is of the essence, and it the situation produces a high degree of pressure. The parameters and understanding provided by bounded rationality theory provide for the plausibility that some individuals would conclude that abandoning their post in response to either fear or concerns for loved ones is a viable solution. As bounded rationality theory suggests, the satisficing option chosen by the decision maker may not look like the most responsible decision to observers outside the context; but inside the context it may be the only subjectively viable solution.

In some cases, within the scope of a disaster, fear is the dominant emotion governing one's response options. While there are different maladaptive responses to fear, the one most germane to this discussion is panic flight. Panic flight is associated with acute fear, loss of control, and nonsocial and nonrational flight (Quarantelli 1954). It is a natural response to intense fear, and though people will not attempt to flee a situation if there is no perceived escape route, they will seize the opportunity to flee if one is presented (Fisher 1998). Quarantelli was one of the first to examine the issue of panic flight and found that, while rare, it is more likely to occur under certain conditions: (1) a prior-held belief that certain situations will lead to panic; (2) insufficient management of the crisis, causing people to feel they are on their own; (3) the perception that the opportunities to escape danger are diminishing; (4) the perception that the only way to save oneself is through flight; and (5) a feeling of isolation and inability to depend on anyone in their surroundings. Ultimately, Quarantelli argues that panic flight is not likely to occur but that it can when a person feels opportunities for gaining assistance are quickly declining. In essence, while unlikely, panic flight is a conceivable reaction for first responders if the right conditions and temperament of the person combine for such a response.

Crisis decision theory, bounded rationality theory, and the concept of panic flight offer valuable insights on factors affecting decision-making processes in the midst of a watershed moment in life. The officers who served during the Katrina disaster encountered unstable environmental conditions, dysfunctional organizational circumstances, and, for many, clashing obligations. In sum, these officers were assessing the situation and weighing their response options—stay and work or flee the city for short or long periods of time—under extreme conditions. The officers' descriptions of the factors that led them to leave their posts illustrate the response assessment and weighing process. The officers considered the direct and indirect effects of the decision within an environment that was beset with uncertainty, limited situational awareness, diminished mental capacity, and tight time constraints. These officers appraised the situation, selected what they perceived as optimal response strategies, and evaluated those strategies while considering the available resources and direct and indirect effects of their choices.

While many of the officers' decision to leave was grounded in an appraisal process that led them to choose their obligations to loved ones over their professional obligations, those who left their posts during the initial phase of the disaster appeared to have made the decision out of fear, which typifies panic flight. There was a general sentiment among the officers who did not abandon their posts that most of the officers who left did so out of fear. Many who were interviewed argued that allowances were made for those who had to go to attend to the needs of their families and loved ones, but those who left out of fear were deemed to have turned their backs on the department. An example of what was regarded as flight in response to fear is articulated by an NOPD sergeant who described how he lost three officers out of a team of fourteen, right after the storm passed over the city: "The rumor had passed the Canal, the Industrial Canal, levee was actually blown and water was actually coming toward our district department, and they said it was going to be like 20 feet of water, which would be higher than the roof: we weren't going to survive. And some of them just felt like they, [they] were going to leave before it got to them. . . . One guy, he never returned." Essentially, the three officers the sergeant described fled their district station because they were fearful their lives were in imminent danger. Two of the officers returned to continue working with the team, but the third officer never returned to the department. Although the floodwaters did eventually reach the station, none of the officers who remained on duty was physically harmed. This case exemplifies how fear can lead some officers to think that the most viable option is flight in the midst of perceived danger—thus, panic flight. The behavior of the two officers who returned to work after the initial flight can be regarded as temporary post abandonment.

While the focus of this discussion has been on post abandonment among the NOPD, as Chapter 3 highlights, how officers deal with the draw to attend to the needs of loved ones during a disaster can vary. A few of the GPD officers that Chapter 3 reported on took creative measures to attend to the needs of their loved ones. Some reportedly took time away from their post during the disaster, but those who took such an action did not define it as post abandonment.

The failure to define such these measures as post abandonment speaks to the difference in perception. In contrast with the NOPD, the GPD came under little to no fire during the Katrina crisis. The department had no known infractions reported against its officers for post abandonment. Any violations committed by the officers were done under the radar of the public and the department. Nevertheless, reports from personal interviews collected by Adams and Turner (2014) note that a small number of officers took time while they were on duty to attend to the needs of their family members or to check on the status of their loved ones. One could argue that these officers were creative in their approach to resolving this conflict (Adams and Turner 2014), while others might suggest that the time they took away from their post to attend to personal duties constitutes role abandonment or what could be called a form of temporary post abandonment. In sum, the act of leaving one's post can take on many different forms, and the characterization of the action of leaving their post to attend to personal needs depends on who is doing the characterization.

For some, taking time away from work responsibilities during a disaster does not constitute an infraction, particularly when the time away cannot be documented as flight. The perceived severity of the infraction may also depend on the amount of time taken: an absence of an hour or two taken to check on personal responsibilities may appear different from twenty-four or more hours. Nevertheless, one could consider these infractions to be temporary or episodic lapses of duty. Whatever the range of time taken to attend to other matters during a time when one is supposed to be on duty during a disaster, it can be interpreted either as an infraction or as a necessary act. The interpretation of the action depends on what constitutes an appropriate action.

Conclusion

The impetus for post abandonment, as well as the amount of time spent away from the department, varied among the officers who left during the Hurricane Katrina disaster. Analysis of post abandonment cases in New Orleans shows that most officers reported working during their assigned shift before Katrina's landfall. In the following days, some left for twenty-four to forty-eight hours, and others left for five or more days. Officers who were not granted formal permission to leave their assigned post were charged with post abandonment by the NOPD. The department sanctioned the officers according to the perceived egregiousness of their actions: officers were either fired or suspended without pay for four months or more. In total, fifty-one NOPD employees were fired—forty-five officers and six civilian employees—for post abandonment (The Abrams Report 2005).

While most of the previous literature written on first-responder behaviors argues that post abandonment is a nonissue among this community, there is evidence that while it is not the norm, it does happen. The reasons for leaving, as well as the duration of the absence, vary greatly. The top officials' perception of the infraction of leaving one's post depended on the amount of time away from departmental duties, coupled with the reasons advanced for leaving. It appears that a few of the officers succumbed to panic flight, while others weighed their options and discerned that it was best to leave their post to attend to the obligations they had to loved ones.

The cases of post abandonment during Hurricane Katrina reviewed in this chapter illustrate that it can sully the relationship between the officers who leave and those who stay on duty for the duration of the crisis. The perceptions of the infractions by the other officers depends on the reasons for leaving and the duration of their absence. Many of the NOPD officers who did not leave their posts felt that those that did leave for what were perceived as illegitimate reasons could not be completely trusted to "have their backs" in the line of duty. This sentiment is problematic when one of the essential principles of policing is solidarity. The break in solidarity represents a direct assault on two of the key cultural maxims that undergird policing: "watch out for your partner" and "don't give up on another cop."

KEY TAKEAWAYS FROM THIS CHAPTER

1. While post abandonment is uncommon, it occurs in different forms that may sometimes elude the attachment of a label, but this does not mean that it does not happen.
2. A number of factors can lead to post abandonment, but the most common factor appears to be role conflict.
3. Open and constant communication from superiors on the status of operations is essential to try to forestall thoughts of role abandonment.
4. Reinforcement of traditional police values may serve to inhibit viewing role abandonment as a viable option during a critical incident.

DISCUSSION QUESTIONS

1. What are the essential differences between role conflict and role abandonment?
2. What external factors (outside the person) contribute to the abandonment of duty?
3. What were some of the essential differences in how officers abandoned their post during the Hurricane Katrina disaster?
4. What were the primary factors that contributed to the abandonment of post during the Hurricane Katrina disaster?

5. How do crisis decision theory and bounded rationality theory help us better understand what affects decision making during crisis events?

REFERENCES

Absence without Leave. 2018. Article 86. *Uniform Code of Military Justice.* Accessed June 4, 2018. http://www.ucmj.us/sub-chapter-10-punitive-articles/886-article-86-absence-without-leave.

Adams, Terri, and Larry Stewart. 2015. "Chaos Theory and Organizational Crisis: A Theoretical Analysis of the Challenges Faced by the New Orleans Police Department during Hurricane Katrina." *Public Organization Review* 15 (3): 415–431.

Adams, Terri, and Milanika Turner. 2014. "Professional Responsibilities vs. Familial Responsibilities: An Examination of Role Conflict among First Responders during the Hurricane Katrina Disaster." *Journal of Emergency Management* 12 (1): 45–54.

Avins, Alfred. 1962. "The Nature of Hazardous Duty in Military Desertion." *Duke Law Journal* 1962 (4): 490–506.

Dobie, Kathy. 2005. "AWOL in America: When Desertion Is the Only Option." *Harper's Magazine* 310 (March 1): 33–44.

Dynes, Russell R. 1986. *The Concept of Role in Disaster Research.* Newark: University of Delaware Disaster Research Center.

Eisenberg, Daniel. 2005. "From AWOL to EXILE." *Time* 165, no. 9 (February 28): 36–37.

Fiori, Stefano. 2011. "Forms of Bounded Rationality: The Reception and Redefinition of Herbert A. Simon's Perspective." *Review of Political Economy* 23 (4): 587–612.

Fisher, Henry W. 1998. *Response to Disaster: Fact versus Fiction and Its Perpetuation: The Sociology of Disaster,* 2nd ed. Lanham, MD: University Press of America.

Folkman, Susan, and Richard S. Lazarus. 1980. "An Analysis of Coping in a Middle-Aged Community Sample." *Journal of Health and Social Behavior* 21:219–239.

Killian, Lewis. M. 1952. "The Significance of Multiple-Group Membership in Disaster." *American Journal of Sociology* 57 (4): 309–314.

Lazarus, Richard S., and Susan Folkman. 1984. *Stress, Appraisal, and Coping.* New York: Springer.

Leventhal, Howard, and Patricia Niles. 1965. "Persistence of Influence for Varying Durations of Exposure to Threat Stimuli." *Psychological Reports* 16:223–233.

March, James. 1978. "Bounded Rationality, Ambiguity, and the Engineering of Choice." *Bell Journal of Economics* 9:578–608.

Patterson, William. 2005. "To Fight or Not to Fight? The Ethics of Military Desertion." *International Journal of Applied Philosophy* 19 (1): 11–25.

Penton, J. C. 1950. "A Study in the Psychology of Desertion and Absenteeism in Wartime and Its Relation to the Problem of Morale." *Operational Research Quarterly* 1 (2): 25–26.

Quarantelli, E. L. 1954. "The Nature and Conditions of Panic." *American Journal of Sociology* 60 (3): 267–275.

Ramsberger, Peter F., and D. Bruce Bell. 2002. "What We Know about AWOL and Desertion: A *Review of* the Professional Literature for Policy Makers and Commanders." Alexandria, VA: U.S. Army Research Institute for the Behavioral and Social Sciences.

Reuss-Ianni, Elizabeth. 1983. *Two Cultures of Policing.* New Brunswick, NJ: Transaction.

Rogers, George Oliver. 1986. "Role Conflict in Crisis with Limited Forewarning." *Journal of Applied Psychology* 3 (1): 33–50.

Rose, Arnold M. 1951. "The Social Psychology of Desertion from Combat." *American Sociological Review* 16 (5): 614–629.

Simon, Herbert A. 1956. "Rational Choice and the Structure of the Environment." *Psychological Review* 63 (2): 129–138.

Sims, Benjamin. 2007. "The Day after the Hurricane: Infrastructure, Order, and the New Orleans Police Department's Response to Hurricane Katrina." *Social Studies of Science* 37 (1): 111–118.

Skolnick, Jerome. 1994. *Justice without Trial: Law Enforcement in the Democratic Society*, 3rd ed. New York: Macmillan.

Sweeney, Kate. 2008. "Crisis Decision Theory: Decisions in the Face of Negative Events." *Psychological Bulletin* 134 (1): 61–76.

Trainor, Joseph E., and Lauren E. Barsky. 2011. *Reporting for Duty? A Synthesis of Research on Role Conflict, Strain and Abandonment among Emergency Responders during Disasters and Catastrophes.* Newark: University of Delaware Disaster Research Center.

Treaster, Joseph B. 2005. "Law Officers, Overwhelmed, Are Quitting the Force." *New York Times*, September 4.

Vargas, Mark. 1987. *A Reevaluation of the Reasons for Enlistment and the Causes of Desertion in the United States Army, 1821–1835.* Master's thesis, University of Maryland–College Park.

Walzer, Michael. 1967. "The Obligation to Disobey." *Ethics* 77 (3): 163–175.

White, Meda Miller 1962. *Role-Conflict in Disasters: Not Family but Familiarity First.* Chicago: University of Chicago.

Wilcox, Victoria L. 1994. "Burnout in Military Personnel." In *Military Psychiatry: Preparing in Peace for War,* edited by L. B. Davis, C. M. Quick, and S. E. Siegel, 30–49. Washington, DC: U.S. Department of the Army and Borden Institute.

Woodbury, E. N. 1921. "Causes for Military Desertion: A Study in Criminal Motives." *Journal of the American Institute of Criminal Law and Criminology* 12 (2): 213–222.

5

When the Police Become the Criminals

Misconduct among Law Enforcement Officers in the Midst of Disaster

You shot because you wanted to be part of something, you thought, was bigger than you. You let your ego control your emotions. You wanted to be viewed as a big man among the other officers. That's the creed of the NOPD, and I hope the jury ignores your lame explanations and renders justice.... To do less is to sanction any cop who decides it is in his best interest to put a load of buckshot in the back of a disabled American in broad daylight.[1]

As Chapter 4 discusses, the pressure of responding to disaster work can cause some officers to engage in maladaptive behavior. In order to gain a better understanding of the circumstances under which such behavior can be triggered, this chapter explores the reported misconduct of NOPD officers during and after the Hurricane Katrina disaster. The above quote was transcribed from the trial of Kenneth Bowen, a former NOPD sergeant. It illustrates the degree to which some officers engaged in unethical and illegal behaviors during the response to the Katrina disaster. Bowen was eventually found guilty of

---

1. U.S. v. Bowen, 969 F.Supp.2d 518, 531 (E.D. La 2012).

six counts of deprivation of rights under the color of law, two counts of using a weapon during the commission of a crime of violence, one count of conspiracy, two counts of obstruction of justice, and one count of civil-rights conspiracy. Bowen was sentenced to forty years in prison; in 2016, his sentence would get reduced to ten years with credit for time served and five years of supervised release.

This chapter places maladaptive responses by first responders in a context that will allow for an examination of the issues that lead to these types of responses and, thus, the ability to mitigate them. To do this, this chapter addresses two integral questions: first, what led to the misconduct of NOPD officers during the Katrina disaster? Second, should this type of behavior be expected during other large-scale disasters?

Police crime includes both illegal acts and acts that may not be unequivocally criminal but are a misuse of official power. To fully comprehend the misconduct of some officers of the police force during the Katrina disaster, it is important to gain an understanding of the definitions and manifestations of what is typically identified as police misconduct. Police misconduct typically falls within one of four categories: police criminal behavior, occupational deviance, police corruption, and abuse of authority (Kappeler, Sluder, and Alpert 1994). While some of these concepts are used interchangeably, they represent differences in the engagement of actions that are in conflict with the official code of ethics that govern any police department. Police criminal behavior applies to behavior that is criminal when committed by anyone, police or civilian. Occupational deviance describes activities that occur on the job that do not conform to departmental standards and encompasses both criminal and noncriminal forms of misconduct that take place while an officer is on duty (Barker and Carter 1994). Police corruption includes the use of police authority and power for personal gain, and abuse of authority occurs when an officer uses excessive force (also referred to as extralegal use of force or police brutality), psychologically abuses a citizen, or violates a citizen's constitutional rights. For the purpose of this discussion we use the term "police misconduct" to describe the general forms of occupational deviance (e.g., theft) and use the terms "police brutality" and "excessive use of force" when describing extralegal physical force (e.g., use of firearms, punching) used against citizens.

Police Behaving Badly: Misconduct within the NOPD

The NOPD has a long history of police misconduct. Chapter 1 discusses the history of the NOPD and reports that the department was no stranger to repeated allegations of abuse of authority or extralegal aggression. Over the years, several news outlets (e.g., *60 Minutes*, *New Orleans Times-Picayune*, and *Washington Post*) have covered sordid stories of brutality and corruption within the department. The following section briefly reviews this history of misconduct within the NOPD to establish a context for the police misconduct that took place during and after the Katrina disaster.

Known for having a number of "officers on the take" during the early 1950s—prostitution and gambling in New Orleans were rampant. The department's reputation continued to plunge throughout the 1950s and 1960s, touting a reputation of using black males as target practice and brutalizing the bodies of black women (Moore 2003). The department's reputation continued to decline through the 1970s, and in 1981, seven NOPD officers were indicted on police harassment and brutality charges by a federal grand jury that resulted in the conviction of three officers (McCarthy 2010). Commonly referred to as the "Algiers Seven," the case involved a series of attacks on the black community over the period of a week that included four murders of innocent victims and several incidents of extreme brutality ("Local History" 2011). Despite the conviction, the misconduct continued, and in the mid-1990s the misconduct came to the attention of the U.S. Department of Justice, which led to a series of FBI sting operations that were designed to weed out the dirty cops.

The 1990s marked a period of significant change within the NOPD. Appointed to the position of NOPD superintendent by

Mayor Marc Morial in 1994, Richard Pennington made the reduction of police corruption one of the primary objectives of his administration. The need to reform the department became acutely evident when he was confronted with the high levels of misconduct of his department minutes after taking over the leadership of NOPD. Pennington has recounted the story of his introduction to the lawlessness of his department numerous times in interviews, remarking that during his swearing-in ceremony an agent from the FBI whispered in his hear that he needed to brief him on the level of corruption in his department (personal communication 2006; "Richard Pennington" 1997). The FBI informed the new superintendent that the department was teeming with criminals, and FBI agents were conducting a sting operation within the department. Embodying the level of corruption in the department was the retaliatory murder of Kim Groves on the day of Pennington's inauguration. Groves had filed a complaint of police brutality against NOPD Officer Len Davis, who conspired to have her murdered. Pennington later stated in an interview, "I thought, my Lord, what am I getting myself into? . . . Sometimes I felt like I was in a tank of barracudas or piranhas" (Webster and Bullington 2016).

Despite the ongoing FBI operations that started in 1994, one of the most notorious criminal acts committed by an NOPD officer occurred in 1995. Officer Antoinette Frank went on a killing spree at a Vietnamese Restaurant where she occasionally moonlighted as a security guard. Using a key stolen from the restaurant, Frank entered the store with an accomplice and killed off-duty police officer Ronald A. Williams and two members of the restaurant's staff. Frank fled the scene, later returning and acting as if she were unaware of the crime. A survivor who had hidden inside a refrigerator, however, called the police to the scene and shared the story of what took place. Frank was convicted of three counts of capital murder and sentenced to death in 1995 (Filosa 2008a). The Frank case revealed the depth of criminality within the department.

Superintendent Pennington sustained a working relationship with the FBI, seeking assistance with addressing the department's corruption problem, which resulted in the identification and firing of over three hundred officers for police corruption (Anderson and Farber 2006). The department's standing in the community vastly improved during Pennington's eight years with the NOPD. Some argue that the improvement to its reputation was short-lived, as it began a slow decline after Pennington's departure in 2002 (Anderson and Farber 2006). Eddie P. Compass III, a twenty-six-year veteran of the department, replaced Pennington. The start of his tenure coincided with the end of the FBI investigative sting in the department, and the criminal behavior continued. Just two weeks before Katrina's landfall, two NOPD officers were arrested: one for sexual assault and the other for check fraud (Anderson and Farber 2006). (While singling out NOPD's history of corruption, it is important to note that criminal behavior within the ranks is not unique to the New Orleans Police Department.)

Police Misconduct during Hurricane Katrina

According to a number of news outlets (e.g., *CNN*, *New Orleans Times-Picayune*, *New York Times*, and *Washington Post*), several NOPD officers engaged in misconduct during the Katrina disaster that ranged from theft to homicide. Some of these events did not become apparent to the public until months after the disaster. In total, fourteen officers were put on trial for their offenses; all were convicted, but sentences were reduced and officers were acquitted as a result of prosecutorial misconduct (Thompson 2017).

The early reports of police misconduct centered on incidents of theft. News outlets across the United States showed photos and video footage of officers pilfering items from stores, such as a Wal-Mart located in the Lower Garden District of the city ("New Orleans Probes" 2005). The NOPD reported that they were aware of reports of theft during the early stages of the disaster (Nossiter 2005). According to an interview conducted by the *Washington Post*, the spokesperson for the department contended that "out of 1,750 officers we're looking into the possibility that maybe 12 officers were involved in misconduct" (Nossiter

2005). Upon reflection over the incident, Superintendent Warren Riley made a distinction between taking essential (e.g., food and jeans) and nonessential items from stores, as officers were granted permission to take essential items needed by the officers in the department. Four of the twelve officers accused of looting were suspended for ten days without pay for failing to stop the looting and not for the looting they conducted themselves. Seven months later, a spokesperson for Superintendent Riley provided this statement about the officers: "It was determined that all four officers had received permission from their commanders to get clothing for fellow officers who were soaking wet" ("New Orleans Police" 2006). Nevertheless, suspicions remained about officers taking nonessential items ("Crimes after Katrina" 2005).

Other news stories surfaced of officers stealing cars from a local Cadillac dealership. Some reports claimed the officers commandeered the vehicles to substitute for the cars they lost to floodwaters. Superintendent Riley said in an interview, "We had one district that did not have any cars, and there were some officers who actually patrolled in Cadillacs" (Abrams Report 2005). Other news outlets suggested that some of the officers who took vehicles used them to flee the city (Horne 2006).

There were other reports of more malicious acts of misconduct by members of the NOPD. Review of public records indicate that NOPD officers shot six people over the course of four days under suspicious circumstances, and there were other news reports of police brutality (e.g., Maggi 2010, *Times-Picayune*; McCarthy 2009, *ProPublica*). The timeline and map at the end of this chapter show the timing and geographic location of the reported acts of excessive use of force by NOPD officers during the Katrina disaster. While it is not known what exactly set off the firestorm of police aggression, a series of events took place that may have fanned the flames of aggression among some of the officers.

First, within a couple of days of Katrina's landfall, the news coverage switched from a focus on the victimization and despair of the city's stranded residents to intense coverage of reported acts of looting and violence in the city. The countless narratives characterized the city as being out of control, with widespread murder, rape, child abuse, carjacking, and assault (Carr 2005; Coates and Eggen 2005a). Headlines such as "A City of Despair and Lawlessness" (Coates and Eggen 2005a) and "Relief Workers Confront 'Urban Warfare'" (Lawrence and Lavandera 2005) dominated the newspapers and television reports. While many of these stories were later found to be greatly exaggerated ("Crimes after Katrina" 2005; Guariano 2015; Pierre and Gerhart 2005), the picture of chaos painted by the media affected the response of outside agencies to the disaster and of agencies operating within the city. As Carr (2005) notes in a *New York Times* article: "Disaster has a way of bringing out the best and the worst instincts in the news media. It is a grand thing that during the most terrible days of Hurricane Katrina, many reporters found their gag reflex and stopped swallowing pat excuses from public officials. But the media's willingness to report thinly attributed rumors may also have contributed to a kind of cultural wreckage that will not clean up easily." The absence of reliable communication systems not only allowed rumors to dominate the news, it also affected the rhetoric espoused and believed by members of the force within the department. What's more, it was later discovered that some of the misinformation that was shared with the media came from police officials and specifically Superintendent Eddie Compass (Joseph 2006). Some believe that NOPD's mishandling of the media helped exacerbate the challenges faced by the department and the city in general (anonymous NOPD interview September 2007) and slowed federal response (Brezina and Phipps 2008; Cooper 2005; PBS News Hour 2005).

Adding to the perception of mass chaos was the attempted killing of an NOPD officer during a stop-and-frisk search on the 2600 block of Gen. De Gaulle Drive on August 31, 2010 (Filosa 2010). Officer Kevin Thomas of the 4th District stopped four men he suspected of looting and conducted a pat-down search (Filosa). The men perceived the stop as harassment and a dispute broke out between him and the suspects; during his testimony during the court hearing of one of the suspects, as

Thomas reported, "He felt I was harassing him" (Filosa). Subsequently, the suspects shot Thomas in the head as one of the men fled on foot from the crime scene. Thomas survived the shooting, but the incident established a different tone of concern in the department, heightening the perception of danger and chaos in the city. The heightened media coverage of events prompted Mayor Ray Nagin, late in the afternoon on August 31, to call a meeting with Warren Riley, deputy superintendent at the time, instructing him to "take back the city" and shift the department's focus from search and rescue efforts to addressing the looting and violence in the city (McGreal 2010; New Orleans Office of the Independent Police Monitor 2014). Mayor Nagin was quoted as stating, "Let's stop the looting. Let's stop the lawlessness and let's stop this crap now" (Harper 2012, p. 304). Governor Kathleen Blanco doubled down on the mission of stomping out the "lawlessness" with her assertion of the firepower of the National Guard who were present in the city: "[The soldiers] are fresh back from Iraq, well trained, experienced, battle-tested and under my orders to restore order in the streets. They have M-16s, and they are locked and loaded. These troops know how to shoot and kill, and they are more than willing to do so if necessary, and I expect they will" (Harper 2012, p. 304). The call to establish order was intended to set a tone of a no-nonsense approach to crime in the city (Harper 2012).

Soon after the call to "take over the city," a cluster of excessive-use-of-force cases took place. Public records indicate that NOPD officers shot seven people over the course of four days under suspicious circumstances, and there were other reports of police brutality. The first recorded act of violence took place at 1 p.m. on September 1, just one day after the Thomas shooting and the call for law and order in the city. Keenon McCann, a thirty-two-year-old African American male, was shot in the chest multiple times by members of the NOPD SWAT team in search of a stolen truck carrying bottled water. Officers on the scene claimed the suspect was in possession of a weapon, but no weapon was found upon his arrest (Thompson, McCarthy, and Maggi 2009). McCann ultimately survived the shooting and later filed a lawsuit against the NOPD for his injuries; this case never went to trial, however, because he was murdered in 2009 (Thompson et al.).

Later in the afternoon of September 1, the second incident occurred during a traffic stop of two suspects driving a stolen vehicle. Ernest "Ricky" Bell and Robert Williams were instructed to pull over while driving a stolen limousine they claimed was taken for evacuation purposes (Russell 2010). The officers believed the two were involved in a shootout with other officers earlier in the day. While only two officers from the 6th District made the initial stop, eyewitnesses, including a reporter and two photographers (despite being forced to hand over their cameras, one of the photographers retained photos of the incident), assert that hundreds of officers arrived on the scene (Russell 2010). Reports from the eyewitnesses indicate that the suspects were severely beaten, the severity of which is illustrated by the loss of Williams's teeth, which were kicked out of his mouth. After the beating, the two were left on the street to fend for themselves.

In the evening of September 1, three officers in the French Quarter reportedly battered retired schoolteacher Robert Davis, without cause. Davis asserted that he stopped an officer to ask a question about curfew requirements, but his question was greeted with aggression (Harper 2012). An article in the *Times-Picayune* pointed out that another "officer then ran up behind Davis, threw him against a wall and punched him. At that point, the officer behind Davis called him a racial slur, and added, 'You know I can kick your ass'" (McCarthy 2010). The assault was videotaped by a *CNN* associate. The assaulting officer contended that Davis hit him in the chest with his elbow; Davis was arrested for public intoxication, battery, and resisting arrest. Those charges were dismissed, but Davis filed a civil suit against one of the officers and won his case in 2009. Of the three officers involved in the incident, one committed suicide and the other two were dismissed from the department (Harper 2012; Maggi 2009).

The fourth incident of excessive use of force occurred around 9:30 P.M. on September 2, when Danny Brumfield, a forty-five-year-old African American man, was shot and killed outside the Convention Center. The police involved in the incident reported that Brumfield jumped on the hood of the police car, landed on his feet, and lunged toward the passenger side of the car carrying what looked like a shiny object. The victim's family, however, reported that Brumfield was almost hit by the police car, after which he started yelling at the officers about the arrival of buses that were scheduled to take stranded victims to other locations. An autopsy report showed that Brumfield died from a gunshot wound to his back at close range, a fact that contradicted the officers' story. Brumfield's family filed a civil suit, but only one officer was convicted, and that for perjury, as the officers claimed they got out of their car to check the victim's pulse, but eyewitnesses disputed that claim. The witnesses claimed the offending officers left Brumfield on the street to die.

The fifth incident, one of the best-known episodes of violence, also took place on September 2. Henry Glover, a thirty-one-year-old African American man, was shot by an officer. In response, he ran, collapsing in the street about one hundred yards from where he was shot ("Henry Glover" 2010). The officer who shot Glover argues that he was carrying an object in his hand and attempted to break into a store. Glover's brother, Edward King, witnessed the incident and flagged down a car driven by a bystander named William Tanner. Assuming that they would not make it to a medical center in time, the two rushed Glover to a local elementary school, where the NOPD Special Operations Center had set up camp, to seek assistance (Simerman 2015). When they arrived, the police on the scene accused them of looting, then handcuffed and physically assaulted them, later forcing the two to leave the makeshift police department ("Henry Glover" 2010). Meanwhile, Glover lay bleeding in the car, never having been attended to by the officers. Tanner reported that the officers took the body and fled the scene in a police car, and it was later reported that the body was found burned in a police car near the makeshift camp set up by the SWAT team. In 2010, a federal grand jury found three officers guilty of Glover's death.

Perhaps the most infamous act of violence was the sixth act, which occurred on the Danziger Bridge on September 4. Nine officers arrived on the scene in a rental truck responding to a distress call from 911 that claimed an officer was down under the Danziger Bridge. The officers claimed they issued a warning shot, and fired their weapons only in response to the threats posed by the individuals on the bridge. The evidence pointed to a different set of circumstances, however. Among the people who were shot were high school student James Brissette and Ronald Madison, a mentally challenged man who died as a result of bullet wounds to his back. In total, six individuals were shot, including two women. In 2006, the state of Louisiana brought charges against seven of the police officers involved in the Danziger Bridge incident—four for murder and three for attempted murder. In 2008 the state charges were dropped, but two years later the U.S. Department of Justice investigated the incident. In total, four of the officers were indicted for the shooting of six unarmed citizens—two of them dead. These officers and two supervisors were charged with plotting to cover up the criminal acts (Maggi 2009). After several years, four of the indicted officers were sentenced from seven to twelve years for the shootings of the unarmed civilians, and a fifth officer was sentenced for three years for conspiring to cover up the crime (Robertson 2011; Daley and Lane 2016).

Examination of the Causes of Police Misconduct Committed by Officers Serving as First Responders

Upon reviewing the police misconduct, particularly excessive use of force by members of NOPD, several questions come to mind about the underlying causes of these actions and the likelihood of their occurrence in other major crises: (1) What caused the rash of excessive-use-of-force cases during the Katrina disaster? (2) Was the violence a function of the stress experienced by the officers? (3) Was it a result of the call to law and order by authorities? (4) Or was it simply a part of a routine course of action by corrupt officers? The following section outlines plausible explanations for these behaviors in an attempt to address these questions.

Excessive Use of Force Induced by Stress

Although people tend to engage in prosocial activities during disasters, criminal behaviors also occur, some of which appear to be maladaptive responses to stress. In some instances, the feeling of being overwhelmed and powerless leads to negative behavior patterns such as lashing out at those more vulnerable than oneself. One type of incident where a direct link has been shown is the increase in sexual assault cases during disasters (Thornton and Voigt 2012). People also engage in other criminal behaviors, such as looting, cyber looting, use of illegal substances, and various forms of violent behaviors including homicide (Frailing and Harper 2012).

Unfortunately, outside the literature on post-abandonment, there is scant research on maladaptive behaviors of first responders during crisis events. In spite of this, it is well known that policing is considered one of the most stressful occupations and it is assumed that their threshold for stress is higher than others outside the profession, largely because they are routinely subjected to highly stressful situations (Lanterman et al. 2010). Studies have shown, however, that police officers are more likely to engage in maladaptive coping strategies as a result of the stressful nature of their work, which in turn leads to long-term chronic stress (Hurrell 1995) and, thus, a perpetual cycle. The cycle is further aggravated during responses to disasters.

Some investigators have also argued that the police are plagued with feelings of anger and aggression. The anger-aggression theory posits that chronically aroused people respond to threats more aggressively than others. Originally developed by Bernard (1990; 1993), the theory is used to explain violence that disadvantaged populations exhibit in response to minor provocations. Griffin and Bernard (2003) have applied these concepts to the extralegal violence among police officers. They argue that, consistently with Bernard's (1990; 1993) discovery, the police are at risk for expressing anger and aggression when chronically aroused. Consequently, emotionally charged incidents can lead to responses that are rooted in anger and fear, especially when officers are in an environment where they feel threatened. Social isolation, exaggerated fears of threats, and the inability to directly respond to the source of the threat causes individuals to become chronically aroused. This, in turn, can trigger anger and fear and lead to various forms of aggression (Berkowitz 1993). This aggression gets targeted toward members of the public.

Bonifacio (1991) argues that the police have an unconscious reaction to their work. He states, "Every policeman has an unconscious ambivalent reaction to the job. He hates it because he is subjected to degradation and depravity and cannot do anything to stop it" (p. 158). These feelings can lead officers to harbor hostility to the communities they serve, which is heightened during confrontations with the public and engenders protracted arousal. The NOPD officers responding to the Katrina disaster can certainly be described as having been in a state of chronic arousal. For days, these officers were under tremendous stress with no relief in sight; many went without basic provisions while also being isolated from their loved ones. Consequently, it is possible that the extralegal violence the officers committed during Katrina was an expression of the exasperation, fear, and sense of vulnerability some of the officers felt. The shooting of Officer Thomas provided a perceived justification for a heightened "us versus them" mentality, which strengthens in-group bonds and amplifies fear of outsiders—in this case, the public. Consequently, the acts of violence the police committed can be characterized as an emotional reaction to the arousal of a heightened sense of fear.

Excessive Use of Force Caused by the Call to "Law and Order"?

Some scholars have attributed the blitz of police violence during the Katrina disaster to the call to law and order by public officials, including the mayor of New Orleans and the governor of Louisiana. It can be argued that the strong push to reel in the perceived onslaught of violence in the city heightened the defenses of the officers and set in motion a quest to accomplish the enforcement of law with a heavy hand. Previously-reviewed cases—such as the shootings of Keenon McCann and Danny Brumfield—illustrate that the "shoot first and ask questions later" mindset appeared in the reactions of some officers in the cases reviewed in this chapter.

The call to law and order tapped into the previously noted "us versus them" mentality among the officers, which was further amplified by the belief that the officers were at risk of being victimized by the public, engendering fear and leading some officers to use extralegal force. This was evident in each of the previously discussed cases in this chapter. For example, regardless of the perceived threat posed by the suspects Bell and Williams, the arrival of one hundred or so officers on the scene to confront the potential threat of only two suspects indicated that the response was probably more about vengeance for a perceived wrong than about seeking needed back-up assistance. According to Van Maanen's 1978 article "Asshole," police officers often deal out what is referred to as "street justice" to suspects in response to a perceived wrong, which one can argue is epitomized by the brutal beating of Bell and Williams. The "take back the streets" and "armed and dangerous" mantra voiced by the authority figures signaled that a "by any means necessary" approach, including the use of brute force, was encouraged and supported by the authorities.

The call for martial law that pervaded the city also gave the police the opportunity to operate with impunity. Besides the limited presence of the police department, the criminal justice system was basically rendered inoperative during the disaster. Furthermore, the lack of communication capabilities, infrastructural damages, and shifting of the command structure provided the officers with little support to seek out alternative procedures from superiors to execute their duties and fulfill the expectations being placed on them.

Simply Corrupt Officers Engaging in Corrupt Behaviors

According to Van Maanen (1978), once an officer identifies a person as a troublemaker—what he says the officers refer to as an "asshole," it is deemed acceptable in the minds of some officers to render "street justice" on this particular type of individual; thus releasing the officer from moral conflict. Some officers believe that their badge gives them the authority to use force beyond what is necessary for the situation at hand. Officers that fit into this category take a "Dirty Harry"[2] approach to policing and often believe they have the *moral* authority to dispense street justice on offenders (Klockars 1980).

Regardless of the pronouncements made by public officials, the reactions of the officers in each of the incidents of excessive use of force appear to be more about the officers than any calls to "take back the city" by authority figures. Regardless of the perceived green light given to use extralegal force, none of the authority figures explicitly said go out and brutalize or kill members of the public who appear be criminal. Whether it is one or two officers wielding influence over other officers in a single incident, as in the case of the Bell and Williams incident, or an unofficial code of conduct accepted within a district or group of officers, use of extralegal force is a decision made by each individual officer.

While official police codes are ingrained in police officers throughout the training process, the approach a person takes toward his or her work as a law-enforcement officer may not always strictly reflect the official code of ethics espoused by the department. There are three schools of ethical theory that describe how an officer might approach their enforcement of the law: ethical formalism, ethical utilitarianism, and ethical relativism (Pollock 1997). Ethical formalism places emphasis on duty and "going by the book." Full enforcement of the law is sought, which is the legally strict way of policing. Ethical utilitarianism emphasizes the results of one's actions for determining the morality of that action, and therefore the result is deemed to be more important than the characteristics of the action. Consequently, if an illegal action on the part of an officer yields the arrest of an offender, the illegal action is deemed to be appropriate and the actions justified as moral.

---

2. The term is derived from the infamous Dirty Harry movie series of the 1970s starring Clint Eastwood as an unruly police officer. The main character used "any means necessary" in law enforcement, which often involved using brutal force against suspected offenders.

The third school of thought, ethical relativism, argues that what is considered to be ethical varies with who is making the judgment. Further, how and whether the law is enforced depends on the circumstances and individuals involved. Therefore, it may be necessary to enforce the law within a certain context or situation and not in others (Roberg, Novak, and Cordner 2009). It is important to note that this ethical relativism rests on the perception that full enforcement of the law is not a realistic goal (Goldstein 1998).

Most police officers find themselves operating under an ethical realist model (Roberg et al. 2009), wherein they make the best decisions they can within the parameters in which they have to work. Some engage in ethical utilitarianism, wherein they make decisions on the basis of what they deem necessary, whether it is within or outside the law. This is often akin to the "Dirty Harry" problem noted earlier (Klockars 1980).

Skolnick's (1975) work describing the police officer as a craftsman sheds additional light on this issue. He argues that the police see themselves as craftsmen and, at their best, masters of their trade. He goes on to state that they skillfully "draw a moral distinction between criminal law and criminal procedure" (p. 176). According to Skolnick, the police believe that criminal law is intended to control the behavior of criminals; and criminal procedures are in place to control authorities. The difference here is that by the police do not regard criminal procedures to be in the same moral class as criminal law. As a result, police officers who function according to this belief system tend to blur the line between illegal or extralegal police aggression and illegal acts committed in the name of law enforcement. In other words, this value system justifies extralegal actions as a necessary evil, to carry out law-enforcement duties.

This section of the chapter has presented three plausible explanations to the rash of violence carried out by the NOPD during the Katrina disaster—excessive stress, authorities' call to law and order, and basic police corruption. While it is uncertain what actually caused the violence, we know that there were circumstances at play during the disaster that provided ripe conditions for the use of extralegal force against members of the public whom police deemed to be criminal. The question arises, should extralegal use of force be added to the expected maladaptive behaviors during disasters? While the majority of the officers engaged in prosocial activities, the number of officers who did engage in police misconduct during the Katrina disaster signals that the issue of increases in police misconduct may be an issue that police supervisors and administrators should be on the lookout for in times of extreme crisis.

Conclusion

Most NOPD officers upheld the valor of their profession during the Katrina disaster, but there were officers who engaged in negative and maladaptive behaviors during the disaster. The incidents ranged in egregiousness from petty theft to homicide, underscoring the reality that some people, including first responders, do engage in negative behaviors in response to disasters. This finding diverges slightly from the claims of the preponderance of research, which maintains that people will engage in positive behaviors during disasters. Although most officers worked earnestly to fulfill their first responder duties, the six incidents of police misconduct and brutality that were discussed in this chapter illustrate that such misconduct may be indicative of both legitimizing structures and individual propensities toward violence or criminality.

The intensity of the disaster coupled with the direct and indirect effects on the police department and its officers caused a sense of fear, isolation, and uncertainty among the officers that promoted maladaptive behaviors for some of the officers. Added to this mix of emotions was the anger over the loss of a fellow officer gunned down during the crisis, which possibly triggered the "us versus them" mentality that the call to law and order spurred on. Understanding that the angry aggression theory posits that the most chronically aroused people will respond to threats more aggressively than others further illustrates how the toxic cocktail of events and ramped-up emotions could have been the fuel behind the violent acts carried out by the officers. All the same, it is important to understand that officers who had a predisposition to engage in "Dirty Harry" or corrupt police behaviors may commit similar acts regardless of the circumstances, though the conditions during Katrina certainly may have fostered those decisions. In fact, officers who have a tendency to engage in maladaptive coping behaviors, and those with a tendency to engage in "Dirty Harry" tactics, may readily succumb to the pressures of disaster work and seek to exact retribution against the powerless.

For these reasons, it is probable that under similar circumstances, police officers with these tendencies may engage in similar maladaptive behavioral practices in times of crises. Officers who are isolated, fearful, and chronically stressed could exhibit this type of behavior as well, significantly decreasing the number of police officers who will be able to effectively perform first responder duties. Therefore, it is important for supervisors to closely monitor the behaviors of officers who have a history of excessive use of force or other behavioral issues in general, in order to attempt to mitigate instances of these negative behavior patterns during high-consequence events. Chapter 7 explores ways in which ranking officers can abate negative behaviors and encourage resilience among the officers they supervise.

It is important to note that although there were many things that went awry during the Katrina disaster and the subsequent response, including officers engaging in police misconduct and other maladaptive behaviors, most officers did execute their duties and engage in prosocial behaviors. The next chapter discusses the resilience displayed by NOPD officers during the Katrina disaster and the elements that led to positive coping strategies among officers during the response.

KEY TAKEAWAYS FROM THIS CHAPTER

1. It is important to carefully watch for signs of disgruntled officers and officers exhibiting signs of extreme stress. Feelings of such officers may be expressed in maladaptive behaviors during extreme events.

2. One of the major maladaptive responses that an officer can exercise against the public is excessive use of force.
3. Police administrators and public officials have to be careful about the words and phrases they use when giving orders to police officers during critical incidents, as poor word choice can lead some to misunderstand or take a message out of context.
4. Officers who have been known to have engaged in previous misconduct should be carefully monitored during critical episodes, as the individuals may have a propensity to drift toward maladaptive behavior in the face of excessive exposure to stress.

DISCUSSION QUESTIONS

1. What is police misconduct? What are the similarities and differences between police misconduct during disasters and police maladaptive behaviors in response to police stress?
2. What is the "Dirty Harry" problem and how can it affect policing behaviors during disasters?
3. Do you think the history of police conduct among the NOPD had an impact on the misconduct that took place during the Katrina disaster?
4. Among the various cases of police misconduct that took place during the Hurricane Katrina disaster, which behaviors do you think could be exhibited by officers in other disaster scenarios?
5. Of the various explanations given to provide an understanding the impetus of the police misconduct during Hurricane Katrina, which do you believe is most likely the reason for the behavior?

REFERENCES

Abrams Report. 2005. "Inside Allegations That NOPD 'Looted' Cadillacs." *NBC News*, September 30. http://www.nbcnews.com/id/9542398/ns

/msnbc-the_abrams_report/t/inside-allegations-nopd-looted-cadi llacs/?hasFlash=true&.

Anderson, Willoughby, and Daniel Farber. 2006. *This Isn't Representative of Our Department: Lessons from Hurricane Katrina for Police Disaster Response Planning*. Berkeley: University of California–Berkeley Law School.

Barker, Thomas, and David L. Carter. 1994. "Typology of Police Deviance." In *Police Deviance*, 3rd ed., edited by T. Barker and D. L. Carter, 3–12. Cincinnati, OH: Anderson.

Berkowitz, Leonard. 1993. *Aggression: Its Causes, Consequence, and Control*. Philadelphia, PA: Temple University Press.

Bonifacio, Philip. 1991. *The Psychological Effects of Police Work: A Psychodynamic Approach*. New York: Springer.

Brezina, Timothy, and Herbert E. Phipps Jr. 2008. "False News Reports, Folk Devils, and the Role of Public Officials: Notes on the Social Construction of Law and Order in the Aftermath of Hurricane Katrina." *Deviant Behavior* 31 (1): 97–134.

Carr, David. 2005. "More Horrible Than Truth: News Reports." *New York Times*, September 19. http://www.nytimes.com/2005/09/19/business /media/more-horrible-than-truth-news-reports.html?_r=0.

Coates, Sam, and Dan Eggen. 2005. "A City of Despair and Lawlessness." *Washington Post*, September 1. http://www.washingtonpost.com/wp -dyn/content/article/2005/09/01/AR2005090100533.html.

Cooper, Christopher. 2005. "Misinformation Slowed Federal Response to Katrina." *Wall Street Journal*, September 30. http://www.wsj.com /articles/SB112804420733656428.

"Crimes after Katrina May Have Been Overblown." 2005. Associated Press, September 29. http://www.nbcnews.com/id/9503449/ns/us_news -katrina_the_long_road_back/t/crimes-after-katrina-may-have-been -overblown/#.WpsiP6inGUk.

Filosa, Gwen. 2008. "Convicted Killer Antoinette Frank Appears in Court." *New Orleans Times-Picayune*, February 27. http://www.nola.com /news/index.ssf/2008/02/convicted_killer_antoinette_fr.html.

———. 2010. "Hurricane Katrina Aftermath Shooting of Police Officer Described." *New Orleans Times-Picayune*, January 14. http://www.nola .com/crime/index.ssf/2010/01/hurricane_katrina_aftermath_sh .html.

Frailing, Kelly, and Dee Wood Harper. 2012. "Fear, Prosocial Behavior and Looting: The Katrina Experience." In *Crime and Criminal Justice in Disaster*, 2nd ed., edited by Dee Wood Harper and Kelly Frailing, 101–121. Durham, NC: Carolina Academic.

Goldstein. Joseph. 1998. "Police Discretion Not to Invoke the Criminal Justice Process: Low Visibility Decisions in the Administration of Justice." In *The Criminal Justice: Politics and Policies*, 7th ed., edited by G. F. Cole and M. G. Gertz, 85–103. Belmont, CA: Wadsworth.

Griffin, Sean P., and Thomas J. Bernard. 2003. "Angry Aggression among Police Officers." *Police Quarterly* 6 (1): 3–21.

Guarino, M. 2015. "Misleading Reports of Lawlessness after Katrina Worsened Crisis, Officials Say." *The Guardian*, August 16. https://www.theguardian.com/us-news/2015/aug/16/hurricane-katrina-new-orleans-looting-violence-misleading-reports.

Harper, Dee Wood. 2012. "The New Orleans Police Department during and after Hurricane Katrina—Lessons Learned." In *Crime and Criminal Justice in Disaster*, 2nd ed., edited by Dee Wood Harper and Kelly Frailing, 285–310. Durham, NC: Carolina Academic.

"Henry Glover Jury Finds 3 Officers Guilty in Death, Burning of Algiers Man." 2010. *New Orleans Times-Picayune*, December 9. http://www.nola.com/crime/index.ssf/2010/12/henry_glover_verdict_form.html.

Horne, Jed. 2006. *Breath of Faith: Hurricane Katrina and the Near Death of a Great American City*. New York: Random House.

Hurrell, Joseph J. 1995. "Police Work, Occupational Stress and Individual Coping." *Journal of Organizational Behavior* 16:27–28.

Joseph, Channing. 2006. "Police Chief Says He Exaggerated Post-Katrina Crime." *New York Sun*, August 21. http://www.nysun.com/national/police-chief-says-he-exaggerated-post-katrina/38268/.

Kappeler, Victor E., Richard D. Sluder, and Geoffrey Alpert. 1994. *Forces of Deviance: Understanding the Dark Side of Policing*. Prospect Heights, IL: Waveland.

Klockars, Carl B. 1980. "The Dirty Harry Problem." *Annals of the American Academy of Political and Social Science* 452: 33–47.

Lanterman, Jennifer L, Douglas J. Boyle, Joseph Pascarella, and Susan Furrer. 2010. "Police Stress and Access to Confidential Support Services." In *Police Psychology*, edited by J. M. Peters, 57–73. Suffolk, NY: Nova Science.

"Local History: Algiers (Fischer Projects) Massacre and Resistance, 1980–81." 2011. *Nola Anarcha*, July 14. http://nolaanarcha.blogspot.com/2011/07/local-history-algiers-fischer-projects.html.

Maggi, Laura. 2009. "Lack of Communication during Katrina Proved Crippling." *New Orleans Times-Picayune*, September 15.

McCarthy, Brendan. 2010. "Infamous Algiers 7 Police Brutality Case of 1980 Has Parallels to Today." *New Orleans Times-Picayune*, November 7. http://www.nola.com/crime/index.ssf/2010/11/algiers_7_police_brutality_cas.html.

McGreal, Chris. 2010. "New Orleans Police on Trial over Killing in Chaos following Hurricane Katrina." *The Guardian*, February 19.

Moore, Leonard C. 2003. *Carl B. Stokes and the Rise of Black Political Power*. Urbana: University of Illinois Press.

New Orleans Office of the Independent Police Monitor. 2014. *Hurricane Katrina: The Remaining Legacy; A Story of Uninvestigated Police Shootings and Human Rights Deprivations*. New Orleans, LA: Office of the Independent Police Monitor. http://tbinternet.ohchr.org/Treaties/CAT/Shared%20Documents/USA/INT_CAT_CSS_USA_18551_E.pdf.

"New Orleans Police Officers Cleared of Looting." 2006. Associated Press, March 20. http://www.nbcnews.com/id/11920811/ns/us_news-katrina_the_long_road_back/t/new-orleans-police-officers-cleared-looting/#.WpshgainGUl.

"New Orleans Probes Police Role in Looting." 2005. Associated Press, September 29. http://www.nbcnews.com/id/9535751/ns/us_news-katrina_the_long_road_back/t/new-orleans-probes-police-role-looting/#.V5O79zfosug.

Nossiter, Adam. 2005. "New Orleans Probing Alleged Police Looting." *Associated Press*, September 30. http://www.washingtonpost.com/wp-dyn/content/article/2005/09/29/AR2005092901975.html.

Pierre, Robert, and Ann Gerhart. 2005. "News of Pandemonium May Have Slowed Aid." *Washington Post*, October 5.

Pollock, Joycelyn M. 1997. "Ethics and Law Enforcement." In *Critical Issues in Policing: Contemporary Readings*, 3rd ed., edited by R. G. Dunham and G. P. Alpert, 337–354. Prospect Heights, IL: Waveland.

"Richard Pennington Says He Was Warned about Len Davis Corruption on Day He Was Sworn in as Police Chief." 1997. *New Orleans Times-Picayune*, March 16. http://www.nola.com/crime/index.ssf/1997/03/richard_pennington_says_he_was.html.

Roberg, Roy, Kenneth Novak, and Gary Cordner. 2009. *Police and Society*. Cary, NC: Oxford University Press.

Robertson, Campbell. 2011. "Officers Guilty of Shooting Six in New Orleans." *New York Times*, August 5. http://www.nytimes.com/2011/08/06/us/06danziger.html.

Russell, Gordon. 2010. "Looking for the Truth about the Beatings of 2 Men by Police in the Chaos after Katrina." *New Orleans Times-Picayune*, August 8. http://www.nola.com/crime/index.ssf/2010/08/looking_for_the_truth_about_th.html.

Simerman, John. 2015. "Appeals Court Drops Charge, Orders New Sentencing for Former NOPD Officer Who Burned Henry Glover's Body in a Car on the Algiers Levee." *New Orleans Advocate*, August 1. http://www.theadvocate.com/new_orleans/news/article_69c6ed59-83c6-594b-ac07-1cb68ae4dc66.html.

Skolnick, Jerome. 1975. *Justice without Trial*, 2nd ed. New York: Wiley.

Thompson, A. C., Brendan McCarthy, and Laura Maggi. 2009. "Did New Orleans SWAT Cops Shoot an Unarmed Man?" *ProPublica*, December 15. https://www.propublica.org/article/did-new-orleans-swat-cops-shoot-an-unarmed-man-1215.

Thompson, Dee. 2017. "Cases Related to Hurricane Katrina Police Misconduct in New Orleans Settled." *Louisiana Record*, January 2. http://louisianarecord.com/stories/511065030-cases-related-to-hurricane-katrina-police-misconduct-in-new-orleans-settled.

Thornton, William E., and Lydia Voigt. 2012. "The New Orleans Police Department during and after Hurricane Katrina—Lessons Learned." In *Crime and Criminal Justice in Disaster*, 2nd ed., edited by Dee Wood Harper and Kelly Frailing, 37–72. Durham, NC: Carolina Academic.

Van Maanen, John. 1978. "The Asshole." In *Policing: A View from the Street*, edited by P. K. Manning and John Van Maanen, 221–237. Santa Monica, CA: Goodyear.

Webster, Richard, and Jonathan Bullington. 2016. "The Murders of 1994: Lessons from New Orleans' Deadliest Year." *New Orleans Times-Picayune*, June 16. http://www.nola.com/crime/index.ssf/2016/06/new_orleans_murder_nopd_police.html.

6

Resilience in the Face of It All

> The public expects us to know what to do, and we expect our supervisors to know what to do, but when you're faced with something as bad as what no one has ever experienced before all that went out the window and everyone just fly [sic] by the seat of our pants. But, I don't know, either you're going to pick it up or you don't, you make decisions along the way, you don't worry about the consequences, 'cause if you do something without permission you might get in trouble, but in a situation like that who you're gonna ask. They'd rather you just make the decision; it's probably going to be a good one.
>
> —Anonymous NOPD Officer

Policing is a highly stressful occupation, but it becomes even more stressful during a disaster, as exhaustion, distress, and uncertainty typify the disaster workers' experience. In spite of this, first responders are required to function at full capacity, with little to no rest. The words of the police officer above underscore the precarious nature of disasters, and the fact that first responders are only human and are susceptible to the same human frailties as civilians. Nevertheless, they are expected to be able to make critical decisions in the midst of the crisis. The pressures one faces, coupled with the important role they play during extreme crises, point to the need to foster resilience during disasters.

This chapter is designed to familiarize readers with the concept of resilience and the adaptive responses law-enforcement officers exhibit when exposed to high-consequence events. The essential questions addressed in this chapter are (1) What are the definitions of resilience? (2) How do law-enforcement officers cultivate a sense of resilience in times of crisis? (3) What role does resilience play in the culture of law-enforcement agencies? Case studies are used to highlight real-world instances of resilience and coping mechanisms used by law-enforcement officers when responding to disasters. The first responders examined in this book provide a window into their lived experiences and an opportunity to comprehend what factors aided them in their ability to make it through harrowing circumstances. As Paton, Smith, and Violanti (2000) argue, it is vital to identify the mechanisms extant during disasters that foster resilience and vulnerability. This chapter draws on interviews with police officers who responded to the Hurricane Katrina disaster in New Orleans, Louisiana, and Gulfport, Mississippi, to examine these important issues. The New Orleans and Gulfport police departments were selected as the foci of this chapter because of the degree to which the Katrina disaster affected them both directly and indirectly. Review of the adaptive and maladaptive challenges these officers faced provide important insights into short-term coping strategies the officers employed in times of extreme crisis.

What Does It Mean to Be Resilient?

Resilience is defined in many ways, but a particular few provide context for the discussion in this chapter. One of the most comprehensive definitions is offered by Dunning (1999), who posits three forms of resilience: (1) dispositional resilience, personal characteristics that affect response; (2) cognitive resilience, an individual's ability to create sense and meaning from difficult situations; and (3) environmental resilience, characteristics of the environment from which the individual derives resilient traits. Paton et al. (2000) defines it as "An active process of self-righting, learned resourcefulness and growth—the ability to function psychologically at a level far greater than expected given the individual's capabilities and previous experiences" (p. 173).

Taking a more streamlined approach to defining resilience, Luther, Cicchetti, and Becker (2000) maintain that resilience is "a dynamic process encompassing positive adaptation within the context of significant adversity" (p. 543). Herrman et al. (2011) understand resilience to be largely related to mental health; they refer to "resilience to positive adaptation, or the ability to maintain or regain mental health, despite experiencing adversity" (p. 259). Masten (2001) defines it even more simply as "Good outcomes in spite of serious threats to adaptation or development" (p. 228). All these definitions provide important clues about what constitutes resilience; but, for the purposes of this chapter, Paton et al.'s (2000) and Luther et al.'s (2000) definitions will be used to guide the discussion, because the stories examined in this chapter—drawn from the qualitative data collected by the authors—include the personal reflections of first responders and not a clinical or psychological analysis of their experiences.

Achieving Resilience

Resilience in the face of a catastrophic event becomes possible with the use of coping mechanisms. When a threat confronts a person, an internal appraisal process begins that leads to the selection of a coping method. The implementation of a coping method or a combination of coping methods lays the foundation for resilience. When individuals are exposed physically or emotionally to a threatening situation, they engage in one of two forms of coping behaviors: maladaptive behavior or adaptive behavior.

The two major maladaptive behavioral responses that the disaster literature document are panic flight and disaster syndrome. As Chapter 4 notes, panic flight is associated with acute fear, loss of control, and nonsocial and nonrational flight. It occurs as a result of a set of conditions that make a person feel as if the only viable response is to flee the situation they are facing. While there have been reported cases of panic flight among the public, the literature shows that it is a rare response during and immediately after a disaster event.

Disaster syndrome, the other maladaptive behavioral response commonly mentioned in the literature, refers to a cluster of conditions, largely characterized by a state of shock and typified by docility, disoriented thinking, and lack of sensitivity to cues from the immediate environment (Tierney, Lindell, and Perry 2001). Studies have shown that the onset of disaster syndrome is rare but more likely to occur in sudden-onset disasters with widespread physical destruction, harrowing injuries, and death (Fritz and Marks 1954). The condition is typically transient and tends to affect only a small portion of the affected population.

Panic flight and disaster syndrome are behavioral responses that happen at the onset of a disaster, but other maladaptive responses occur during and after a disaster, for example, avoidance behavior, alcohol abuse, and drug abuse.

While individuals do certainly employ maladaptive behavioral responses as a means of surviving through a crisis, as Herrman et al. (2011) note, resilience can arise only as a consequence of positive adaptation and the implementation of adaptive behavioral responses at the height of the crisis. Research has also shown that although victims and first responders experience a variety of emotional and physical symptoms of distress during a critical incident, they are generally able to function and develop coping mechanisms to act responsibly during the disaster (Tierney et al. 2001), and they rarely lose control of their senses and actions entirely in response to a crisis event (Clarke 2002; Quarantelli 2001). Rather, research has found that people tend to engage in adaptive, altruistic, and protective behaviors rather than maladaptive and negative behaviors during disasters (Bourque, Russell, and Goltz 1993; Johnson 1988; Keating 1982). As Quarantelli (1975) states, "Human behavior under extreme stress is controlled rather than impulsive, uses appropriate means for the perceived ends, and is organized and functional for the most part" (pp. 6–7). This is especially true for first responders, as the literature indicates that most are able to function at full capacity, in spite of the challenges they face, and abandonment of duty is rare (e.g., Tierney et al. 2001). In sum, most people are able to adapt to the conditions caused by a critical incident.

According to Lazarus and Folkman (1984b), individuals will assess the situation they face and conclude that it is one of the following: (1) a potentially harmful situation, (2) a challenging but controllable situation, or (3) a situation that presents no threat at all. This is the primary appraisal process. A second appraisal process is the contemplation of potential responses to the threat. Coping is the process of executing that response (Carver, Scheier, and Weintraub 1989). Coping is an important process on the road to achieving resilience. According to Rutter (1981), "Coping mechanisms include an individual's attempts to directly alter the threatening conditions themselves and the attempts to change only his appraisal of them so that he need not feel threatened. That is, coping must have the dual function of problem-solving and of a regulation of emotional distress" (pp. 344–345).

The contemplative process will determine which method of coping one will choose. After this assessment, an individual will begin to employ either a problem-focused or an emotion-focused coping method (Lazarus and Folkman 1984b). Problem-focused coping seeks methods of either solving the problem or alleviating its consequences (Roussi et al. 2007; Schnider, Elhai, and Gray 2007). It is an effort to act on the source of the stress (a person, an environment, or the relationship between them) and change one or more components of the dynamic (Compas and Epping 1993). It also involves elements of planned problem solving and confrontation.

It has been argued that problem-focused coping predominates when individuals believe that something can be done about a situation, whereas emotion-focused coping predominates when it is believed that the crisis has to be endured (Folkman and Lazarus 1980). Emotion-focused coping seeks to manage negative feelings through the regulation of the emotional state (Lazarus and Folkman 1984b; Compas and Epping 1993). Emotion-focused coping involves denial/avoidance, distraction or minimization, wishful thinking, self-control of feelings, seeking meaning, self-blame, and expressing or sharing feelings. It also includes a positive reinterpretation of events and seeking out support. Ultimately, emotion-focused coping is geared toward reducing the impact of emotional distress (Carver et al. 1989).

In summary, in the midst of a crisis, individuals who exhibit adaptive behaviors will use one of two forms of coping—

problem-focused coping or emotion-focused coping. Problem-focused coping is rooted in action with the intent to affect the source of stress, and emotion-focused coping typically manifests itself through psychological soothing and the management of feelings. Both forms of coping can lead to resilience in the face of extreme crisis.

Resilience among Law-Enforcement Officers in Times of Extreme Crisis

As Chapter 1 discusses, the literature thoroughly documents the fact that law enforcement is a particularly stressful occupation (Goodman 1990; Violanti, Marshall, and Howe 1985), one that is associated with unique sources of stress that sometimes engender the use of unique coping strategies (Anshel, Robertson, and Caputi 1997). As Asen and Colón (1995) assert, "Few professions can parallel policing in terms of the number and intensity of environmental and personal stressors. In addition to the obvious ever-present potential for physical danger, policing entails numerous stressors. As a result, police suffer from high levels of job burnout, accidents, alcohol and substance abuse and posttraumatic stress syndrome" (p. 46). Because policing is one of the most stressful occupations, many assume that officers' threshold for stress is higher than that of others outside law enforcement, largely because officers are routinely subjected to highly stressful situations. Studies have shown that police officers are more likely than the general public to engage in maladaptive coping strategies, which in turn leads to long-term chronic stress (Hurrell 1995). Moreover, according to Woody (2006), this stress often leads to severe emotional and physical consequences that leave a vast number of officers in need of mental health services.

As previously noted, people respond to stress in a variety of ways and seek to manage their stress using various coping strategies. Some negative responses to job stress include increased alcohol use, which is related to increased psychiatric symptoms (Ballenger et al. 2001). Burnout is another negative response to long-term job stress, and officers typically increase alcohol use when they feel overwhelmed (Sterud et al. 2006). PTSD is another result of exposure to extreme stress. Much of the literature explores negative coping practices of law-enforcement officers, but they also engage in positive behaviors. The next section of the chapter reports on data collected from interviews conducted among first responders to the Hurricane Katrina disaster that provide examples of coping strategies used during disasters.

Surviving Disasters: Resilience in the Throes of Katrina

All the officers interviewed provided insights about the issue of resilience. Though some suggested that maintaining resilience was difficult, most insisted that resilience was nonetheless their primary reason for persevering through the challenges the disaster imposed on them. Emotional- and problem-focused coping strategies facilitated resilience was facilitated through both. The discussion that follows highlights the differences and similarities in the strategies used by the NOPD and GPD officers.

Most of the law-enforcement officers interviewed mentioned engaging in positive coping strategies in response to the pressures of disaster work. A large number, however, reported that they were too busy to consider how to cope with the situation, and thus did not consciously employ positive coping strategies. The officers reported being so focused on the work of disaster response that they did not think about the magnitude of the disaster or how to respond to the situation: they simply did what had to be done. As was stated by some of the officers, "I was on automatic pilot" and "I didn't have time to think." This was a common theme among both the NOPD and GPD officers. This may be referred to as disaster distraction, the act of being so absorbed in the frenzy of disaster response that they do not have time to do much reflection beyond the tasks at hand.

The following statement by an NOPD officer illustrates this:

> I never really thought about the situation. We just did our jobs and worked the streets. Police officers are trained to serve and protect and that is all we did during the

aftermath. No one stopped and thought about the situation. If we did, it would have been difficult to continue to work. When you [sic] going through a stressful situation, it is best that you do not think about the situation but only focus on doing the job. We did not have time to think; but only react to the situation.

Other officers in New Orleans shared this sentiment. For example, one officer said, "I just focused on the job and not the mess in the city. We worked 18 to 20 hours per day after the storm and there was no time to think about anything."

Another common coping response among the law-enforcement officers was the use of support systems. Support was noted both in the form of support from fellow officers as well as familial support. For some officers, talking with their comrades on the force allowed them the opportunity to discuss the circumstances they faced and vent their frustrations. As one officer in New Orleans noted, "We talked to each other and supported each other during the hard times in the city. Many officers sat around after work to debrief about the day events and this really helped a lot of officers. Only police officers can understand other police officers. We are a closed knit [sic] family." Similarly, a GPD officer shared the following: "The department is close-knit and they were able to talk to each other about all that they were experiencing. Benefit of a smaller department—they knew everybody and were concerned with everyone's wellbeing."

Some of the officers looked to leadership in their departments for support. This coping method is illustrated in the following statement by a NOPD officer: "I talked to the older officers for advice and leadership support. Talking to the older officers really helped me cope with the situation. After work, we played cards and talked about the situation and what we needed to do to make it better. This really helped me a lot." Noting the importance of familial support systems, one NOPD officer said, "I talked a great deal with my wife and children and this helped me to deal with the aftermath of the storm."

Some of the officers, notably those in Gulfport, attested additional support outside the police department. A few of the officers mentioned that responders from other agencies served as a source of support. One officer underscored this with the following statement:

> There were so many things going on, of course when you see what we saw you are going to struggle with things . . ., and you know it bears on people, especially police officers, we're the tough guys, we aren't suppose [sic] to let things bother us, things like that. But what I found out and what I saw and what I witnessed was these are the outside agencies would come in . . . a multitude of guys from NY showed up, beautiful bunch of guys, but the bond was so quick, and what it turned out to be was not only were they coming out to help us, and they did help us on the streets maintain order and things like that; but it turned into almost a healing process for our guys. It gave us somebody to talk to, another police officer, not somebody trying to dig into your brain and say it's okay to feel like this and things like that. But they were able to talk about each individual struggle that they were going through and things like that with the officers.

The officer voiced a high level of gratitude for the assistance of outside forces in providing support for their response efforts; but more important, the officer describes how the ability to communicate with officers who had previous experience with a large-scale disaster provided the Gulfport officers with the ability to express their challenges with others who could understand their plight. This provided a bonding experience among the officers.

The GPD experience of sharing among the officers is different from what NOPD officers expressed. This department also had outside agencies come in to provide assistance, but the officers interviewed did not directly express that their interaction with members of these agencies provided opportunities to share their angst. It is interesting that, although none of the NOPD officers interviewed expressed the same sentiments about their experiences with outside agencies, they were more likely than the Gulfport officers to say that talking with fellow officers in the department served as a coping mechanisms through the disaster. However, both NOPD and GPD officers articulated in some form that the interactions they had with other officers, whether they were from within their own agency or an outside policing agency served as a means of support through which they were able to cope with the disaster.

In addition to the use of social support systems, some of the officers mentioned that humor also served as a coping mechanism. One of the NOPD officers who was married to a NOPD officer stated, "[We] make each other laugh about things . . . not so much talking with other people. . . . [We] made each other laugh about it." Echoing this same point, a GPD officer noted that "Laughter was a huge coping mechanism. Had to find things to laugh about."

Others mentioned the use of other activities to cope during the disaster. A few officers mentioned reading and participating in recreational activities as sources of stress relief. An NOPD officer noted that in the weeks after Katrina, he helped set up a makeshift golfing range in the parking lot of a Walmart, launching golf balls as an outlet. Other officers noted that barbecuing was a fun outlet.

Another source of support that the interviewed officers conveyed was their reliance on their spirituality, whether it was through prayer or by relying on their faith. A number of officers noted that their faith helped to alleviate their fears during the crisis. This form of coping was noted among the police officers in both the NOPD and the GPD.

An additional factor cited among the officers interviewed was that of loyalty; this was a common theme among the NOPD and GPD officers. Many of the officers interviewed said that loyalty was what kept them going through the tough times. Some cited their dedication to the department, but most of the officers who discussed loyalty related it to a commitment to their fellow officers. As one GPD officer stated, "What got me through was the man next to me, you came back for your buddies. You didn't come back for—how can I put this? Not that you don't care about the citizens of the city, but you came back because you wanted to help your buddies out and there was a mission to be accomplished." Others noted that their dedication to the citizens is what motivated them to make it through the disaster. As one NOPD officer stated, "Seeing all the people in need, [I] broke down and cried. [You] can't touch and help everyone. [I] tried to help all that I could, focus on helping others not focus on your own problems."

Most of the coping practices to foster resilience that the officers described were positive in nature. However, some officers shared that they used a vice as a coping method. Some reported they either started smoking or smoked more than usual, and others disclosed that they drank alcohol to cope with the disaster. As the following statements illustrate, the consumption of alcohol was used to soothe the pains of disaster work. "Drank a lot, that was for sure, at night when we got off," said one officer. Another officer commented that scotch was his coping method.

It should also be noted that a few of the respondents cited their prior military training as being extremely useful in helping them deal with all the issues they confronted during the disaster. One NOPD officer reported that he "readapted to training from military days; life coping skills learned in military kicked in." Similarly, a GPD officer stated, "I truly readapted to the training I had in my military days. Not necessarily police, law enforcement, but military. . . . Life coping skills that I learned in the military kicked in to preserve my life . . . just because things were so bad."

It should be added that when the interviewed officers were asked directly whether they received any training that helped them during the disaster, the majority reported that other than military training, no training could prepare one for what they experienced. A few did note that the academy training they received provided a foundation for dealing with their experiences. Overall, it was clear that most believed that no training could truly adequately prepare a person for a large-scale disaster.

In sum, the key coping strategies identified include (1) support from coworkers and communication with other officers,

(2) detachment, (3) spiritual practices, (4) communication with significant others, (5) use of vices, (6) recreational activities, (7) application of skills obtained from prior military training, and (8) outward display of dedication to fellow officers. In sum, the officers used both maladaptive and adaptive coping mechanisms.

The factors that facilitated resilience among the NOPD and GPD officers displayed a number of similarities, though with some minor differences. For example, respondents from both the NOPD and GPD indicated that talking with others was very beneficial. The NOPD officers, however, were more likely to report that talking with other officers in their department was beneficial than the GPD officers were. Contrarily, some of the GPD officers reported the benefits of talking with others outside of their department as a source of encouragement.

Overall, most of the respondents indicated using emotion-focused strategies rather than problem-focused strategies. But it is also important to note that one of the major responses—working without stopping—could be characterized as both emotion-focused and problem-focused. The predominant strategies they used included support from others and distraction. Reliance on communication with others (e.g., coworkers, significant others) is related to the expression of emotion and the need for emotional support from others in the midst of a crisis. This idea occurs in the emotional expression thesis, which argues that expressing emotion during disasters is a healthy way to cope (Stanton et al. 1994). The other oft-cited coping strategy—detachment—can be characterized as both an emotion-focused and problem-focused coping strategy. It is emotion-focused because the person is actively abating their feelings to focus on other things; but it can also be problem-focused when the individual is actively working to do their part to alleviate fallout from the disaster. A number of scholars have identified spiritual practices as a useful response to traumatic life events (Bjorck and Thurman 2007; Pargament et al. 1998) and is a form of emotion-focused coping.

The fact that emotion-focused coping strategies were used more often among the police officers examined in this chapter than were problem-focused coping strategies may be a result of the nature of the Katrina disaster. As noted in the introduction, Hurricane Katrina was one of the most devastating disasters to affect the nation, resulting in the dismantling of normal modes of operation for the affected first-responder agencies. It also jolted the consciousness of those in its wake as it created never-before-seen scenarios, as one GPD officer described: "But to be mentally and emotionally prepared for what we saw, there was nothing that could prepare you for that. . . . [W]hen you get down to the beach and there's nothing left and there is dead seals and sea lions the things you saw, the buildings you never would have dreamed could get destroyed. They [were] gone, there's not even rubble, there's just a slab. Nothing really prepares you for that." Hence, the shocking nature of the disaster may have forced many officers out of their comfort zones, requiring a more emotion-focused approach to deal with the chaotic nature of the disaster. In addition, the lack of basic equipment and the inability to rely on normal modes of operation may have limited the use of problem-focused strategies, forcing a reliance on emotion-focused ones. As Adams et al. (2011) described, the reliance on emotion-focused coping strategies during the Katrina disaster may be a sign that these coping strategies are important for the "cultivation of resilience among first responders during a critical incident" (p. 11).

Resilience and Police Culture

The coping strategies described by the law-enforcement officers examined in this chapter paint a picture of how one may respond to a set of difficult circumstances. This provides a window into better comprehending the best practices one may engage in to achieve resilience during a high-consequence event. This next section discusses how resilience is reflected in police culture, which some of the coping methods during the Katrina disaster reveal.

As Chapter 1 discusses, several key cultural precepts undergird policing. The ideals of solidarity, brotherhood/sisterhood, and bravery are embedded in police culture (Skolnick 1994). These concepts encourage camaraderie and loyalty among officers and are accompanied by the following axioms of policing: "watch out for your partner," "don't give up on another cop," and "get the job done" (Reuss-Ianni 1983). These axioms highlight the group nature of police work and the reliance they have on each other as a unit. Some of the sentiments the officers articulated (e.g., talking with other officers, loyalty to other officers) were identified in this chapter as being core reasons why they were able to perform their duties in the midst of horrifying circumstances. It was particularly evident that some of the officers were strongly motivated by the oath of office, as exemplified by one officer, who said, "What motivated me to continue working through the crisis... was the oath I took to serve and protect, and that oath is not just for when it's feasible to you." Many officers made similar statements.

It was also easy to discern that some of the officers had a very strong affiliation with their comrades and had an intense desire to be supportive during and after the disaster. This sentiment was demonstrated in one officer's statement: "Our team, 60 guys, all we have is each other. [We] had to do department's dirty work. Like family, [it] kept us together."

The expression of these core values as coping strategies the law-enforcement officers relied on during the Hurricane Katrina disaster underscores the degree to which these axioms play an essential role in police culture. The reliance on communicating with other officers as well as the desire to not "let their brothers [sisters] down" proved to be important strategies that further reinforced the solidarity among the first responders.

The strategies discussed in this chapter demonstrate that a practical framework for developing resilience in first response should include practices that complement the core values of an agency. In particular, it should be noted that activities that encouraged the brotherhood/sisterhood cultural ethos proved to be an important component in an officer's ability to cope and consequently be resilient during a disaster.

As we continue as a nation to move closer toward maximizing preparation and mitigation efforts for disasters, resilience is a central topic for critical discussions. Resilience of infrastructure, resilience of the economy, resilience of communication systems, and resilience of communities are commonly discussed. Much of the discourse, though, leaves out the issue of resilience in the people who play a vital role in smoothing the way for the community to bounce back when disaster strikes: first responders. If the nation is to truly prepare for future disasters, it is important to include this population in those broader discussions. One of the ways to foster resilience among this population in critical incidents is through providing adequate support systems during a disaster and adequate training prior to a disaster. Departmental support can come in a variety of forms, from food and supplies to the institution of family support systems during high-consequence events. The training feature is also important. As noted earlier, when the officers examined in this chapter were asked whether they received any training that helped them, or if they relied on any particular training during the disaster, many reported that nothing could really prepare one for circumstances that are so catastrophic that they surpass any training possible. Nevertheless, some of the officers acknowledged that they relied on their military training to make it through the challenges the disaster presented. Hence, military-style training may provide an experience that facilitates positive adaptive strategies, ultimately leading to resilience.

Conclusion

Review of the adaptive and maladaptive challenges that the New Orleans and Gulfport police departments faced provided important insights on short-term coping strategies the officers employed. Among the coping strategies that officers employed, communicating openly with fellow officers was cited as the primary effective short-term coping strategy. The need to communicate and connect with fellow officers is an illustration of the brotherhood/sisterhood cultural ethos noted by Skolnick (1994). The development and maintenance of the brotherhood/sisterhood bonds within first-responder communities is an important component to coping through a disaster. Informal debriefings (e.g., talking with other officers) among first responders also represents an important strategy that further builds solidarity and facilitates open communication.

The previous chapters' focus on the expression of a maladaptive behavior—post abandonment and criminal behavior—provides an opportunity to juxtapose maladaptive responses with adaptive responses to crisis. The stories shared by the officers discussed in this chapter suggest that early personal intervention may represent an effective strategy that impedes the onset of negative behavioral responses. Consequently, addressing the vulnerabilities that arise during disasters can serve to promote resilience.

KEY TAKEAWAYS FROM THIS CHAPTER

1. Resilience has many definitions, but the primary theme among them all is the ability to bounce back quickly after exposure to extreme circumstances.
2. Positive coping strategies can promote resilience and ward off harmful responses to extreme stress.
3. People tend to engage in either problem-focused or emotion-focused coping strategies. Neither type of response lends itself to generating more resilience than the other, but people are more likely to use problem-focused coping strategies when they feel they can positively affect the situation at hand.
4. The data reviewed in this chapter suggests that officers may be more inclined to use emotion-focused coping strategies during large-scale disasters that cause massive amounts of destruction and chaos in a community.
5. The reinforcement of police ethos is important for fueling resilience during a critical incident.

DISCUSSION QUESTIONS

1. Many definitions were offered to describe the concept of resilience in this chapter: Which definition do you think is most adequate?

2. Is there a difference between coping and resilience? If so, what is the difference, and if not, how are they the same?
3. Which of the maladaptive behavioral responses to exposure to disasters do you think could be most commonly exhibited by first responders during emergencies?
4. What are the ways in which the police officers quoted in this chapter fostered resilience?
5. Do you think that resilience can be taught? How do you think it is practiced as a component in police culture?

REFERENCES

Adams, Terri, Leigh Anderson, Milanika Turner, and Jonathon Armstrong. 2011. "Coping through a Disaster: Lessons from Hurricane Katrina." *Journal of Homeland Security and Emergency Management* 8 (1). https://doi.org/10.2202/1547-7355.1836.

Anshel, Mark H., Michelle Robertson, and Peter Caputi. 1997. "Sources of Acute Stress and Their Appraisals and Reappraisals among Australian Police as a Function of Previous Experience." *Journal of Occupation and Organisational Psychology* 70: 525–549.

Asen, Julie, and Israel Colón. 1995. "Acceptance and Use of Police Department Employee Assistance Programs." *Employee Assistance Quarterly* 11 (1): 45–54.

Ballenger, James C., Jonathan R. Davidson, Yves Lecrubier, David J. Nutt, Thomas D. Borkovec, Karl Rickels, D. J. Stein, et al. 2001. "Consensus Statement on Generalized Anxiety Disorder from the International Consensus Group on Depression and Anxiety." *Journal of Clinical Psychiatry* 62 (Supp. 11): 53–58.

Bjorck, Jeffrey P., and John W. Thurman. 2007. "Negative Life Events, Patterns of Positive and Negative Religious Coping, and Psychological Functioning." *Journal for the Scientific Study of Religion* 46 (2): 159–167.

Bourque, Linda B., Lisa A. Russell, and James D. Goltz. 1993. "Human Behavior during and Immediately after the Earthquake." In *The Loma Prieta, California, Earthquake of October 17, 1989—Public Response*, edited by P. Bolton, 3–22. Professional Paper 1553-B. Washington, DC: U.S. Geological Survey.

Carver, Charles S., Michael F. Scheier, and Jagdish K. Weintraub. 1989. "Assessing Coping Strategies: A Theoretically Based Approach." *Journal of Personality and Social Psychology* 56 (2): 267–283.

Clarke, Lee. 2002. "Panic: Myth or Reality?" *Contexts* 1(3): 21–26.

Compas, Bruce E., and Joanne E. Epping. 1993. "Stress and Coping in Children and Families." In *Children and Disasters*, edited by C. F. Saylor, 11–28. New York: Springer.

Dunning, Chris. 1999. "Post-intervention Strategies to Reduce Police Trauma: A Paradigm Shift." In *Police Trauma: Psychological Aftermath of Civilian Combat*, edited by J. M. Violanti and D. Paton, 269–286. Springfield, IL: Charles C. Thomas.

Folkman, Susan, and Richard S. Lazarus. 1980. "An Analysis of Coping in a Middle-Aged Community Sample." *Journal of Health and Social Behavior* 21 (3): 219–239.

Goodman, Alan M. 1990. "A Model for Police Officer Burnout." *Journal of Business and Psychology* 5 (1): 85–99.

Herrman, Helen, Donna E. Stewart, Natalia Diaz-Granados, Elena L. Berger, Beth Jackson, and Tracy Yuen. 2011. "What Is Resilience?" *Canadian Journal of Psychiatry* 56 (5): 258–265.

Hurrell, Joseph J. 1995. "Police Work, Occupational Stress and Individual Coping." *Journal of Organizational Behavior* 16:27–28.

Johnson, Norris R. 1988. "Fire in a Crowded Theater: A Descriptive Analysis of the Emergence of Panic." *International Journal of Mass Emergencies and Disasters* 6:7–26.

Keating, J. P. 1982. "The Myth of Panic." In *Hotel Fires, behind the Headlines*, edited by J. Keating, 89–107. Quincy, MA: National Fire Protection Association.

Lazarus, R. S., and S. Folkman. 1984a. "Coping and Adaptation." In *The Handbook of Behavioral Medicine*, edited by W. D. Gentry, 282–325. New York: Guilford.

———. 1984b. *Stress, Appraisal, and Coping*. New York: Springer.

Luther, Suniya S., Dante Cicchetti, and Bronwyn Becker. 2000. "The Construct of Resilience: A Critical Evaluation and Guidelines for Future Work." *Child Development* 71:543–562.

Pargament, Kenneth I., Bruce W. Smith, Harold G. Koenig, and Lisa Perez. 1998. "Patterns of Positive and Negative Religious Coping with Major Life Stressors." *Journal for the Scientific Study of Religion* 37 (4): 710–724.

Paton, Douglas, Leigh Smith, and John Violanti. 2000. "Disaster Response: Risk, Vulnerability, and Resilience." *Disaster Prevention and Management* 9 (3): 173–180.

Quarantelli, E. L. 1977. "Panic Behaviour: Some Empirical Observations." In *Human Response to Tall Buildings*, edited by D. J. Conway, 336–350. Stroudsburg, PA: Dowden, Hutchinson and Ross.

———. 2001. "The Sociology of Panic." In *International Encyclopedia of the Social and Behavioral Sciences*, edited by N. Smelser and P. B. Baltes, 11020–11030. New York: Pergamon.

Reuss-Ianni, Elizabeth. 1983. *Two Cultures of Policing*. New Brunswick, NJ: Transaction.

Roussi, Pagona, Vagia Krikeli, Christiana Hatzidimitriou, and Ifigeneia Koutri. 2007. "Patterns of Coping, Flexibility in Coping, and Psychological Distress in Women Diagnosed with Breast Cancer." *Cognitive Therapy and Research* 31:97–109.

Rutter, Michael. 1981. "Stress, Coping and Development: Some Issues and Some Questions." *Journal of Child Psychology and Psychiatry* 22 (4): 323–356.

Schnider, Kimberly R., Jon D. Elhai, and Matt J. Gray. 2007. "Coping Style Use Predicts Posttraumatic Stress and Complicated Grief Symptom Severity among College Students Reporting a Traumatic Loss." *Journal of Counseling Psychology* 54:344–350.

Skolnick, Jerome H. 1994. *Justice without Trial: Law Enforcement in the Democratic Society*, 3rd ed. New York: Macmillan.

Stanton, Annette. L., Sharon Danoff-Burg, Christine L. Cameron, and Andrew P. Ellis. 1994. "Coping through Emotional Approach: Problems of Conceptualization and Confounding." *Journal of Personality and Social Psychology* 66 (2): 350–362.

Sterud, Tom, Øivind Ekeberg, and Erlend Hem, E. 2006. "Health Status in the Ambulance Services: A Systematic Review." *BMC Health Services Research* 6 (1): 82–91.

Tedeschi, Richard G., and Lawrence G. Calhoun. 1996. "Post-traumatic Growth Inventory: Measuring the Positive Legacy of Trauma." *Journal of Traumatic Stress* 9:455–471.

Tierney, Kathleen, J., Michael K. Lindell, and Ronald W. Perry. 2001. *Facing the Unexpected: Disaster Preparedness and Responses in the United States*. Washington, DC: John Henry.

Violanti, John M., James R. Marshall, and Barbara Howe. 1985. "Stress, Coping, and Alcohol Use: The Police Connection." *Journal of Police Science and Administration* 13 (2): 106–110.

Woody, Robert Henley. 2006. "Family Interventions with Law Enforcement Officers." *American Journal of Family Therapy* 34 (2): 95–103.

7

Picking Up the Pieces

Life after a Disaster

> I think about . . . the people who died. . . . When I have the flashbacks it's like the day before . . . the smell just pops in my nose. . . . [I] look back to think about what I could have done differently.
>
> —Anonymous NOPD officer

The sentiment the officer above expresses provides a window into the experiences of first responders who find it difficult to continue with business as usual after disasters. As we have previously emphasized, it is sometimes inevitable for a large-scale disaster to affect those responding to it both professionally and personally. As a result, as Chapter 3 stresses, first responders often suffer from both direct and indirect victimization effects of a disaster, while they are mandated to provide necessary services to the public. Such duality complicates their ability to function effectively as first responders and it can also prolong the recovery process, as they are expected to attend to the needs of the public while trying to attend to their own personal and professional needs.

This chapter discusses how law-enforcement officers attempt to reassemble their lives both professionally and personally after a disaster. This topic is explored through the examination of survey data and case studies of the NOPD, the GPD, and the Constitución Police Department officers. While the 2011 Super Outbreak was a major disaster, it is not included in this discussion. Because the geographic impact of tornadoes is specific to the path of the storm, fewer officers responding to them are at risk for being direct victims of it and hence less likely to suffer the same emotional strains as the officers who respond to hurricanes, earthquakes, and tsunamis. To examine the nature of the impact on the officers and how they recovered from the disaster, the chapter addresses the following questions: (1) What are the key challenges law-enforcement officers face after a disaster? (2) What are the various ways in which disasters have affected the professional and personal lives of law-enforcement officers? (3) What factors have aided law-enforcement officers after experiencing the impact of a disaster?

Professional and Personal Challenges

Professional Challenges

> St. Charles Parish deputies informed New Orleans police of the suicide Saturday, Pfeiffer said. It was yet another tragedy among tragedies, and an indication of the emotional scars left on the city. "People are tired, depressed," said Lieutenant Chris Mandry, of the city's SWAT team. "There is total despair, and there is no light at the end of the tunnel. You've got people who believe their lives are over." (O'Brien 2005).

As noted before, the professional challenges an officer can face during and after a disaster depend on the level of damages to the infrastructure and the rest of the community at large and the department. Disasters, and particularly natural hazards, can affect the terrain, air quality, infrastructure, and economic and social dynamics of a community. They can severely damage buildings, limit communication, and impinge on the efficacy of police departments (Harrald 2006). A disaster can also lead to a loss of personnel, changes in the command structure, and a shift in duties to perform. Ultimately, a disaster can make major changes to the normal operational protocols of a police department. This in turn can affect the functions of each officer and his or her perceptions of the role to perform during and after a disaster. Such conditions can cause officers to question their career decisions and their ability to continue working under such stressful situations (Thomas-Riddle 2001). During a disaster, a police officer can find himself or herself shifting from law-enforcement responsibilities to duties such as search and rescue, retrieval of the deceased, or distributing needed resources to survivors.

Performing this wide array of tasks poses a challenge to officers, as they continually shift between roles outside their normal duties while being physically, mentally, and emotionally exhausted. As Chapter 3 notes, the shifting from one role to another can lead to role strain. Review of disaster cases examined in this book demonstrates that most officers are able to function effectively within the confines of the chaos. Some, however, find it quite difficult to operate professionally, as exemplified by one officer's reflection on his experience during the Hurricane Katrina crisis in New Orleans:

> The entire operation was completely unorganized. I made it to the station where everything was in complete chaos. The command staff did not have a plan and there was no leadership. I was distraught from the incident at my home, but they wanted me to patrol the streets. I was not mentally ready to work and needed time to regroup but was told that I did not have the luxury of time.
>
> I left the city due to the fact that everything was in chaos. I could not locate my supervisor and I was not given any directives as to the proper course of action to take after the storm. Basically, it was every man for himself. I had to sleep on the sidewalk outside of the office. Also, I had to leave to take care of my family.

The sentiments this officer expressed illustrate that for many it is arduous to navigate the chaos that ensues during a disaster.

The chaos a disaster causes also requires officers to function in an unpredictable set of circumstances. While law-enforcement officers are trained to function under extreme circumstances, a disaster presents challenges and circumstances that people generally do not occur in the line of duty. Officers can be exposed to sights they aren't used to seeing, such as large numbers of dead bodies, displaced buildings, and scattered debris. As one GPD officer who served during the Hurricane Katrina disaster commented, they are not used to seeing dead body after dead body. Another officer with the NOPD echoed this point: "Seeing all the people in need . . . [I] broke down and cried. . . . [You] can't touch and help everyone." At times disasters push officers to their psychological and emotional brink. Further, while they are meeting psychological challenges, they are also at their limits physically. These multiple pressures can heighten stress levels and overwhelm an officer. As Greene (2001) notes, "Anyone (police officer, emergency responder, or an actual or vicarious witness of a death scene) can reach and exceed the saturation point when exposed to the highly inflammatory emotional and sensory stimuli associated with dead bodies and death scenes. No one is immune. Each police officer, like any human being, can be pushed beyond the limit of his psychological experience and endurance, to a point at which he becomes overwhelmed."

Being pushed to the physical and psychological limits can cause a host of side effects, including acute stress, posttraumatic stress disorder (PTSD), and depression. It can also affect the officer's ability to effectively carry out their law-enforcement duties. In addition, being pushed to the brink can affect an officer's perception of the role of a law-enforcement officer during and after a disaster. Some officers experience a greater sense of dissatisfaction with their jobs after a disaster, while others experience a greater sense of purpose with their role as law-enforcement officers as a result of serving as a first responder. Some officers, in fact, are energized by the intensity of a disaster. Such officers not only are able to focus their attention on the demands of the situation and perform their tasks as they are assigned (or as they become evident) but even become keenly attuned to the role of a rescue worker. The "heroic role as a rescue worker," to borrow from Killian (1952), may serve as a means of role enhancement (Ahrens and Ryff 2006; Sieber 1974) for some officers, whereby their perceptions of their role as law-enforcement officers are strengthened during a crisis. This version of the heroic role reinforces a law-enforcement officer's identity, which can mitigate feelings of role conflict during crisis events (Adams and Turner 2014). The role may also reveal that some officers' identity is strongly rooted in their role as a law-enforcement officer, as Chapter 3 discusses.

While some officers are able to thrive in an extreme crisis, others unfortunately are not able to perform well under such intense circumstances. An example of how disasters can negatively affect the role and functions of the police can be gleaned from some of the experiences of the New Orleans police officers during the Katrina disaster, many of whom reported a sense of frustration in performing their role as first responders during chaotic conditions with a dearth of resources and inconsistent leadership. Some of the officers who abandoned their post during the Hurricane Katrina disaster noted that the chaos caused them to feel isolated and overwhelmed. Many felt it challenged their professionalism, and a number struggled with living up to their professional mandates while dealing with inner turmoil. The inner turmoil they experienced was exacerbated by the personal challenges they faced during the disaster.

Personal Challenges

Disasters can turn the personal world of an officer's life upside down. This is particularly true for large-scale disasters that leave behind a wide footprint of destruction. Those who live within the boundary of the disaster zone may suffer from a loss of housing, connections to local and family ties, and other social and interpersonal networks. First responders who are personally affected by a disaster often confront issues similar to those of their fellow citizens. The officers who were on duty during Hurricane Katrina experienced the pressures of trying to fulfill their professional responsibilities while having major concerns about how to address their own personal needs. The level of devastation caused by the disaster triggered concerns for the safety of loved ones, property, and the general way of life for people who lived within the affected communities. Added to this are the realities of their professional world—an increase in responsibilities, decreases in resources, and damaged infrastructure—that complicated their ability to perform their duties and dramatically intensified stress levels.

An example of how a disaster can uproot the lives of an officer is illustrated in the experiences of the New Orleans officers in the wake of the Hurricane Katrina disaster. Since many of the officers' homes were declared unlivable, the department provided alternative housing on a cruise ship for a large segment of the force until other arrangements for housing could be made. To add to this inconvenience, many officers in both New Orleans and Gulfport had to live for months without the comfort of their loved ones, as the nature of the situation required the evacuation of entire segments of the cities. Many family members who evacuated did not return for months after the disaster, and some never returned. As one officer noted, "Biggest stress factor was that officers couldn't get away from the situation. Didn't have a place to go home to in some situations. You would work seven days [a week], sixteen-hour shifts—wears on anyone." Frustrated by the complications of working in a dynamic environment as well as missing the comfort of their loved ones, a number of officers eventually left their departments to join their families, establishing new lives for themselves in other locations outside the city.

All these circumstances together exacerbate the stress levels of officers and can affect their psychological state. It is not uncommon for first responders to experience depression, acute stress, or PTSD as a result of the stress in disaster work. Law-enforcement officers have been characterized as the most stressed populations within the United States in what is likely the most stressful occupation in the world (Violanti 2001). Police officers deal with intense situations every day. But the level of stress experienced during a disaster surpasses even that everyday experience. For a police officer whose job requires a quick response to stress-laden events, their primary goal is to gain and maintain continuous control of the situations they face (Anshel 2000; Van Maanen 1978). In a disaster, however, they must function in a new and dynamic environment that cannot be controlled and is continuously evolving.

One officer who worked during the 2010 earthquake disaster in Constitución Chile described his experience this way:

> We evacuated people for about one hour. We moved all the residents to a safe area on top of a hill and then went down to the coast to evaluate the situation. . . . While me and other two Carabineros were doing this the first wave came in. The sea dragged me about eight hundred meters inland and I struggled for about forty minutes in the water. . . . While in the water, my feet were entangled in some plastics. The wave dragged me until I was washed away to a hillside.

In the middle of performing rescue activities, suddenly it is his own life he must save. Clearly, this officer was subject to extreme stress.

Depression, acute stress, and PTSD have been cited as psychological conditions that may develop as a response to extreme duress (Fullerton, Ursano, and Wang 2004). Depression is a condition in which a person exhibits a loss of interest or enjoyment in daily activities, low mood, and other physical, cognitive, and psychological conditions (Penninx et al. 2013). A number of studies have found depression to be one of the side effects of disaster work. Beaton et al. (1998) found a comorbid diagnosis among firefighters after they engaged in a critical incident. Violanti et al. (2006) found depression among police officers exposed to extreme stress. Biggs et al. (2010) found that 26 percent of the disaster workers who responded to the 9/11 World Trade Center terrorist attack were tested and reported to have symptoms of depression. Another study conducted by West et al. (2008) examined symptoms of depression and posttraumatic stress disorder among the NOPD personnel who provided law-enforcement and relief services to affected communities after Hurricane Katrina, finding that 26 percent reported symptoms consistent with depression. Similarly, a study by Fullerton et al.

(2004) found that not only are disaster workers at a higher risk of depression, they also seek care for emotional problems at a rate nearly four times that of an unexposed comparison group. In their study, nearly 40.5 percent of the exposed workers in the thirteen-month study met criteria for at least one of a list of diagnoses that included acute stress disorder, PTSD, and depression.

The other condition commonly associated with exposure to disasters is acute stress disorder, which is regarded as a precursor to PTSD (Bryant 2011). Acute stress disorder results from exposure to one or more traumatic events and can become apparent within two days to four weeks after exposure to trauma (Bryant 2011). Symptoms of the disorder include severe anxiety, dissociative expressions (e.g., memory loss, feeling detached from one's self and emotions, lack of continuity between thoughts and identity), emotional unresponsiveness, and inability to experience pleasure. A number of studies on disaster workers have found that they are at risk of acute stress (Biggs et al. 2010; Fullerton et al. 2004). Other studies have shown that those exposed to the potential of physical harm, loss of home and community, environmental destruction, emotional demands, loss of family contact or support, loss of sleep, fatigue, hunger, or extreme weather conditions are at the greatest risk for a traumatic stress response (West et al. 2008).

The psychiatric conditions acute stress disorder and traumatic stress response are both related to PTSD. According to the criteria of PTSD as described by the Diagnostic and Statistical Manual of Mental Disorders V, the condition arises in response to the traumatic events officers experience in a disaster, but in response to their daily routines as well (Tucker, Van Hasselt, and Russell 2008). PTSD is characterized as "a pathological anxiety disorder resulting after exposure to a traumatic event" and its stressors. Such stressors can be direct personal experience of an event, including actual or threatened death, serious injury, or other threats of harm to another person. In addition, PTSD can manifest as a result of a person learning about the unexpected or violent death, serious harm, or threat of death or injury to a family member or close associate. The onset of these conditions can occur immediately after or up to a year after experiencing a traumatic stressor, such as those experienced by first responders participating in rescue efforts.

A number of studies have examined the prevalence of PTSD among disaster victims—including first responders and members of the public—with most finding that more than 10 percent of the study's participants suffer from the condition. According to a report from the Centers for Disease Control and Prevention on the effects of Hurricane Katrina, 19 percent of the police officers surveyed in the NOPD reported PTSD symptoms, and 26 percent reported depressive symptoms (West et al. 2008). In addition, a study conducted by Guo et al. (2014) of professional and nonprofessional rescue workers who served in the 1999 Chi-Chi Earthquake in Taiwan found that there was a high prevalence of PTSD one month after the earthquake took place. The results showed that disaster rescue work is highly stressful for first responders and may cause mental health problems, even among highly trained professional rescuers. Similarly, a study that examined the prevalence of PTSD and comorbid symptoms among professional firefighters in Germany found that 18.2 percent had symptoms related to PTSD (Wagner, Heinrichs, and Ehlert 1998). Likewise, Durham, McCammon, and Allison (1985) looked at seventy-five rescue, fire, and medical personnel who were participated in rescue efforts after a building explosion and found that 80 percent of them had at least one symptom of PTSD. Another study examined the mental health of police responders after the 9/11 terrorist attack over a three- to four-year period and found a high prevalence of PTSD among them, especially among women officers (Bowler et al. 2012).

Acute stress, depression, and PTSD are but some of the many conditions that law-enforcement officers suffer as a result of the extreme stress of serving during disasters. Enduring a critical incident causes some to reevaluate their lives in ways they never had prior to the event. Some officers may, for instance, experience a greater sense of dissatisfaction with their career choice as a result of the disaster experience. A few officers who served during the Hurricane Katrina disaster reported that the love they once felt about their work diminished after the disaster.

For some, the stress of the disaster, coupled with their personal loss, generated frustration with their job. Others expressed that they felt let down by the lack of support they received from the department and the community at large.

Another potential side effect officers can experience as a result of working during a disaster is the inverse of PTSD: PTG. Instead of experiencing negative side effects as a result of the critical incident, some experience personal growth. Tedeschi and Calhoun (2004) defined PTG as "positive psychological change experienced as a result of the struggle with highly challenging life circumstances" (p. 1). PTG describes the experience of individuals whose development, at least in some areas, surpasses what was present before the crises occurred. The individual experiences important changes that go beyond pretrauma levels of adaptation. It is a deeply profound experience of improvement for some people. PTG has a quality of transformation—or a qualitative change in functioning—unlike the apparently similar concepts of resilience, sense of coherence, optimism, and hardiness. Overall, PTG occurs alongside attempts to adjust to highly negative circumstances that can engender high levels of psychological distress (Tedeschi and Calhoun 2004).

The difference between some officers' mental health conditions in response to serving in a disaster depends on the confluence of a variety of factors related to the personal and professional challenges they experience as a result of the disaster. The degree to which the professional and the personal challenges cause emotional pain, disrupt established norms, and affect daily operations determines the impact the incident has on the professional (Gospodinov and Burnham 2008). Two of the major factors that can mitigate the negative effects of the stresses caused by a disaster are the coping mechanisms the officers use (see Chapter 6) and the amount of social support they receive.

Rebounding after a Disaster

A person who endures the life-altering effects of a disaster often faces with the daunting task of putting the pieces of their lives back together afterward. Law-enforcement officers are not immune from the complexities associated with dealing with life after a disaster. The ability of an officer to find a place of normality, or a new normal, depends on the professional and personal circumstances the officer faces as a result of the disaster, as this section discusses.

Disasters are disconcerting, often engendering a variety of emotional and physical challenges (Norris et al. 2002) that can lead to feelings of helplessness, inadequacy, and frustration. Law-enforcement officers are not immune to feelings of despair. Trained to function under risky circumstances, they are only human and are susceptible to fear-induced cognitive processes (e.g., acute stress disorder, PTSD, panic flight) that are typical of responses to extreme stress in the aftermath of a disaster.

Interviews conducted with the officers who served during the disasters examined in this book displayed one of two basic responses to the organizational challenges caused by a disaster. Officers demonstrate either a general acceptance of the impacts generated by a disaster or a sense of ambivalence toward the changes. The nature of the disaster determines the changes officers face at the organizational, community, or landscape level. Each sort of change poses a different set of challenges and requires different modes of action or inaction to accommodate the changes.

Review of the data collected on officers who worked during natural disasters illustrates that organizational level changes can range from nonmonumental deviations such as changes in shift times to major changes such as relocation of department headquarters or precincts or changes in leadership. Organizational changes can affect the equilibrium of the officers and negatively affect how they view themselves and the department. Some officers are challenged by changes to their normal routines, others see the change as either necessary or temporary and adapt to the change. An example of how a change that some may consider minor can affect the psyche of an officer is illustrated with a review of officers' responses to the required change of NOPD's uniform after Hurricane Katrina. After Hurricane

Katrina, Superintendent Warren Riley ordered a change in the color of the department's uniform from powder-blue shirt and black pants to an all-black uniform. The department leadership made the decision because some of the uniforms were misplaced during the disaster, which leadership decided posed a risk of impersonation. While a number of officers readily accepted the change, this caused a great deal of dissent among the ranks and reportedly lowered morale for many of the officers. A few years later, Superintendent Riley reverted to using the old uniform to boost morale (McCarthy 2010). Uniforms represent an important part of police culture. They not only symbolize the identity of the organization, they also embody the identity of the wearer and are emblematic of the role of the police to serve and protect society against crime (De Carmargo 2012). Although something as simple as changing the color of an entire units' shirt may seem trivial, studies have shown such changes have psychological effects on both the individual and the public (see De Carmargo 2012). A small but symbolic change of departmental policies can have a major impact on morale of the force. As one NOPD officer stated, "Once they allowed us to go back, once we were able to go back to our old uniforms, then there was a lot more pride in putting that uniform on. It was like restoring us back to where we were." Changes that affect the symbolism or the ideology of a department can deeply affect the sense of community and morale of the officers, and some may reject modifications that threaten the ties that bind them as a community.

As we have noted in earlier work (e.g., Adams and Turner 2014), officers who are more accepting of the changes caused by the disaster exhibit a sense of embracing their role as heroic figures and take a great deal of pride in their ability to endure the pressures of the job at the height of a disaster and in its aftermath. They demonstrate a tendency to embrace the role of providing a service to the community in a time of ultimate need. This sense of being a part of a collective that was responsible for providing a much-needed service to victims encourages officers to develop a positive response to the crisis. The acceptance of the heroic role reinforces important cultural ideals entrenched in police culture, particularly the ideals of solidarity, brotherhood/sisterhood, and bravery that are embedded in police culture (Skolnick 1994). A number of law-enforcement officers have voiced aspects of these axioms as motivating for their ability to adapt to their changing circumstances caused by the disaster. When asked "What motivated you during the Katrina disaster," one officer responded, "Basically [the] people around [me] . . . [working] with partner I've been with my whole career . . . joking smoking, drinking. We are like a family."

These ideals include a variety of axioms that represent these ideals, for example, "watch out for your partner," "don't give up on another cop," and "getting the job done" (Reuss-Ianni 1983). A number of law-enforcement officers have voiced aspects of these axioms as motivational factors in their ability to adapt to their changing circumstances caused by the disaster, as exemplified by one officer in Chile:

> The Carabineros [Chilean police force] is very special; any Carabineros member could have done what I did. I told the president of the Republic that I did this work because it was my responsibility. I also did it for my discipline and dedication to serve the people. It is not about others helping us, we are the ones who have the responsibility to help. Even though we lost half of the Quirihue's [city 51 miles from Concepción] Carabineros facilities we never stop working. Our active participation makes people feel safe and protected by the police.

Another key ingredient that fuels an officer's ability to adapt to the sudden and sometimes dramatic changes within their professional world is the degree to which they identify with the department. The officers who express that the unit or team of officers with which they work are like family, or a second family, are inclined to feel a greater sense of support from their fellow officers. These feelings of support reinforce their identities as police officers, which serves as a buffer against stress caused by the disaster.

A positive identification with the department or coworkers also provides officers with a primary or secondary source of social support (secondary to loved ones or other social circles). Social support can be received from ties with family members, friends, and other social circles. As Chapter 6 highlights, the use of social support systems can be a significant factor in dealing with stress (Haarr and Morash 1999). Hence, officers who experience social support may fare better after a critical incident than those who do not receive social support (Brewin, Andrews, and Valentine 2000). Social support is a significant factor in developing an understanding of how to effectively mitigate psychological distress after being exposed to extreme stress (Glass et al. 2009). Furthermore, research shows that interventions aimed at increasing optimism, social support, and coping strategies can foster positive changes after a traumatic event (Prati and Pietrantoni 2010). In addition, studies have reported that social support has a positive effect on health when stress levels are extremely high (Berkman et al. 2000); and social support serves as a suppressor of stress after a natural disaster (Cook and Bickman 1990; Murphy 1987; Norris and Kaniasty 1996). Other researchers have found lack of social support to have a negative impact on stress levels after a disaster (Kaniasty and Norris 2001). A person's perception of the social support the person receives may lessen the impact of a stressful incident on individuals (Wind et al. 2011).

The police department in which an officer operates can serve as a primary source of support both during and after a disaster. The support services offered can provide officers with tools to foster resilience. But the number and type of services provided by a department does not necessarily translate into their officers feeling supported. Some scholars note that perceived support is more important than received support (Prati and Pietrantoni 2010). The perception of actual or possible support contributes to resilience after a traumatic event.

While departmental support is not always the cure-all for officers, many officers do rely on each other both during and after a critical incident. Among the officers involved in the

Hurricane Katrina disaster in New Orleans who were surveyed, 41 percent stated that they could rely on their fellow officers for social support. Research on police culture emphasizes that solidarity, a form of social support, is a key component of the culture and helps to sustain the officers through the challenges of being law-enforcement officers. This characteristic is heightened during times of extreme crisis. As one officer from Gulfport remarked, "We were a family; there was an officer in Bay St. Louis that hadn't heard from his family and we went there with him after he got off of work to help him find them.... They were alive after two days, part of the time on the roof." This is an illustration of police officers providing emotional support for their fellow officers.

The social bonds these officers forge as a result of their common experiences after a disaster can be lifelong. While there is a common belief that police officers in general function within a realm of complete solidarity—and this is indeed one of the major aspects of police cultural ethos—nothing solidifies this unity like the experience of going through a major crisis together. As one member of the NOPD SWAT team reported, "The SWAT team is [a] close-knit family and we supported each other during the crisis. I talked to the guys every day about the situation and we gave each other a lot of support and courage."

While many officers are able to find support among their colleagues, Evans, Pistrang, and Billings (2013) argue that some officers are reluctant to share emotionally with their coworkers because they are expected to cope with the stress of their jobs (see also Howard, Tuffin, and Stephens 2000). Rather than talking about such matters with their comrades, officers engage in "emotional talk" with their loved ones (Evans et al. 2013). Studies have shown that such support from loved ones is extremely important (Arnberg et al. 2012). A number of police officers of the NOPD who served during Hurricane Katrina noted that support from family members and loved ones served to mitigate some of the stresses associated with serving during the disaster (Adams et al. 2011).

The use of social support systems is a significant factor in dealing with stress (Haarr and Morash 1999). Research finds that social support has a positive effect on health when stress levels are extremely high (Berkman et al. 2000); and social support serves as a suppressor of stress after a natural disaster (Norris and Kaniasty 1996). Kaniasty and Norris (2001) also find the lack of social support to have a negative impact on stress levels after a disaster. The perception of the social support received may serve to lessen the impact of a stressful incident on individuals (Fordham 1999). Note, however, that other scholars have found a weak connection between social support and stress (Cook and Bickman 1990; Murphy 1987).

Another important factor that is linked to how an officer will respond to the stress during a crisis is the ability to cope with the changes and pressures the disaster causes. While there are a variety of ways in which one can respond to extreme stress, the coping strategies chosen can either foster resilience or lead to negative behavioral practices. As Chapter 6 emphasizes, in general, people engage in either adaptive or maladaptive coping practices. Adaptive coping strategies allow people to engage in practices that mitigate the impact of stress, such as seeking social support or participating in positive stress-reducing activities such as yoga or meditation. Maladaptive coping strategies would include using alcohol or drugs, smoking, or engaging in other negative behavior to reduce stress. Unfortunately, the abusive of alcohol in response to the stress of policing is not uncommon and has been associated with a number of psychiatric symptoms (Ballenger et al. 2001).

In addition to social support and effective coping strategies, as Chapter 6 notes, religious beliefs or spiritual practices are also linked to successfully rebounding after a disaster. Studies have shown that individuals who have a strong belief system often engage in adaptive coping strategies and fare better than their counterparts when undergoing extreme stress. In a study conducted by Adams et al. (2011), over 30 percent of the NOPD officers who served during Hurricane Katrina reported that engaging in a spiritual practice (e.g., prayer) helped them make it through the crisis. In sum, spiritual practices serve as an effective means of picking up the pieces of one's life after a disaster.

Another important coping strategy that is commonly used among law-enforcement officers is humor. Studies show that humor is typically used as a buffer against the stressors of this profession. As one Gulfport police officer who served as a first responder during Hurricane Katrina noted, "Laughter was a huge coping mechanism. [I] had to find things to laugh about." Samson and Gross (2012) argue that humor diverts attention from negative emotions and can promote positive emotions (see also Evans et al. 2013). Evans et al. further argue that humor serves to reinforce the masculine identity and provides a communication vehicle to discuss difficult manners. Hence, humor appears to be a vehicle for coping and for reinforcing the police identity.

Case Study: Andrew Rivers[1]

This section of the chapter reviews the post-disaster story of NOPD officer Andrew Rivers. The journey to become a law-enforcement officer is often marked by three pulls to the profession: childhood dream, job security, and the desire to help the community (Foley, Guarneri, and Kelly 2008; Lester 1983; Raganella and White 2004). For Rivers, it was the job security as well the opportunity to help others that attracted him to the profession; he saw it as an opportunity to join the ranks of a respected occupation. Rivers had served in a middle-rank position in the NOPD for over fifteen years at the time of Katrina's landfall. He describes himself as a dedicated officer, one who takes pride in wearing the uniform and serves the public. He rose through the ranks and was serving in a middle-rank position when Katrina struck the city.

Prior to the hurricane's landfall, Rivers concerned himself with the task of securing places of refuge for his officers in various hotels around the city. Once secure, they hunkered down and braced for the impact of the storm. As the storm moved

---

1. The identity and rank of the person have been changed to protect his anonymity.

out of the city, he confirmed that his officers were safe and they began the normal task of performing reconnaissance. In contrast with previous hurricane experiences, as the officers walked the city streets the morning of August 30, 2005, the scene was disconcerting. Rivers writes, "So, the next morning I was anxious, I couldn't stay in the hotel so I got up pretty early and got dressed, got my gear and I walked outside. When I walked outside it was like a lull quiet, that's when it kind of started to sink in that this was something totally different than any of the storms I had ever worked in." What River describes is a scene that was shocking to the senses; the level of destruction surpassed that of previous hurricanes. In spite of the scenes before him, Rivers shared that he was not emotionally shaken. He remarked,

> Well, [Katrina] wasn't really stressful because the nature of police work in general, it's a lot of being able to think and make decisions in split seconds. But for that particular incident, I worked storms before and I was kind of used to the aftermath—trees down, damage and destruction to houses and buildings—that was OK. Just being able to get the people who worked for me together, to make sure everybody was okay, and then knowing what my role was as a supervisor to give them information as it was passed down to me and make decisions on what we needed to do wasn't stressful for me.

Thus, he described himself as being resilient, that he could handle his role as a first responder in the midst of this extraordinary event. He also notes that while most of his other officers who worked under him were resilient, a few officers felt overwhelmed by the threats that unfolding events posed. Consequently, although all his officers made it through the storm unscathed, he lost 20 percent of his team to post abandonment. Rivers reported that his officers' post abandonment did not affect him emotionally, as be believed "Either you're with us, or you're not."

What caused the most emotional distress for Rivers was that he felt NOPD and the city at large neglected to take care of the men and women who served during the disaster. He believed that the department let them down, that they were basically on their own, and that they could not have their basic needs addressed—such as supplies of water, food, clothing, and shelter:

> The thing that caused me the most stress was that, knowing I worked for the city of New Orleans, I was a police officer, I put my life on the line for years prior to the incident. We had no planning, there was just . . . it was like we were left to fend for ourselves. We had no food—I brought enough to maintain myself for a couple of days, just for me. But for the entire district we had no food, no water, we had no sleeping facilities: we basically slept where we could.

The absence of support from a department that he once took pride in persisted in the months following the disaster and ultimately led to disillusionment about the profession. The cynicism Rivers felt caused him to feel unmotivated as an officer. Nevertheless, he was able to hide his inner feelings from his fellow officers and performed his duties successfully enough to receive a promotion. But he lacked the motivation to seek other promotions and continued to hold a deep sense of resentment toward some of the higher-ranking officers who he felt let him down. He also voiced feeling underappreciated for the work he and his fellow officers performed during the disaster. He found that he was quick to get upset with the citizens with whom he came in contact on the job. Rivers stated, "I had a lot of rage built up and anger, a lot of just-don't-care attitude, and it just progressed."

Unfortunately, his feelings of anger did not end at work, as he was quicker to display dissatisfaction at home as well. The degree to which he reprimanded his children increased and he found his temper was greater and he was quick to argue with his wife. Subsequently, distance grew between him and his loved ones; he did not share his inner struggles with his wife, nor did he want to make connections with his friends or even fellow officers. Rivers said, "Personally, I didn't want to be bothered with anybody; I didn't want any friends, I didn't need any friends, I didn't need anybody, any associates. I just wanted to be left alone. I guess being left alone I wouldn't have to reveal myself, my pain, and my hurt." As time went on, he became aware that part of his frustration was a result of feeling trapped in a profession with which he no longer connected. He felt, as he described it, "inadequate."

In an attempt to rebuild his life and expand his professional options, Rivers decided to go back to school and earn a bachelor's degree. He continued his education to eventually earn a master's degree and was in pursuit of a doctorate degree at the time of his interviews. The pursuit of higher education had a profound effect on Rivers. He stated the following: "Interacting with other people in a classroom environment—professors and reading and studying and researching more—gave me more of an identity of where I wanted to be and what I wanted to do with my life." The process of earning an education opened his world and gave him a sense of purpose.

An additional benefit of advancing his education was his introduction to the concept of PTSD. One day, while reading about PTSD, he reviewed a checklist of symptoms and realized he met all the criteria on the list. It was then that it hit him: he was suffering from the condition. Rivers decided that day that he was going to change his life, and he actively took steps to alter his worldview. He began to see that he was slowly returning to who he was prior to Katrina as the burdens of Katrina's aftermath began to lift from his shoulders. He started to open up and talk about his disaster experience with his wife and fellow officers at work. This was a 180-degree change from his previous wishes to distance himself from others and to avoid discussing what happened. Over time, he saw that he was more pleasant with the people with whom he came into contact and more pleasant at home.

When asked what he would want people to consider when thinking about the aftermath of a disaster and its impact on first responders, Rivers said, "We are men and women who actually stood up to take the job of policing corruption and crime in the city, and they need to understand that police officers are people first: they only put on a uniform, . . . but under that uniform is a person who has feelings—who has needs." Rivers' story highlights the fact that the road to recovery for police officers who experience disasters is not a straight path. Rivers went years without a diagnosis of his frustrations and depression and suffered in silence without support from professionals. It was the serendipitous experience of taking a course that covered PTSD that finally freed him from his pain. Prior to the course, Rivers spent countless days emotionally marred by the experience of Katrina. This prompts the question: how many other first responders are suffering in silence from the wounds of despair caused by disasters?

Conclusion

Serving as a first responder during a disaster can be an arduous endeavor. The disaster itself can pose health risks, physical safety risks, and emotional challenges. Added to this are the complexities of working in a very dynamic and unpredictable environment. It is also important to note that the size and temporal dimensions of a disaster play a profound role in how it affects first responders. All the police officers examined in the book confronted stressful and strenuous circumstances, and the Katrina disaster placed a tremendous load of long-term burdens on the officers. It can be argued that the officers with the Constitución Police Department also endured a lengthy recover process, but the immediate assistance they received from the Carabineros helped to reduce the level of chaos within the department and affected communities.

Law-enforcement officers are susceptible to all the frailties associated with the human condition. Serving as a first responder during a disaster can pose both short- and long-term professional and personal challenges to individuals serving in this capacity. For some officers, a disaster brings them face-to-face with some of the underlying fears associated with policing. While the fast pace and need for quick and decisive thinking reflects the reality of policing in some communities, changes in the landscape, dearth of equipment, and damaged infrastructure pose another level of challenges to their law-enforcement skills. Some are able to adapt and respond in the required manner with few outward professional impacts, but others cannot do the same. Even those who are able to thrive in their roles as first responders during a disaster sometimes confront physical and emotional exhaustion. And as illustrated by the post-Katrina story shared in the case study in this chapter, some first responders find themselves frustrated and disillusioned by the profession they once loved. This is reflected in the attrition rates of two of the police departments examined in this book—the NOPD lost approximately 27 percent of their force after Katrina, and the story is similar for the GPD.[2]

The fallout from disaster work affects not only the work life of first responders, but also their personal lives. The experience of serving as a disaster responder can affect them in a multitude of ways, including altering interpersonal relationships, putting a strain on family ties, and increasing health risks. As we describe in Chapter 1, police culture is one that is largely sustained by the interpersonal relationships developed within the department, and solidarity and trust are important in the ethos of policing. For some officers, the experience of working with their comrades during a disaster serves to strengthen the bonds between them, while a disappointing experience during the crisis can lead some to distance themselves from their fellow officers. As the case study illustrated, Rivers lost respect for his superiors and he shunned interaction with his fellow officers to avoid talking about what happened during Katrina.

The desire to avoid talking about the disaster experience with one's coworkers is sometimes carried over into one's life outside the job. In general, the intensity and risk associated with policing lead to the custom of keeping work life separate from home

---

2. There were no reports of attrition in response to the Superstorm Outbreak, and no attrition data was reported for the Chilean police departments examined.

life and is primarily practiced to protect loved ones from worrying about safety issues. This practice reinforces the ethos of secrecy that typifies police culture and serves to strengthen the bonds between the officers. As the officer in this chapter's case study indicated, however, the inability to share the trials and tribulations of a disaster experience with others at both work and home can heighten isolation and stress. This, in turn, can place strains on relationships with family members and friends outside the force. For some, it can lead to the dissolution of relationships.

For some officers whose families are not in tune to the requirements of their roles as first responders, the separation between one's work life and personal life sometimes poses relationship challenges. As Chapter 3 notes, family members who provide support and offer a sense of understanding about the nature of the officer's work responsibilities serve as positive support for the officers. When support is lacking, it can pose serious relationship challenges, particularly if one is dealing with the emotional and the psychological remnants of disaster work.

Depression, acute stress, and PTSD are some of the side effects of disaster work. The onset of these conditions can change a life, and unfortunately many first responders go undiagnosed and untreated. For many first responders who suffer from these conditions, the road to recovery is often long and crooked. One of the underlying messages from this chapter's case study is that many who are plagued with these conditions go untreated and suffer in silence.

While the stress of disaster work can be overwhelming, there are strategies an officer can employ to help mitigate the threats to their wellbeing. Interacting with a social support system, using positive coping strategies, and engaging in spiritual practices can all serve to mitigate some of the negative effects of serving as a first responder. Using humor to buffer the horrors of the situations faced during a disaster can also serve as a means of reducing stress among officers.

Overall, it is important to note that while some officers who are exposed to a disaster are affected both professionally and personally, research has shown that most officers are able to effectively pick up the pieces of their life after a disaster. Although the life they knew before the disaster may never return to the predisaster state, most are able to experience some sense of normality sometime after the crisis. For some, the process can take several years, as exemplified by the officer examined in the case study in this chapter.

KEY TAKEAWAYS FROM THIS CHAPTER

1. When police officers serve as first responders to large-scale disasters, they are more likely to be both direct and indirect victims of the incident. This can severely affect their ability to regain a sense of normality in their lives, as both their professional and personal worlds may be severely changed by the circumstances generated by the disaster.
2. Exposure to a considerable amount of destruction, loss of life, and human suffering can be emotionally taxing on an officer, and it is important for peers and superiors to carefully watch over other officers and also for the high-ranking officers to carefully watch over each other.
3. While many people feel overwhelmed by disaster work, some get energized by the work. These individuals should be tasked to play key roles in the disaster response efforts.
4. It may take years for some officers to regain a sense of normality in their professional and personal lives after being exposed to a disaster. Some may regain normality in one area of their life before another or never return to a state of normality.

DISCUSSION QUESTIONS

1. What are some of the external and internal challenges faced by police officers during disasters?

2. What are the short- and long-term effects of disaster work on the professional and personal lives of police officers?
3. While disasters can affect police officers professionally and personally, do you think it's possible for one to be affected professionally and not personally by a disaster or vice versa?
4. Which factors appear to cause the most distress among police officers who have served during significant disasters?
5. What policing ideals do you believe can serve as inspiration during extreme crisis events?
6. How do the differences in how police are organized in the United States versus Chile affect the differences in the challenges faced by the police officers who experienced the disasters examined in this chapter?

REFERENCES

Adams, Terri, Leigh Anderson, Milanika Turner, and Jonathon Armstrong. 2011. "Coping through a Disaster: Lessons from Hurricane Katrina." *Journal of Homeland Security and Emergency Management* 8 (1). https://doi.org/10.2202/1547-7355.1836.

Adams, Terri, and Milanika Turner. 2014. "Professional Responsibilities vs. Familial Responsibilities: An Examination of Role Conflict among First Responders during the Hurricane Katrina Disaster." *Journal of Emergency Management* 12 (1): 45–54.

Ahrens, Christina, and Carol Ryff. 2006. "Multiple Roles and Well-Being: Sociodemographic and Psychological Moderators." *Sex Roles* 55 (11–12): 801–815.

Anshel, Mark H. 2000. "A Conceptual Model and Implications for Coping with Stressful Events in Police Work." *Criminal Justice and Behavior* 27 (3): 375–400.

Arnberg, Filip K., Christina M. Hultman, Per-Olof Michel, and Tom Lundin. 2012. "Social Support Moderates Posttraumatic Stress and General Distress after Disaster." *Journal of Traumatic Stress* 25 (6): 721–727.

Ballenger, James C., Jonathan R. Davidson, Yves Lecrubier, David J. Nutt, Thomas D. Borkovec, Karl Rickels, D. J. Stein, et al. 2001. "Consensus Statement on Generalized Anxiety Disorder from the International Consensus Group on Depression and Anxiety." *Journal of Clinical Psychiatry* 62 (Supp. 11): 53–58.

Beaton, Randal, Shirley Murphy, Clark Johnson, Ken Pike, and Wayne Corneil. 1998. "Exposure to Duty-Related Incident Stressors in Urban Firefighters and Paramedics." *Journal of Traumatic Stress* 11 (4): 821–828.
Berkman, Lisa F., Thomas Glass, Ian Brissette, and Teresa E. Seeman. 2000. "From Social Integration to Health: Durkheim in the New Millennium." *Social Science and Medicine* 51 (6): 843–857.
Biggs, Quinn M., Carol S. Fullerton, James J. Reeves, Thomas A. Grieger, Dori Reissman, and Robert J. Ursano. 2010. "Acute Stress Disorder, Depression, and Tobacco Use in Disaster Workers following 9/11." *American Journal of Orthopsychiatry* 80 (4): 586–592.
Bowler, Rosemarie M., Matthew Harris, Jiehui Li, Vihra Gocheva, Steven D. Stellman, Katherine Wilson, Howard Alper, et al. 2012. "Longitudinal Mental Health Impact among Police Responders to the 9/11 Terrorist Attack." *American Journal of Industrial Medicine* 55 (4): 297–312.
Brewin, Chris, Bernice Andrews, and John D. Valentine. 2000. "Meta-analysis of Risk Factors for Posttraumatic Stress Disorder in Trauma-Exposed Adults." *Journal of Counseling and Clinical Psychology* 68 (5): 748–766.
Bryant, Richard A. 2011. "Acute Stress Disorder as a Predictor of Post-traumatic Stress Disorder: A Systematic Review." *Journal of Clinical Psychiatry* 72:233–239.
Cook, Jerome D., and Leonard Bickman. 1990. "Social Support and Psychological Symptomatology following Natural Disasters." *Journal of Traumatic Stress* 3:541–556.
De Camargo, Camilla. 2012. "The Police Uniform: Power, Authority and Culture." *Internet Journal of Criminology* 1:1–58.
Durham, Thomas W., Susan L. McCammon, and E. Jackson Allison Jr. 1985. "The Psychological Impact of Disaster on Rescue Personnel." *Annals of Emergency Medicine* 14 (7): 664–668.
Evans, Rachel, Nancy Pistrang, and Jo Billings. 2013. "Police Officers' Experiences of Supportive and Unsupportive Social Interactions following Traumatic Incidents." *European Journal of Psychotraumatology* 4 (1). https://doi.org/10.3402/ejpt.v4i0.19696.
Foley, Pamela. F., Cristina Guarneri, and Mary E. Kelly. 2008. "Reasons for Choosing a Police Career: Changes over Two Decades." *International Journal of Police Science and Management* 10 (1): 2–8.
Fullerton, Carol S., Robert J. Ursano, and Leming Wang. 2004. "Acute Stress Disorder, Posttraumatic Stress Disorder, and Depression in Disaster or Rescue Workers." *American Journal of Psychiatry* 161 (8): 1370–1376.
Glass, Kerrie, Kate Flory, Benjamin L. Hankin, Bret Kloos, and Gustavo Turecki. 2009. "Are Coping Strategies, Social Support, and Hope Associated with Psychological Distress among Hurricane Katrina Survivors?" *Journal of Social and Clinical Psychology* 28 (6): 779–795.

Gospodinov, Encho, and Gilbert Burnham. 2008. *The Johns Hopkins and International Federation of Red Cross and Red Crescent Societies Public Health Guide for Emergencies*, 2nd ed. Geneva, Switz.: International Federation of Red Cross and Red Crescent Societies.

Guo, Jing, Ping Wu, Donghua Tian, Xiaohua Wang, Xiulan Zhang, and Zhiyong Qu. 2014. "Post-traumatic Stress Disorder among Adult Survivors of the Wenchuan Earthquake in China: A Repeated Cross-sectional Study." *Journal of Anxiety Disorders* 28 (1): 75–82.

Haarr, Robin N., and Merry Morash. 1999. "Gender, Race and Strategies of Coping with Occupational Stress in Policing." *Justice Quarterly* 16 (2): 303–336.

Harrald, John R. 2006. "Agility and Discipline: Critical Success Factors for Disaster Response." *Annals of the American Academy of Political and Social Science* 604 (1): 256–272.

Howard, Christina, Keith Tuffin, and Christine Stephens. 2000. "Unspeakable Emotion: A Discursive Analysis of Police Talk about Reactions to Trauma." *Journal of Language and Social Psychology* 19 (3): 295–314.

Kaniasty, Krzysztof, and Fran H. Norris. 2001. "Social Support Dynamics in Adjustment to Disasters." In *Personal Relationships: Implications for Clinical and Community Psychology*, edited by B. R. Sarason and S. Duck, 201–224. New York: Wiley.

Killian, Lewis M. 1952. "The Significance of Multiple-Group Membership in Disaster." *American Journal of Sociology* 57 (4): 309–314.

Lester, David. 1983. "Why Do People Become Police Officers: A Study of Reasons and Their Predictions of Success." *Journal of Police Science and Administration* 11 (2): 170–174.

McCarthy, Brandon. 2010. "Infamous Algiers 7 Police Brutality Case of 1980 Has Parallels to Today." *New Orleans Times-Picayune*, November 7. http://www.nola.com/crime/index.ssf/2010/11/algiers_7_police_brutality_cas.html.

Murphy, Lois Barclay. 1987. "Further Reflections on Resilience." In *The Invulnerable Child*, edited by E. J. Anthony and B. J. Cohler, 84–105. Guilford Psychiatry Series. New York: Guilford.

Norris, Fran H., and Krzysztof Kaniasty. 1996. "Received and Perceived Social Support in Times of Stress: A Test of the Social Support Deterioration Deterrence Model." *Journal of Personality and Social Psychology* 71 (3): 498–511.

O'Brien, Keith. 2005. "Amid Horror, 2 Officers Commit Suicide: 'World Can't Understand.'" *Boston Globe*, September 5. http://archive.boston.com/news/nation/articles/2005/09/05/amid_horror_2_officers_commit_suicide/.

Penninx, Brenda, Yuri Milaneschi, Femke Lamers, and Nicole Vogelzangs. 2013. "Understanding the Somatic Consequences of Depression: Biological Mechanisms and the Role of Depression Symptom Profile." *BMC Medicine* 11 (129). https://doi.org/10.1186/1741-7015-11-129.

Prati, Gabriele, and Luca Pietrantoni. 2010. "The Relation of Perceived and Received Social Support to Mental Health among First Responders: A Meta-analytic Review." *Journal of Community Psychology* 38 (3): 403–417.

Raganella, Anthony J., and Michael D. White. 2004. "Race, Gender, and Motivation for Becoming a Police Officer: Implications for Building a Representative Police Department." *Journal of Criminal Justice* 32 (6): 501–513.

Reuss-Ianni, Elizabeth. 1983. *Two Cultures of Policing*. New Brunswick, NJ: Transaction.

Samson, Andrea C., and James J. Gross. 2012. "Humor as Emotion Regulation: The Differential Consequences of Negative versus Positive Humor." *Cognition and Emotion* 26 (2): 375–384.

Sieber, Sam. 1974. "Toward a Theory of Role Accumulation." *American Sociological Review* 39 (4): 567–578.

Skolnick, Jerome. 1994. *Justice without Trial: Law Enforcement in the Democratic Society*, 3rd ed. New York: Macmillan.

Tedeschi, Richard G., and Lawrence. G. Calhoun. 2001. "Why Should We Care about Stress? What's the Big Deal?" *PoliceOne*, October 7. https://www.policeone.com/archive/articles/43292-Why-Should-We-Care-About-Stress-Whats-The-Big-Deal/.

———. 2004. "Posttraumatic Growth: Conceptual Foundations and Empirical Evidence." *Psychological Inquiry* 15 (1): 1–18.

Tucker, Abigail S., Vincent B. Van Hasselt, and Scott A. Russell. 2008. "Law Enforcement Response to the Mentally Ill: An Evaluative Review." *Brief Treatment and Crisis Intervention* 8 (3): 236–250.

Van Maanen, John. 1978. "The Asshole." In *Policing: A View from the Street*, edited by P. K. Manning and John Van Maanen, 221–237. Santa Monica, CA: Goodyear.

Violanti, John M. 2001. "Post traumatic Stress Disorder Intervention in Law Enforcement: Differing Perspectives." *Australasian Journal of Disaster and Trauma Studies* 2001 (2).

Violanti, John M., Desta Beyene Fekedulegn, Tara A. Hartley, Michael E. Andrew, Luenda E. Charles, Anna Mnatsakanova, and Cecil M. Burchfiel. 2006. "Police Trauma and Cardiovascular Disease: Association between PTSD Symptoms and Metabolic Syndrome." *International Journal of Emergency Mental Health* 8 (4): 227–237.

Wagner, Dieter, Markus Heinrichs, and Ulrike Ehlert. 1998. "Prevalence of Symptoms of Posttraumatic Stress Disorder in German Professional Firefighters." *American Journal of Psychiatry* 155 (12): 1727–1732.

West, Christine, Bruce Bernard, Charles Mueller, Margaret Kitt, Richard Driscoll, and Sangwoo Tak. 2008. "Mental Health Outcomes in Police Personnel after Hurricane Katrina." *Journal of Occupational and Environmental Medicine* 50 (6): 689–695.

8

Moving Forward

The Role of Management in Mitigating the Challenges that Law Enforcement Officers Face

> Mistakes are learning tools, for individuals to be sure, but also for organizations. Unlike an individual, whose mistakes usually generate direct feedback and clear signals about needed behavior changes, organizational mistakes generate diffuse feedback in every direction, both within and beyond the organization. Signals regarding corrective action can easily, and even deliberately, be missed. We have too much invested in the success of all of our organizations to dwell very long on their failures. We are similarly invested in our public organizations and particularly our law enforcement agencies, whose functions are so critical.
> —O'Hara, Why Law Enforcement Organizations Fail

One of the primary objectives of this book has been to present the experiences of law-enforcement officers acting as first responders during natural disasters. The synthesis of the experiences of these officers has provided a view of the challenges they faced, their best practices, and the most pressing concerns that arose during high-consequence events. Our analysis provides an opportunity to develop practical solutions to those issues that can be the most debilitating to response efforts. To this end, this chapter presents lessons learned and recommendations for law-enforcement agencies seeking to adopt and implement practices that can mitigate some of the potential negative impacts of disasters on their departments. The topic is explored using data collected from interviews with psychologists, emergency managers, and the top brass of law-enforcement agencies who have worked during and after disasters. The essential questions addressed in this chapter are

1. What are the important lessons learned about how disasters affect law-enforcement officers?
2. What are some of the protocols law-enforcement agencies can put in place to mitigate the potential adverse impacts of disasters on their officers?
3. What operational protocols can be established to foster resilience among officers during times of extreme crisis?
4. How can policing agencies train officers to be more resilient during periods of extreme stress?

Lessons Learned

The data collected from the law-enforcement agencies reveal key insights into how departments are affected by adverse conditions during disasters. First, they provide understanding of the challenges officers faced in the heat of battle during the disaster preparation, mitigation, and response phases. Second, they provide insights into the organizational challenges faced by first-responder agencies before, during, and after disasters. This section discusses lessons about the impact of disaster work on first responders and lessons about its impact on first responder organizations.

First-Responder Lessons

While each worker has his or her own story about the impact of the event on their lives, a few key findings are common to them.

Lesson One: The Outer Persona of an Officer May Not Match the Inner Emotions

One of the most valuable lessons learned pertains to the need to see beyond the outward persona of law-enforcement personnel, which is often presented as an indestructible veneer. Officers can be just as vulnerable to the effects of disasters as are ordinary citizens. As Chapter 7 illustrates, many officers were emotionally affected by their experiences as first responders. Many concealed their difficulties, masked their inner turmoil. Like all human beings, law-enforcement officers are often able to hide their fragilities and emotions. Unfortunately for some, their inner turmoil turns outward in a show of short temper or anger toward their family members or the citizens they interact with while enforcing the law. As one officer noted, "It really kind of started a cycle of me [getting] into a state of depression. I had a lot of rage built up about anger a lot of just-don't-care attitude, and it just progressed." When one attempts to suppress their emotions, it can erupt in inconvenient ways, affecting others in both their personal and their professional lives.

Lesson Two: The Impact of Disaster Work Can Extend Long after the Response and Recovery Phases of Disaster Work

Some officers can rebound after experiencing a traumatic event, continuing with their lives as if the event were merely a bump in the road. For others, however, the sting of the event lingers well beyond the events of the disaster. As Chapter 7 stresses, the path to recovery can be exceptionally long. Several of the officers interviewed reported that the images and smells of the disaster work continued to haunt them more than five years after the disaster.

Lesson Three: Police Culture Hinders Some Self-Helping Behaviors

The third lesson is that facets of police culture (e.g., isolation) make the process of disaster recovery more convoluted for the officers than for other people, as the organizational culture of policing do not embrace participation in many of the things that will help alleviate stress. Police culture supports and even encourages a type of reclusion, and it is normal for officers to isolate themselves from people outside the profession. It is also typical for officers to avoid sharing details of the dangers they encounter on the job with their loved ones. They do so in part to protect their loved ones from fearing the hazards they face, but the practice serves to isolate the officers further. These behaviors can hinder, and in some cases completely diminish, the healing process. For instance, a few of the officers indicated they isolated themselves from others both in their professional and their personal lives and actively tried to ignore their inner emotional struggles. For many of the officers, time seemed to heal their wounds; for others, it took self-reflection and a recognition of their emotional issues years after the event to resolve the hidden anxiety or anger they experienced as a result of the disaster.

The paradox in the isolation that officers resort to is that it serves to intensify their stress instead of reducing it. Some useful techniques for aiding first responders in their recovery are discussed in the next section. Most of the techniques center on communication.

Organizational Lessons

The Hurricane Katrina disaster, followed by Hurricane Rita, served as red flags to the nation's mitigation, preparation, response, and recovery plans for natural and manmade disasters. Over the past several years, first responder organizations have placed a large effort on tightening the loose ends that these disasters made evident and strengthened their systems of response. Some of the efforts have included developing mutual aid agreements with neighboring jurisdictions, establishing redundancy in communication systems, and developing response protocols that are flexible and reflective of the types of risk responder organizations may face. The following are lessons learned about planning to mitigate adverse impacts of disasters.

Lesson Four: First Responder Agencies Have to Be Flexible

The unpredictable nature of disasters makes it necessary for both leaders and line officers to be up to the tasks of performing roles other than those they are used to during high-consequence events. As Chapter 2 emphasizes, major disasters have caused temporary loss of vital systems that emergency response depends on (e.g., communication systems, roadways). Consequently, alternative resources have to be found and employed quickly to carry out the mission of the organization. For example, during the Katrina disaster, the NOPD had to utilize a mutual aid channel system and messengers after losing access to telephonic means. The use of the old-school methods provided a means of addressing the telecommunication gaps and illustrates how organizations may need to revert to more primitive ways to accomplish tasks. It is essential for organizations to be prepared to function with technological outages and without their customary equipment.

Another effect of damaged telecommunication systems is a loss of contact between officers and their superiors. Hence, it is sometimes necessary for lower-ranking officers to take on leadership roles. Stepping up to the plate to make difficult decisions may seem like an obvious skill for police officers, but, as Chapters 3 and 4 illustrate, some patrol officers can feel overwhelmed when confronted with having to decide for themselves what steps to take during a disaster and to use their discretion in a nonroutine policing situation.

Lesson Five: Organizational Culture Can Either Support or Hinder Resilience

Organizational culture can promote either frustration or resilience during and after a crisis event. As Chapter 2 asserts and O'Hara (2005) echoes, a law-enforcement department's solid foundation of culture, values, ethos, standard operating procedures, and overall practices is fundamental, but, ironically, it can contribute barriers against performance and response during disasters.

One of the core frustrations among the first-responder communities examined in this book was inadequate support from their departments prior to, during, and after the disaster. Prior to a disaster, officers would like to see more development at the organizational level with trainings and guidance focused on preparing them for crises: (1) ensuring that they are all trained on the emergency operations and continuity-of-operations plans, (2) investing in courses to assist with further development of critical thinking and discretionary decision-making skills during a disaster, and (3) greater support of their mental and emotional states during and immediately after the disaster. During the disaster, supporting officers by obtaining information about the safety of their loved ones is an integral component of eliminating a powerful stressor that, as demonstrated here through officer testimonies, was a significant barrier to officers' full concentration on the response efforts and, in some cases, led to officers abandoning their posts in search of this information. It is crucial for law-enforcement agencies to be involved in the process as police officers begin to put the pieces back together professionally and personally. This requires more than ensuring that resources are available and operable; the department must dedicate at least some organizational resources to responding to the emotional, mental, and physical needs of officers and their families. The perceived lack of support from a department lowers the morale of officers and causes some to become disillusioned by their disaster experience. Those who view their department in a positive light are less likely to develop animosity toward their home agency or disaster work in general.

An additional manner in which a department can provide support among its officers is to ensure that their basic needs are addressed during and after a disaster. The lack of access to basic sustenance (e.g., food and water) during the disaster can exacerbate stress levels and intensify feelings of despair. While it may be impossible to have all such resources on hand when a sudden disaster occurs, advance preparations can make provisions for reserve supplies. This would help to foster perceptions of support and consequently cultivate resilience among the officers.

Perceptions of support can also be generated by addressing the officers' basic concerns for the welfare of their loved ones. This issue was the number-one concern among the officers. First responder agencies can take lessons from the Chilean national police force, which has a program that provides immediate care for its officers' family members. This simple action relieves concern about the welfare or whereabouts of officers' family members, as it did during the major earthquake and tsunami in 2010. Some police departments in the United States have developed similar programs to help ease the minds of their officers when they are serving during critical incidents.

Lesson Six: Organizations Have to Normalize Help-Seeking Behaviors

The second organizational lesson is that law-enforcement agencies have to actively promote officer participation in mental health treatment after a critical incident. Police culture is known for embracing traditional masculine behavioral norms that promote toughness, fierce independence, and suppression of emotions. These patterns are active whether or not the organization has a significant female population. These norms can deter officers from seeking the help they need at some of the most critical times in their lives. As Chapter 7 notes, it remains customary for police officers to eschew professional counseling, whether the help is from an outside psychiatrist or someone on staff. Sometimes the reason is the cultural norms previously discussed, but sometimes officers fear that seeking help will harm their reputation and affect their standing within the department. Therefore, it is imperative that police officials issue mandates for officers to participate in counseling after a disaster. In addition, agencies should work to actively debunk the notion that seeking psychological help puts their future opportunities on the force at risk.

Stress: The Number-One Enemy

As Chapter 7 notes, the stress from a critical incident such as a natural disaster can have long-term effects. According to Blacklock (2012), "Critical incident stress is argued to be more debilitating than physical trauma because it can continue long after physical healing has transpired, causing a continuing loss of emotional control" (p. 2). When officers' usual coping mechanisms fail during a critical incident and continue to fail long after, they need to be equipped with practical adaptive alternatives they can deploy when needed.

A reluctance to explore and engage such alternative measures could become debilitating for law-enforcement agencies over time. The impact of traumatic events on police officers manifests itself in both their personal and their professional lives. Although not all officers in a disaster will experience symptoms, the harsh reality is that it is also impossible to predict with certainty which officers will experience them and to what extent. Furthermore, though it is also impossible to predict the pervasiveness of the effects, some scholars argue that it is not uncommon. As Van Hasselt et al. (2008) explain, "Anecdotal accounts provided by clinicians in the field suggest that nearly one-third of police officers suffer from PTSD or post-trauma stress responses that can seriously affect physical and mental health" (p. 134). Many officers continue to feel the effects of stress after experiencing a critical incident. As highlighted in the "Lessons Learned" section of this chapter, some officers can hide their inner turmoil in some ways, but it can manifest itself in other ways that can be damaging to the officer and the department. Failure to prepare officers for what they might experience or identify their inner struggles are a potential liability for the agencies, as stress effects can increase the propensity to take frustrations out on citizens, ultimately creating a risk for abusive behaviors.

Preparing Officers for the Emotional Strains of Critical-Incident Stress

Preparation for crisis response most often involves ensuring that strategic, tactical, and operational plans are written; resources are staged; and personnel are accounted for, trained, and credentialed. It also involves making sure that intergovernmental and interorganizational policies and memoranda of understanding are written and signed and already in place in the event of an overwhelming strain on resources (Kowalski 1995). Rather than as an afterthought in the initial hours of the response, preparation for and response to the first responder's stress-induced symptoms must be an ongoing departmental priority.

As police officers' bodies receive training to meet the physical demands of their jobs, so too must their minds and emotional states receive training. Providing effective vehicles for proper coping is essential, as Lazarus and Launier (1978) suggest: "The ways people cope with stress [may be] even more important to overall morale, social functioning, and health/illness than the frequency and severity of episodes of stress themselves" (p. 308). Mitigating the potential effects of stress is of vital importance to preserving the well-being of officers.

As departments seek to alleviate the effects of stress associated with responding to critical incidents, some areas can serve as a primary focus. Currently, the literature cites three approaches to mitigating the psychological impact of critical incidents on first responders: preincident stress education; psychological first aid during the initial response, including defusing and critical-incident debriefing; and extensive follow-up after the incident.

Preincident Stress Education

Preincident stress education serves a very distinct purpose. Just as required physical training builds the physical resilience of first responders, stress education builds psychological resilience in advance of critical incidents that threaten to cause negative psychological. According to Guenthner (2012), resilience is a state and not a trait and can be taught and learned. Therefore, it is intervention at an early stage that will lead to higher levels of durability and resilience in first responders. Resilience during watershed moments has emerged as one of the defining factors enabling responding officers to implement adaptive coping mechanisms and maintain high levels of functionality during critical incidents. Stress education equips first responders with not only the tools to identify when they are suffering from acute stress but also the tools to choose an appropriate coping strategy.

The proper execution of effective preincident stress education programs will inevitably lead to the solidification of a more resilient department. Officers who receive preincident stress education and who later respond to critical incidents are not only better able to avoid adverse impacts of stress but are also more likely to recover quickly from the effects of acute stress when responding (Kureczka 1996).

A preincident stress education program should include the ability to identify all the variables that are associated with particular critical incidents (Beaton et al. 1998). Preincident stress programs are designed to improve cognitive and behavioral responses by ensuring that officers understand both the full range of adverse outcomes from a critical incident and methods of effective stress recognition and stress reduction (Flannery and Everly 2004; Kowalski 1995; Linton, Kommor, and Webb 1993). While there is a baseline set of expected emotional and mental reactions to critical incidents, being able to identify specific triggers associated with certain threats and hazards is also helpful.

Lessons learned from law-enforcement departments that have dealt with extreme crises and those issues that have proven to be the most probable and impactful should inform the creation and implementation of preincident stress programs as an important preemptive step in mitigating the negative side effects of disaster work. It is at this level that preincident preparation most decreases the likelihood that the department will have to allocate additional resources to mentally and emotionally rehabilitate its officers after a critical incident (Kowalski 1995).

Much can be done to prepare officers for critical incidents, but it is also imperative that they have support systems during and after a disaster. The following section discusses psychological first-aid tools during a disaster.

Defusing and Psychological First Aid during the Crisis

It is during the response period that officers are more likely to experience symptoms of critical-incident stress, and it is during this time that first responders require immediate intervention

(Linton et al. 1993). Within hours of reporting for duty to a critical incident, first responders must understand the gravity and reality of the situation to respond effectively, which means taking an assessment of the incident and its potential for devastation. In addition to crisis duties, this evaluation assesses the ordinary, noncrisis professional duties and the obvious impact that the incident has on their personal lives. It is at this moment that the officer can become overwhelmed. As the multiple roles that the officer occupies begin to take shape around the critical incident and concomitant emotions arise, the officer must recognize those emotions. Ideally, the ability to recognize those emotions has been taught during preincident stress education and training.

The next step for the officer is to employ psychological first aid to increase the likelihood of being able to utilize effective coping mechanisms. Designed specifically as an early intervention tool to enhance resiliency and promote self-help, adaptive coping, and problem solving, psychological first aid is a function of providing emotional stabilization and comfort for disaster-affected populations (Guenthner 2012). Executing psychological first aid involves employing a method known as defusing, an unstructured debriefing that encourages a brief conversation about the crisis event (Kowalski 1995), which occurs within hours of the critical incident. Emotional defusing gauges the extent to which adaptive coping mechanisms are being employed and limits the probability of stressful reactions spinning out of control (Blacklock 2012; Linton et al. 1993; Theophilos, Magyar, and Babl 2009). Defusing occurs within three hours after an event and can last up to an hour (Kowalski 1995).

Critical-Incident Stress Debriefings

Many agencies offer critical-incident stress debriefings (CISD) during a disaster to mitigate the effects of critical-incident stress. Researchers have found CISDs to be useful ways to reduce stress among disaster and rescue workers (Mitchell and Everly 1996; Hokanson and Wirth 2000). CISDs are a more extensive and formal form of diffusion; they are conducted when a hazardous incident appears to substantially affect a group of first responders (Kowalski 1995; Linton et al. 1993). CISDs are staged during the first seventy-two hours of a critical incident (Blacklock 2012) and provide an avenue for first responders to engage in discussions about the situation. The CISD provides perspective on the incident for first responders assessing the impact of the critical incident on their coworkers, including identifying who is using or might use maladaptive coping mechanisms (Davis 1996). According to Mitchell, Sakraida, and Kameg (2003), CISDs are useful for those who are experiencing normal stress reactions during an unusual traumatic incident and allow people to verbalize their distress using relevant concepts about stress reactions before they form false interpretations of the experience. They increase the responders' ability to execute necessary response duties during the critical incident.

The value of the debriefing process has been questioned (Begley 2003; Kennedy 1996), but a number of studies have demonstrated that if the responders are given CISDs within the first few days of a critical incident they are less likely to suffer short- or long-term effects of the stress (Mitchell 1988). During the Hurricane Katrina disaster, the 2010 earthquake and tsunami disaster, and the 2011 Super Outbreak disasters, many of the police officers participated in CISDs in the form of talking with their commanders and other officers at the end of their shifts. As Chapter 6 notes, many reported that the talks they had with other officers were essential to their survival. But when officers spoke about the counseling services or more formal methods of counseling, some shared negative stories about the process. In sum, the worth of regular counseling is greeted with mixed responses but remains necessary.

For all the helpfulness of preincident stress education programs in building resilience and of psychological first aid and CISDs in mitigating psychological impacts after a critical incident, sometimes additional assistance is needed. After a critical incident, resources should be directed toward postincident response initiatives (Guenthner 2012). Postincident response (e.g., legal and financial aid, referrals to therapists) assist the recovery process for individuals, organizations, and communities (Flannery and Everly 2004).

Another form of support provided to officers includes services commonly referred to as critical incident support teams or peer-to-peer counseling.

Peer-to-Peer Support Teams

Peer-to-peer counseling or critical incident support teams are characterized by officers playing an active role in providing emotional support to their fellow officers. "Cops helping cops," as embedded in police culture, meets the ideal of solidarity and brotherhood/sisterhood (Skolnick 1994). This ideal includes a variety of axioms such as "watch out for your partner," "don't give up on another cop," and "getting the job done" (Reuss-Ianni 1983). Looking out for each other and not turning your back on another officer are core elements of policing. Hence, officers providing emotional support to each other fits within the cultural framework of what is comfortable for this population. As one author notes, "With this built-in trust that police officers have for each other, peer counseling becomes a 'natural'" (Klein 1989, p. 1). Professional mental health counselors train those who participate in the peer-support process. The level of confidentiality required of the peer-support officer makes it imperative for officers selected as peer supporters to have "the unequivocal respect and trust of their peers in emergency services" (Linton et al. 1993) and that racial, gender, and multicultural diversity is maintained among the peer-support team (Kureczka 1996).

Peer-support officers are typically received better by their peers than outside counselors because they are believed to be able to understand the challenges police officers face and the increase in emotional, psychological, and physical demands in responding to extreme crises. For this reason, other first responders can open up about their perspectives on the event and place those emotions within the context of other areas of strain police work. The use of peer-support teams provides an avenue for officers to talk in a sympathetic context about the traumatic event they have endured. The assumption is that law-enforcement officers are more comfortable sharing their experiences with others who share similar professional experiences and point of view. That peer-support officers "speak the same language" as their peers makes it easier for officers to feel comfortable sharing their experiences (Money et al. 2011). Training includes ways to recognize symptoms of stress from the critical incident and the use of maladaptive coping mechanisms (Kureczka 1996). Officers trained in this capacity can provide psychological first aid and other defusing services to fellow officers during an event. Peer-support officers can be instrumental in identifying those officers who might need to be assessed for more enhanced psychological attention at the same time as helping to ensure that other officers employ adaptive coping mechanisms.

Some police departments have already instituted peer-to-peer support programs. In some departments, this peer-to-peer support occurs immediately after exposure to a critical incident. Another key component of assisting officers after a critical incident is the employee assistance program.

Employee Assistance Programs

Most police departments have employee assistance programs that offer ongoing services to staff members. Employee assistance programs are commonly designed to provide education, intervention, and support services to police officers and their families to help meet personal and work-related challenges that officers endure as a result of having a highly stressful occupation (Theophilos, Magyar, and Babl 2009). Some of the services provided are stress management training, family crisis intervention, grief counseling, and individual counseling. Many employee assistance programs offer additional services, with the essential mission of providing psychological support and stress management training to meet the needs of the officers.

After a critical incident, officers should be encouraged to use the services offered by the employee assistance program, particularly counseling services delivered by a trained psychiatrist or psychologist. Typically, departments have either a trained professional on staff or a consultant who provides services as needed. Often even officers who have experienced traumatic incidents underutilize these services. The primary reason behind the underuse of these services is the fear officers have of being perceived as being weak or in need of emotional and psychological support, as we have often observed herein. Many officers believe that if their superiors or fellow officers find out that they are seeking counseling, they may be considered mentally unstable, which could make them a risk to the department and their fellow officers. This fear is a major impediment to seeking counseling.

Many of the officers interviewed about their disaster experiences reported that although they are told that the information they share with the counselor will remain private and that their visits will not be reported to their superiors, they are fearful that their visits will not remain confidential. This lack of trust is a further impediment to seeking needed assistance. Some unions have a psychologist who counsels officers, which may be perceived as less likely to lead to repercussions.

Recommendations to Management

The unpredictable reality that the day-to-day stress of police work may combined with the event greater stress of a crisis event places a massive burden on police administrators to prepare in advance to enhance resiliency and decrease the probability of adverse emotional and psychological impacts. In extreme cases, the compounded stress that police officers face affects their ability to perform their duties during a response to a critical incident but after the response phase of the disaster has ended (Blacklock 2012). It is imperative that police administrators place a priority on the psychological wellbeing of their officers and on mitigating negative psychological impacts on them. Departments must be proactive and design policies for the development of a mental health critical incident response program—doing so can reduce instances of burnout, dereliction of duty, and critical-incident stress. Providing adequate mental health care can also build morale and protect the department from litigation that can result from failing to implement such a program (Guenthner 2012; Kureczka 1996). Such programs must be designed to fit the unique qualities and characteristics of a police department (He, Zhao, and Archibald 2002).

According to Kowalski (1995), an effective emergency response plan includes a focus on managing the impact of stress on first responders. Managers too can benefit from such programs, not just the rank and file. Kowalski (1995) and Blacklock (2012) note that police administrators also are susceptible to critical-incident stress, and moreover, it is imperative that they be in good mental health in order to support their officers. People serving in leadership positions are just as susceptible to the impact of extreme stress. As one first responder who served in a leadership position interviewed by Adams and Toge (unpublished manuscript) in Japan noted, "I took a drink before leaving" for work during the Fukushima disaster. While he was able to function in his capacity as a leader during the disaster, the coping method he used was maladaptive. In sum, though he was serving in a leadership position filling an important role in the response and recovery efforts, he too was severely affected by the stress of the disaster.

The above-noted official was just one of many officials who were personally affected by the loss and devastation that resulted from the Fukushima disaster. But he was one of the few in leadership positions who openly admitted to have been affected by the events. Others noted they felt the impact of the disaster long after the debris was clear and the response plans were in place. A person in a leadership position who responded to the Katrina disaster noted that "sometimes I would just go home and sit in my closet," referring to the act of wanting to shut out the rest of the world who could not understand his experiences. One could argue that those who serve in leadership positions have a double burden of maintaining a solid exterior for those they lead on the job—and sometimes in their personal lives too—all while trying to hide their own inner struggles. As one officer noted,

> I was a sergeant at the time, so it was one of those things, so that if I cracked, I knew the troops were going to crack. There were times when I broke down and cried, the situation was that sad, but never ever in front of my family, never ever in front of the troops. That was one of those, you're driving . . . where it's pitch black and dark and no one is around and you let yourself go for a few minutes, collect your thoughts and get back to work. But, with the position I was in. . . . I didn't want anybody to, you know—know.

These examples illustrate that those who serve in management roles are not immune to the negative impacts of disaster work: they too can benefit from having mental health assistance. As someone who organizes first responder missions stated, "If someone tells you they are not affected by this work, they are lying."

Consequently, it is vital that mental health care is made a top priority for all who serve in the capacity of first responders. Kowalski (1995) notes that for this to happen there has to be a collaboration between mental health professionals and emergency services personnel and an education program that describes critical-incident stress and makes a clear case for implementing interventions. Time, space, and resources have to be allocated for the mental health professionals, and there must be substantial follow-up and support for workers even after the event.

Cultivating Resilience

As the data in this book have shown, for some first responders the ability to respond was inextricably linked to their resilience. The training and overall professional physical and psychological preparation of first responders are essential for an effective response. The more trained, prepared, skilled, and equipped a first responder is, the more likely the execution of response duties will be second nature. First responders clearly must be able to respond effectively in situations that would typically temporarily paralyze a non–first responder. The findings have revealed that emotional, mental, and psychological strains affect police officers when they are responding to a large-scale crisis. While the strains may not be on the same scale as those on an untrained non–first responder, and while the amount of time it takes to affect the first responder may be delayed, the simple truth is that they are nonetheless affected.

As the research has shown, while responding to crisis situations, first responders need to make rapid decisions about whether to employ adaptive or maladaptive coping responses while under duress from the physical and psychological stresses with which they must cope. There is no doubt that the average police officer will jump into action and respond to their internal trauma. But the decision of *how* they deal with the emotions that emerge is just as crucial as how they react to the crisis at hand.

The normalization of adaptive and effective coping skills for first responders must be treated as just as critical as standardizing how an officer is to respond to a robbery or a car accident. Established, formalized, and implemented protocols and procedures that treat emotional and mental responses to crises are as important as the protocols for the physical response. A psychological injury has proven to be just as debilitating as a physical injury. How first responders deal with the emotional and mental aspects of their response must not be framed as "I will just have to think about that later." Police officers should be equipped with the mental and emotional strategies to determine what coping mechanisms they must immediately deploy when faced with a critical incident.

Educating police officers about the possible mental and emotional side effects that stem from responding to a crisis not only allows them to recognize those symptoms in themselves, it fosters an ability to look out for destructive patterns of behavior among their fellow officers. It is imperative that officers have the capacity to recognize maladaptive coping mechanisms being employed by their fellow officers. Police officers are trained to be stewards of security and protection when it comes to their fellow officers. They are taught that the physical safety of a fellow officer is a top priority. The same logic and training must be applied to the mental and emotional wellbeing of other officers. As research has shown, maladaptive emotional and mental responses to an extreme crisis event can also manifest as inappropriate or unsuitable physical reactions, which in turn can result in physical harm to a responding officer and the officer's partner. Thus, giving officers the ability to identify negative emotional response patterns in themselves and in others has a compounding effect that increases organizational safety and effectiveness.

Police departments should encourage education, training, and credentialing in peer support and other counseling services for officers to the same degree that they encourage other specialized training (e.g., special operations and SWAT). In many of the cases examined in this book, while resources were limited, response skills were ample. The first responders had been trained to execute response missions successfully and in many cases performed them without the presence or direction of a superior. The fundamental role that the peer support played in providing motivation, support, understanding, comfort, inspiration, and connection demonstrates that, while the response skills were sufficient, the necessary training of first responders in mental health basics should also have been adequate.

Training officers to assess their own mental, emotional, and psychological reactions, as well as those of their fellow officers, becomes particularly paramount if the crisis reaches a level of impact that those described herein did. As the impacts of critical incidents grow, access to mental health professionals may be limited. These limits could exist for many reasons. If mental health professionals are not routinely a part of the initial response team (which they most typically are not), then their presence will have to be formally requested through the incident commander. The incident commander will then have to identify trained professionals, locate them after the crisis, and make arrangements for them to be transported to the response location. Therefore, provisions for ensuring that the mental health of the first responder community should be considered at the same level as provisions for ensuring they have sleeping quarters, adequate food and water, and access to physical resources for meeting the needs of the population that they will be serving. The main priority at the time of the incident is often acquiring other first responders to assist with the demands of disaster response: by the time the mental health professionals do arrive on the scene, the first responders have already gone into survivor mode. Combining this situation with the need to meet similar needs for other first responders who will likely join the crisis scene to assist with the response efforts and life safety missions, it is no mystery why providing access to mental health professionals on the site is imperative.

As first responders rotate shifts during the response efforts and are given time to reset, a crucial window of opportunity begins closing as decisions about which coping strategies they will employ have already been formed. Having already begun to implement the coping strategy, whether maladaptive or adaptive, intervention by a mental health professional to help determine or redirect coping strategies becomes increasingly difficult. This could especially be the case if first responders have already identified their optimum coping mechanism that helps them focus on getting through the response portion of the disaster. The aid they identify can be garnering the support of fellow officers, relying on alcohol or other vices, engaging in religious or spiritual practices, or one of several other options. Delivering early treatment is important to help thwart negative reactions to stress. As Gupton et al. (2011) explain, "Effective trauma intervention serves to normalize an individual's reactions and experiences, as well as to promote emotional processing" (p. 3). This is especially true if the intervention is applied early in the crisis response.

Police administrators and management should consider the conditions under which they would be able to secure and deploy the assistance of a mental health professional at a crisis scene. This step is especially important if the decision has been made to not import basic counseling skills into the training regime of its officers. This process includes assessing the following:

1. How much time (hours, days, weeks) would it take to identify and deploy a mental health care professional to a crisis scene in my jurisdiction?
2. Are there any policies, procedures, or protocols that dictate how my department could go about providing these services in an emergency? When was the last time these guiding documents were reviewed and updated?
3. Will the service provider be internal to our organization? If so, does this person have a respectable reputation (professional and personal) within the department?
4. If the service provider is external to our organization, does he or she have a sound understanding of the job duties and requirements associated with first responders in law enforcement?
5. If the service provider is external to our organization, does he or she have any existing contracts with neighboring response organizations that could cause a potential problem or conflict with obligations to the other response team during the same crisis?
6. Has the department identified an alternative source of payment of the service provider fees if a presidential disaster declaration does not cover the emergency, critical incident, or disaster?

It is important that the identified mental health professionals have experience working with police officers or are aware of police culture. Tanigoshi, Kontos, and Remley (2008) assert the following: "Efforts must be taken by mental health counselors to first understand and consider the unique culture and variables that exist within law enforcement. Collaborative efforts among counselors and law-enforcement personnel are a vital and necessary component in the implementation of a tailored wellness program that is culturally specific and exclusively designed for law-enforcement officers" (p. 72) The inability to identify with police culture can frustrate officers receiving counseling. One of the primary reasons police officers respond to peer counseling is that they feel the person providing the counselors understands them and their profession. Hence, it is imperative that the right counselors be identified.

Innate Resilience

Humans have an inherent ability of to begin journeys of mentally and emotionally self-correcting immediately after a critical incident. Most typically, first responders in our study described ad hoc debriefing sessions with fellow officers and management as the greatest help. They explained how having the ability to talk about the impact of the incident with colleagues afforded them a sense of security and allowed them to partially hit the reset button to approach their response duties with a renewed sense of purpose.

It is essential to emphasize that most police officers interviewed demonstrated resilience during the disaster they faced. Whether it was ingrained in them during their time at the academy, cultivated in them through their relationships with veteran officers, or taught to them by mental health professionals or personal struggles, they already had some level of built-in resilience. What this research has found is that the levels of psychological and emotional resilience for most first responders were higher than one might have imagined in the extraordinary circumstances they tackled. Their ability to innately implement coping practices that facilitated their ability to face some of the most horrifying disasters in history demonstrates a high degree of resilience.

While these officers performed what, they considered to be informal practices used only as a means of survival, it is the responsibility of police administrators and management to formalize these practices. The burden is on management to ensure that their police departments not only are aware of the ways in which they can begin the emotional and mental healing process immediately after a critical incident, but also provide training for their officers to identify those in need of assistance. First responders are trained to respond to the needs of the public first. Beyond being the first line of defense for citizens, they also inadvertently become the first line of defense for and first responders to their fellow officers during a crisis. Before any mental health professional can provide assistance, before loved ones can express their support, before police administrators can validate their actions and encourage them to proceed, before any new media can express the public's appreciation for their efforts, first responders must first turn to their fellow officers to find the courage and the will to continue. Whether it is expressing sadness about the crises that has occurred or feelings of regret for being involved in response efforts instead of ensuring the safety of their family, first responders must rely on each other. In this light, peer support training for all officers becomes invaluable and necessary.

Conclusion

The goal of this chapter was to present a review of the lessons learned from the life experiences shared by the officers examined in this book. The chapter addressed four important questions about the lessons learned about how disasters affect law-enforcement officers who serve as disaster workers, as well as the protocols police agencies can use to mitigate the negative effects of disaster work. The chapter also explored the operational protocols and training options that law-enforcement agencies can institute to foster resilience.

This chapter highlighted the importance of recognizing that police officers often suffer in silence and will probably suppress the effects of disaster work. This suppression of emotions and feelings can have effects that last years beyond their disaster experience. One of the major factors that affected officers' ability to be open about their inner turmoil is the very culture of policing. Police culture encourages the suppression of emotion, and officers often feel they will be chastised or ostracized for seeking help from professional counselors. Therefore, many choose to endure the pains of disaster work by themselves. Consequently, it is necessary for policing agencies to be flexible during times of crisis, proactively foster resilience, and actively encourage help-seeking behaviors.

Many mitigation practices police departments can engage in before, during, and after a critical incident foster resilience and minimize the harmful effects on police officers. Preincident mitigation activities stress education as an essential component in building psychological resilience before a critical event. The practice of defusing and CISDs are important steps departments can take to mitigate the potential psychological trauma of disaster work during the incident. Peer-support teams and employee assistance programs can also serve as important vehicles for providing emotional support to officers during an incident.

The institutionalization of beneficial mitigation practices is an essential part of any effective emergency management plan. The provision of opportunities to engage in positive mental health practices is vital to any emergency management plan. The normalization of healthy behaviors in response to crisis events is necessary for officers to maintain resilience through the response and recovery phases of a disaster.

KEY TAKEAWAYS FROM THIS CHAPTER

1. Police administrators can play an essential role in the mitigation of maladaptive feelings among officers during and after a disaster. Their ability to see the needs of the officers and prepare to address the needs before a critical incident is important for effectively managing the officers on the force during a disaster.
2. It is essential for commanding officers to understand that while some officers find it easy to ask for assistance, many suffer in silence and their recovery can be lengthy as a result.
3. Police culture often hinders help-seeking behaviors, and police administrators should work to normalize the practice of asking for assistance.
4. While highly bureaucratic, it is crucial for police organizations to have the ability to make quick changes to

its functions and hierarchical order of decision making in times of crisis.
5. It is imperative for police departments to develop pre-disaster preparation and provide adequate training to officers. This training should include the introduction of adaptive coping strategies.
6. It is vital that police departments provide outlets for police officers to destress during disasters, which may include providing peer support, debriefings, and employee assistance programs.

DISCUSSION QUESTIONS

1. Of all the lessons learned discussed in this chapter, which two do you believe appear to be the most important for preserving the mental health of police officers?
2. What are the essential mitigation practices a policing agency can put in place before an event to minimize the impact of disasters on their officers?
3. What operational protocols do you think can help foster resilience among police officers during a disaster? Which do you believe the officers will most readily accept?
4. Peer-support teams appear to be a useful practice for providing support to officers. Why do you think it has been a popular approach among the law-enforcement community?
5. Do you think resilience is innate or can a person be trained to be resilient?

REFERENCES

Adams, T. M., and M. Toge. Unpublished Manuscript. *The Impact of the Fukushima Disaster on Fire Fighters*.
Beaton, Randal, Shirley Murphy, Clark Johnson, Ken Pike, and Wayne Cornell. 1998. "Exposure to Duty-Related Incident Stressors in Urban Firefighters and Paramedics." *Journal of Traumatic Stress* 11 (4): 821–28.
Begley, Sharon. 2003. "Is Trauma Debriefing Worse Than Letting Victims Heal Naturally?" *Wall Street Journal*, September 12. http://online.wsj.com/article/0,,SB10633129057000400,00.html.

Blacklock, Eddie. 2012. "Interventions following a Critical Incident: Developing a Critical Incident Stress Management Team." *Archives of Psychiatric Nursing* 26 (1): 2–8.

Davis, Jeffrey A. 1996. "Sadness, Tragedy and Mass Disaster in Oklahoma City: Providing Critical Incident Stress Debriefings to a Community in Crisis." *Accident and Emergency Nursing* 4 (2): 59–64.

Flannery Jr, Raymond B., and George S. Everly Jr. 2004. "Critical Incident Stress Management (CISM): Updated Review of Findings, 1998–2002." *Aggression and Violent Behavior* 9 (4): 319–329.

Guenthner, Daniel H. 2012. "Emergency and Crisis Management: Critical Incident Stress Management for First Responders and Business Organisations." *Journal of Business Continuity and Emergency Planning* 5 (4): 298–315.

Gupton, Herbert M., Evan Axelrod, Luz Cornell, Stephen F. Curran, Carol J. Hood, Jennifer Kelly, and Jon Moss. 2011. "Support and Sustain: Psychological Intervention for Law Enforcement Personnel." *Police Chief* 78 (8): 92–97.

He, Ni, Jihong Zhao, and Carol A. Archbold. 2002. "Gender and Police Stress: The Convergent and Divergent Impact of Work Environment, Work-Family Conflict, and Stress Coping Mechanisms of Female and Male Police Officers." *Policing* 25 (4): 687–708.

Hokanson, Melvin, and Bonnita Wirth. 2000. "The Critical Incident Stress Debriefing Process for the Los Angeles County Fire Department: Automatic and Effective." *International Journal of Emergency Mental Health* 2 (4): 249–257.

Klein, Robin. 1989. "Police Peer Counseling: Officers Helping Officers." *FBI Law Enforcement Bulletin* 58: 1–4.

Kowalski, Kathleen Madland. M. 1995. "A Human Component to Consider in Your Emergency Management Plans: The Critical Incident Stress Factor." *Safety Science* 20 (1): 115–123.

Kureczka, Arthur. W. 1996. "Critical Incident Stress in Law Enforcement." *FBI Law Enforcement Bulletin* 65: 10–16.

Lazarus, Richard S., and Raymond Launier. 1978. "Stress-Related Transactions between Person and Environment." In *Perspectives in Interactional Psychology*, edited by L. A. Pervin and M. Lewis, 287–327. New York: Plenum.

Linton, John C., Martin J. Kommor, and Clifford H. Webb. 1993. "Helping the Helpers: The Development of a Critical Incident Stress Management Team through University/Community Cooperation." *Annals of Emergency Medicine* 22 (4): 34–39.

Mitchell, Ann M., Teresa J. Sakraida, and Kirstyn Kameg. 2003. "Critical Incident Stress Debriefing: Implications for Best Practice." *Disaster Management and Response* 1 (2): 46–51.

Mitchell, Jeffrey. T. 1988. "Stress. The History, Status and Future of Critical Incident Stress Debriefings." *JEMS* 13 (11): 46–47.

Money, Nisha, Monique Moore, David Brown, Kathleen Kasper, Jessica Roeder, Paul Bartone, and Mark Bates. 2011. "Best Practices Identified for Peer Support Programs." Defense Centers of Excellence: For Psychological Health and Traumatic Brain Injury. https://www.mental healthamerica.net/sites/default/files/Best_Practices_Identified_for_Peer_Support_Programs_Jan_2011.pdf.

O'Hara, Patrick. 2005. *Why Law Enforcement Organizations Fail: Mapping the Organizational Fault Lines in Policing.* Durham, NC: Carolina Academic.

Ostrov, Eric. 1986. "Police/Law Enforcement and Psychology." *Behavioral Sciences and the Law* 4 (4): 353–370.

Reuss-Ianni, Elizabeth. 1983. *Two Cultures of Policing.* New Brunswick, NJ: Transaction.

Rutter, Michael. 1981. "Stress, Coping and Development: Some Issues and Some Questions." *Journal of Child Psychology and Psychiatry* 22 (4): 323–356.

Skolnick, Jerome. 1994. *Justice without Trial: Law Enforcement in the Democratic Society*, 3rd ed. New York: Macmillan.

Tanigoshi, Holly, Anthony P. Kontos, and Theodore P. Remley. 2008. "The Effectiveness of Individual Wellness Counseling on the Wellness of Law Enforcement Officers." *Journal of Counseling and Development* 86 (1): 64–74.

Theophilos, Theane, Joanne Magyar, and Franz E. Babl. 2009. "Debriefing Critical Incidents in the Paediatric Emergency Department: Current Practice and Perceived Needs in Australia and New Zealand." *Emergency Medicine Australasia* 21 (6): 479–483.

Van Hasselt, Vincent B., Donald C. Sheehan, Abigail S. Malcom, Alfred H. Sellers, Monty T. Baker, and Judy Couwels. 2008. "The Law Enforcement Officer Stress Survey (LEOSS) Evaluation of Psychometric Properties." *Behavior Modification* 32 (1): 133–150.

Vesely, Rebecca. 2013. "Deal with Post-traumatic Stress Disorder." *Workforce Management* 92 (6): 12–12.

Index

Absenteeism, 32, 39, 70, 93
Acute stress, 35, 38–40, 42, 161, 167, 169–172, 174, 186
Adaptive Responses, 7–9, 64, 145, 147–149, 156, 160, 209
Altruistic behavior, 7, 67, 148

Bell, Ernest "Ricky," 130
Blanco, Kathleen, 57, 59, 68, 129
Bounded Rationality Theory, 114–115, 120
Brissette, James, 132
Brown, Michael, 57, 59
Brumfield, Danny, 130, 135

Carabineros, 22–23, 40, 63, 90, 170, 176, 184
Chilean Earthquake, 39, 41, 49; Investigation Police, 22; Navy, 52
CNN, 109, 126, 130
Cognitive dissonance, 62, 93
Communication capabilities, 39, 47, 54, 60, 135; failure, 111; loss 39, 50, 52–54, 69–70, 196
Compass, Eddie P. III, 126, 128
Conflict(ed), 12, 14, 31, 52, 76–91, 93–96, 103–104, 110, 117, 123, 136, 212

Coping, 1, 5, 7, 33–32, 34, 43–44, 64–65, 71, 92, 103, 113, 120, 133, 139, 142, 146–152, 154–163, 173, 177, 179–180, 186, 188–190, 199–200, 202, 203, 205, 207, 209, 211, 213, 216–218
Counseling, 198, 203–206, 210–212
Criminal, 20, 22 67–68, 122–123, 125–127, 133, 136–138, 160
Crisis, 5–7, 23, 25, 27, 29–30, 34, 38, 42, 47, 54–56, 58, 60–61, 65, 67–69, 71, 75, 79–80, 86, 89, 92, 94–95, 99–102, 104, 111, 113–115, 117, 119, 120–121, 133, 138, 142, 145–146, 148–150, 154, 156, 158, 160, 166, 168, 175, 178–179, 185, 187–188, 191, 193, 196, 199, 201–202, 205–206, 209–212, 214, 215–217
Crisis Decision Theory, 113–115, 130
Cultural maxims, 119

Danziger Bridge, 131–132
Davis, Robert, 130
Dirty Harry, 136–137, 139–140
Disaster syndrome, 35, 147–148

Earthquake, 80, 165, 172
Ebbert, Terry, 55, 60
Extralegal police aggression, 137

Family role, 79–80, 92, 95, 110
FBI, 124–126
Fear, 31, 34–35, 62, 67, 89, 106, 111, 115–117, 133–135, 138–139, 147, 154, 174, 184, 195, 198, 206
First-responder agencies, 13, 53, 81; community 2, 9, 70, 96, 101, 103, 210
Floodwaters, 14, 20, 24, 48–49, 60, 62–63, 94, 107, 116, 127
Fritz, Charles, 46
Fugate, W. Craig, 1, 10, 27, 42

Glover, Henry 131
GOPE, 22, 89–90
Gulfport Police Department, 13, 19, 20, 48, 51, 59, 86, 153–154, 159; Disaster, 12
Gulfport Police Officer, 37, 59, 89–91, 146, 153
Gulfport, Mississippi, 20, 22, 51, 61, 146, 169

Hazardous, 56, 103, 203
Heroic, 6, 78, 95, 167–168, 175

Infractions, 67, 117–119
Infrastructure, 38, 63, 69, 85, 158, 165
Infrastructure damage, 18, 47, 49, 53–54, 65, 85, 165, 169, 185
Internal conflicts, 74, 78, 83, 94

Madison, Ronald, 132
Maladaptive behavioral practices, 179; behavioral responses, 7, 40, 98; behaviors, 35, 39, 93–94, 122, 133, 138–140, 147–148; challenges, 146, 159; emotional and mental responses, 210; feelings, 215; response(s), 8, 35, 67, 115, 123, 133, 140, 147–148, 160–161; coping behaviors, 139, 179; coping mechanisms, 203, 205; coping responses, 209; coping strategies, 150, 156, 179
Martin, Alan Chief, 25
McCann, Keenon, 129, 135
Media, 105, 128–129, 214
Mental health, 38, 103, 147, 172–173, 198–199, 204, 206–208, 211–216; services (care), 32, 38

Misconduct, 8, 20, 22, 39, 61, 67–68, 70, 122–126, 132, 138–140
Mitigation, 2, 26–30, 39–40, 52–53, 57, 62, 71, 158, 193, 195, 215–216
Morale, 31, 34, 37, 93, 175, 197, 200, 207
Morial, Marc, 125

Nagin, Ray, 11, 68, 129
National Emergency Training Center, 25
National Guard, 59–60, 68, 129
New Orleans Police Department, 13, 20–22, 25, 36, 40, 45, 48, 49, 50, 54–55, 59, 63, 68, 88, 95, 101–102, 105, 110, 117, 118, 122, 124–126, 128, 130–132, 137, 140, 156, 170, 172, 174, 181, 185, 196
New Orleans Police Department Police Officers, 36, 56, 62–63, 65–68, 74, 75, 86, 88, 92–94, 97, 105–107, 111, 112, 116, 118–119, 123–129, 132, 134, 138–139, 145, 151–156, 164, 167, 168, 169, 175, 178–181
Ninth Ward, New Orleans, 45, 48, 55
NOAA, 12–13, 16–17

Occupational deviance, 123–124
ONEMI, 26, 56
Operational protocols, 7, 39, 46, 165, 214
Organizational challenges, 69, 174

Panic flight, 113, 115–118, 147–148, 174
Paramilitary, 29, 31, 55
Peer-counseling, 204; support, 204, 205, 215–216
Pennington, Richard, 21, 125–126, 143
Personal challenges, 165, 168, 173, 184
Personal identity, 76
Police brutality, 20, 32, 123–125, 127, 129, 138; corruption, 20–21, 40, 123–126, 137; criminal behavior, 123; misconduct, 8, 20, 22, 68, 124, 126, 132, 138–139; training, 23, 29, 31, 33, 47, 50, 62, 65, 89, 136, 155, 159, 197, 200, 202, 205, 210–211, 213–214, 216
Professional Challenges, 51, 85, 165, 173

Psychological trauma, 31, 215; effects, 35, 40, 175
PTSD, 8, 34–38, 40–44, 151, 163, 167, 169–174, 183–184, 186, 190–191, 199, 218

Red Cross, 52–53, 190; American, 52, 190; Chilean, 53
Resilience, iii, iv, vii, 7,9, 64, 139, 145–149, 150–151, 153, 155–163, 173, 177, 179, 190, 193, 196–197, 200, 203, 208, 213–216
Resources, 2, 28, 30, 34, 38–39, 46–47, 53, 56–57, 59, 62–63, 65, 69–70, 78, 83, 94, 114, 116, 166, 168–169, 196–197, 199–201, 203, 208, 210–211
Riley, Warren, 45–46, 48–49, 105, 127, 129, 175
Role abandonment, 61, 78–79, 81–82, 84, 94–97, 101–103, 117, 119; conflict, vii, 8, 31, 61, 66–67, 69, 74–82, 84–89, 94–100, 102, 110, 119–121, 168, 188; expectations, 79–80, 84, 96; obligations, 77, 80–81; strain 8, 61, 66–67, 69, 74–75, 77–78, 81–85, 88–89, 92, 94–99, 103, 166

Salvation Army, 52
Satisficing, 114–115
Social isolation, 134

Social Support Systems, 54, 177–178
Solidarity, 113, 119, 157–158, 160, 176, 178, 185, 204
Stress, 5–8, 30–44, 53, 62, 65–66, 68–69, 72, 77, 93, 97–99, 108, 120, 132, 133, 137, 139–140, 142, 145, 148–152, 154, 160–164, 166–167, 169–174, 176–182, 184, 186, 188–191, 193–195, 197–203, 205–209, 211, 215–218
Superstorm Outbreak, 16–17, 26, 30, 39–40, 70, 185
Survival, 34, 203, 213

Thomas, Kevin, 128
Trauma, 31, 34, 38, 66, 171, 198, 199, 209, 211, 215
Tsunami, 3, 11, 18, 23, 26–27, 29–30, 39, 46, 51–53, 70, 84–85, 89–91, 198, 203
Tuscaloosa, AL, 3, 11, 16–18, 21–22, 25, 37, 41, 44, 46–47, 52, 54, 56, 60, 70, 85–86; Police Department, 54

U.S. Army, 59–60, 71, 121; U.S. Army Corps of Engineers, 19, 23; Immigration and Customs Enforcement, 59; Military, 59–60

Washington Post, 67, 124, 126
Williams, Robert, 130, 135–136